Battleships
1856-1977

This edition © 1977
Phoebus Publishing Company/·
BPC Publishing Limited
169 Wardour Street
London W1A 2JX

Part published in *Battleships 1856–1919*
© 1977 Phoebus Publishing Company
BPC Publishing Limited

Made and printed in Great Britain by
Waterlow (Dunstable) Limited

ISBN 0 7026 0070 9

Written by Antony Preston
Illustrated by John Batchelor
Edited by Christy Campbell
Designed by Jeff Gurney

Antony Preston was born in England and
educated in South Africa where he studied
at the University of Witwatersrand. He
worked for some time at the National
Maritime Museum, Greenwich, primarily
on Admiralty records. He is Technical
Editor of *Navy International* and has
written numerous articles and reviews on
warship design and aspects of 19th and
20th century naval history for various
specialised journals and periodicals.
Among his books are *Send a Gunboat*
(with John Major), *V & W Destroyers*,
Battleships of World War I, *Submarine:
A History of the Underwater Fighting
Vessel*, *Navies of the Second World War*,
and the translation from the German of
Ships of the Imperial Japanese Navy (with
J D Brown).

John Batchelor, after serving in the
RAF, worked for three British aircraft
firms in their technical publications
departments. He then contributed on a
freelance basis to many technical
magazines, as well as the boys' magazine
Eagle, before starting what was to be a
marathon task of over 1,000 illustrations
for Purnell's *Histories of the Second World
War* and *First World War*. He takes every
opportunity to fly or sail, shoot with, or
climb over and photograph any piece of
military equipment he can find.

INTRODUCTION

In 1914 the ultimate deterrent was the battleship. In the fifty years since the first ironclads, the combination of steel armour plate and the hitting power of the big gun had produced the most powerful weapon the world had ever seen.

This book details the development of the battleship from sailing ships armed with muzzle-loading guns, through the fascinating nineteenth-century period of tactical and design experimentation to the First World War itself and the high-tide of the battlefleets' power. Antony Preston's expert and highly readable text charts the rise of the steel leviathans from the Crimea to Tsushima. Then Britain's revolutionary *Dreadnought* stoked up the naval race, left unresolved in the fog of Jutland in 1916.

The scuttling of the High Seas Fleet at Scapa Flow and the triumphant lines of British and American battleships that steamed past in review seemed to mark the high point of the battleship's power at sea. The great Battle of Jutland, however, had failed to win the war in an afternoon and new challengers, the submarine and aircraft, were waiting in the wings.

Before the Second World War the battleship had to adapt to the constrictions of disarmament treaties and the new threats to its supremacy, but the rebirth of the German Navy and the Japanese challenge in the Pacific rekindled faith in the power of the big gun. The Second World War tested that faith and from Taranto to the destruction of the greatest battleship of all time, the *Yamato*, it was found to be misplaced.

Meanwhile some of the most fascinating ships ever built had been tested in action and this book is a brilliant evocation of the greatest ships that fought at sea from the strange products of the Washington Treaty to the reborn *New Jersey* firing 16-in broadsides off the coast of Vietnam.

CONTENTS

The Battle of Navarino Bay, October 20, 1827. In the last major fleet action fought by wooden sailing ships, the Turkish fleet was destroyed by the combined British, French and Russian fleets

Birth of the Battleship

THE FIRST IRONCLADS

The battleship epitomizes naval warfare in a way that no other warship can. Many people associate the passing of the battleship with the decline of navies, and yet it had a short life. The first 'ironclad,' the *Gloire*, was begun only in 1858, just over a century ago, while the *New Jersey*, the last battleship to see action, was decommissioned in 1968. When Drake and Howard fought the Spanish Armada in 1588 'ship-of-the-line' was a term unknown to them, and the 'great gun' had not yet come to dominate warfare at sea. Although the requirements of eighteenth-century warfare were to foster the growth of warships, the battleship as we know it had no reason to exist until such time as guns threatened to destroy the traditional ship-of-the-line. Until that day dawned the seas were ruled by majestic two- and three-deckers, armed with tiers of smooth-bore guns on the broadside. It was these ships which fought the great sea battles of the Napoleonic Wars, culminating in Trafalgar, and the outstanding example of the type, the 100-gun ship HMS *Victory*, can be seen today at Portsmouth.

The first step in the evolution of the modern battleship came in 1822, when a French artillery colonel, Henri Paixhans, published his ideas about using shell-guns at sea. The French Navy had only just sus-tained a shattering defeat at the hands of the Royal Navy, the British having captured or destroyed enough French ships to make up a fair-sized navy in its own right. Both sides had relied almost solely on the cast-iron smooth-bore ship-gun, firing a solid iron shot. At any distance the stout wooden walls of a two- or three-decked man-o'-war sufficed to keep out cannon-balls, and it was only at short distances that guns could act as 'ship-smashers'. France had only the remnants of her once-large navy, and Paix-hans knew that there could be no question of building enough big ships to equal or overtake the Royal Navy.

What he wanted was a devastating weapon which could give France an advantage in quality, and he was sure that he had the answer in the shell-gun. With hollow explosive shells instead of solid shot, Paix-hans argued, a small warship could inflict tremendous destruction on the largest wooden warships; if France were to build a large number of these small (and therefore cheap) warships she could nullify the British three-to-one preponderance in ships by making them all obsolete.

Many writers are under the impression that Paixhans invented the shell-gun. This is not true, as the shell had been a naval weapon since the seventeenth century in the form of the mortar-bomb. What Paix-hans did was to adapt the principle of the fuzed delayed-action projectile on the 'long' ship gun. The great value of a hollow cast-iron sphere filled with gunpowder was that it could so easily set fire to a wooden ship if it burst inside the hull. Nothing was feared as much as a fire aboard a wooden ship, with its tarred cordage and its enormous quantity of combustible material, and even the threat of fire was enough to make the captain of a three-decker wary of taking on a ship capable of setting him alight. Sailors remembered with a shudder that Admiral Brueys' flagship *l'Orient* had been lost with all hands during the Battle of the Nile because she had had an 'infernal machine' aboard, or so it was believed.

Unlike many visionaries Paixhans had an attentive audience, for the French Navy wanted to erase the stain of the recent catastrophe. In 1824 the first *canon-obusier* was adopted by the Navy, and tests against target hulks showed that in most cases the explosion of shells caused a fire. If all had gone as planned the French would have immediately become the world's leading navy. But of course Paixhans, like so many theorists, had assumed that the opposition would be hypnotised by the awesome destructive power of his shell-gun. The

Napoléon was one of the first examples of the screw-propelled ship-of-the-line. Although fully rigged, she was designed from the start for steam propulsion

The iron-hulled floating battery HMS Terror *on the slip at Palmer's shipyard, Yarrow in 1856, too late for the Crimea. The period of British supremacy in iron shipbuilding was beginning*

Royal Navy met the French challenge by designing its own shell-guns, with the result that French warships were now just as vulnerable to damage. By the end of the 1840s it was normal for a three-decker to have a mixed battery of about 40% shell-guns and 60% firing solid shot. Apart from the understandable temptation to retain a proven weapon for as long as possible, the solid-shot gun fired further and more accurately; the hollow shell was difficult to cast with perfect balance, and the fuze made for erratic flight.

In addition to the shell-gun, another invention had a profound effect on the traditional wooden ship-of-the-line. The Royal Navy first tried to put a steam engine in a small sloop in 1814, but without success. Undeterred by this the Admiralty sanctioned the building of six paddle vessels in 1821 – a remarkably far-sighted step. But there was no doubt that the paddle-wheel was not the right method of propulsion for ships relying on massed broadside guns. Apart from reducing the area on the broadside which could carry guns, the paddle-wheel was highly vulnerable to damage. Not until the screw-propeller was perfected in the early 1840s did the Admiralty feel confident enough to embark on building a steam-powered battle fleet. But once the screw-propelled HMS *Ajax* went to sea in the autumn of 1846 the pace of conversion was only limited by the cost. By 1854 both France and Great Britain had either converted ships under construction or had designed new steam-powered wooden ships with propellers, and other navies were following their example. The outstanding examples of this type were the British *Agamemnon* and the French *Napoléon*, both fast for their day and well armed, but still curious hybrids. Some observers feared that a naval action was likely to last minutes rather than hours, with both sides consumed by fire and blast as the explosive shells tore through the wooden hulls.

Shell-Guns in Action
Actually the record of shell-guns in action proved rather disappointing. Their first recorded use was at the Battle of Yucatan, fought in April 1843 between the fledgling Texan Navy and a Mexican squadron. As if this does not sound unlikely enough, two weeks later at the Battle of Campeche two Texan sailing brigs defeated the same squadron, including an English-built iron steamer, the *Guadelupe*. It was the first action involving an iron ship and the only

known case of sailing ships defeating steamers. In both actions the heavier Mexican shells inflicted casualties but failed to destroy the Texan ships. In November 1853 the 'massacre' of Sinope occurred, in which six Russian ships-of-the-line took some hours to sink ten Turkish frigates and smaller warships. Naval and public opinion, anxious both for a war against Russia and for a scare about a new horror weapon, harped on the fact that the Turkish ships caught fire and blew up, without mentioning that at Navarino in 1827 a Turkish squadron, similarly trapped without hope of escape, had also been destroyed by fire.

By itself Sinope did not cause the introduction of armour protection, but it acted as a tremendous spur to progress. As early as 1835 the French had tried to produce iron plate which was proof against shells, and the Royal Navy in the early 1840s carried out trials with an iron-hulled steamer, the *Ruby*. The quality of iron at this period was not sufficiently good to allow it to be used as armour; under the shock of impact it shattered into flying shards which were as deadly as the fragments of the original shell. Like the French, the British concluded that they could not recommend the use of iron in warships, and, although this is derided as a triumph of prejudice over scientific advance, their admirals were

The wooden-hulled battery Devastation, *ironclad veteran of the bombardment of Kinbourn Kosa*

right. But the science of metallurgy was making giant strides, notably in England, and in only ten years many of the drawbacks were eliminated. As a result, when the call came in 1854 for a sure method of protection against shellfire, iron was found to be satisfactory. The reason for this was partly that wrought iron now had greater tensility and partly because it was used in such a way as to absorb the stresses set up by the impact of a shell.

The lesson of Sinope was followed by the unsatisfactory performance of the Anglo-French ships against the Russian fortifications at Sevastopol in 1855. The Allies found that they could avoid serious damage from the red-hot and explosive shells fired by the forts, but only at a price of staying so far out that their own fire against the batteries was ineffective. What was needed was a means of taking ships in close, and it was this rather than any exaggerated fear of the Russian Fleet which inspired the French *Directeur de Matériel* to draw up plans for a 'floating battery.'

Floating Packing-cases
The first proposals were to pack the hollow sides of a ship with iron solid shot, but after consultation with their British allies the French constructors decided that 100-mm wrought-iron plates were far more suitable. The result was that in the autumn of 1854 the first five floating batteries were laid down in France. Their names were *Congreve* (to flatter their English allies), *Devastation*, *Foudroyante*, *Lavé* and *Tonnante*. The Royal Navy ordered a further five of almost identical design: the *Aetna*, *Glatton*, *Meteor*, *Thunder* and *Trusty*; they were unwieldy craft like floating packing-cases, with bluff bows and sterns, feeble machinery to drive them at no more than 4 knots, and three masts with barque-rig to assist the engines. Their massive timber hulls had a strake of wrought iron 110 mm (4.3 in) thick at its maximum, sloping to half that thickness at its upper edge, but it covered the length of the hull. The French batteries had a length of 53 m (174 ft) over all, a beam of 13.14 m (43 ft) and drew 2.88 m (9½ ft) of water. The single gun deck carried sixteen 50-pdr guns, and two 18-pdr carronades.

The French quintet commissioned in the summer of 1855, nearly a year after they had been laid down, and their English sisters were ready in April (minus the *Aetna*, which caught fire on the stocks, launched herself and had to be written off as a total loss). But the French were less dilatory in getting their batteries out to the Black Sea, with the result that the *Devastation*, *Lavé* and *Tonnante* arrived in time for the big attack on Kinbourn Kosa, a complex of five forts guarding the approaches to the mouths of the Dnieper and Bug rivers, near Odessa.

On the morning of 17 October, 1855 these 'formidable engines of war' came into action at a range of 900-1200 yds. Despite being hit by red-hot shot and shell from the Russian guns their armour proved invincible, although 28 casualties were caused by shot and splinters going through the gun-embrasures and the overhead hatch. What was more to the point, Kinbourn surrendered after an hour-and-a-half, a dramatic reversal of the normal supremacy of forts over ships. The British batteries arrived too late, despite the fact that the French ships had travelled nearly as far, from Brest, Rochefort and Lorient on the Atlantic coast.

'THE BLACK SNAKES OF THE CHANNEL'

Despite their instant fame the floating batteries were not battleships. Their lack of speed and manoeuvrability meant that they could never control the seas in the way that other warships could. But they had proved the principle of using armour to keep out shells, and the next step was to build a seagoing armoured ship. The French, fired with enthusiasm for the new idea which they had developed, started work immediately. In this they were aided by the fact that they possessed in Dupuy de Lôme one of the finest naval architects of the century. As the new *Directeur de Matériel* for the French Navy, de Lôme had the backing of the *Conseil des Travaux* and the Emperor Napoléon III. De Lôme had already proposed an ironclad 12 years before, and had achieved fame as the designer of the fast steam-powered two-decker *Napoléon* in

Gloire, with her steam power and iron plating, made the rival navy across the Channel suddenly seem obsolete. The ironclad race was on and the all-iron hulled battleship was only a few years away

1850. Early in 1857 all work on conventional wooden ships-of-the-line stopped, and by March 1858 the French were ready to start work on four ironclad warships.

The four ships were the prototype *La Gloire*, her sisters *Invincible* and *Normandie*, and a slightly larger vessel, *La Couronne*. The most famous of these was the *Napoléon*, and built of timber in the conventional manner, but protected by iron plating. This plating varied from 4.7 in on the waterline to 4.3 in thickness at gun-deck level, and was calculated to keep out the new Model 1855 16-cm (6.5-in) shell, which

was fired from a rifled muzzle-loading gun known also as a 50-pdr. Although even her admirers could not call her a beautiful ship, as she was squat and plain in appearance, the *Gloire* was a sound, workmanlike design which gave the French Navy a head start, and she rightly deserves her place as the first true battleship.

Across the Channel, the Royal Navy was still wallowing in the wave of unpopularity which washed over both services as a result of the revelations of muddle and incompetence during the Crimean War. The news of the laying down of four French ironclads in March 1858 caused a 'naval scare' in Parliament. As ever, Press and Parliament did little to assist the Admiralty in coming to a sensible decision. At one stage the French ships were described as 'huge polished steel frigates,' and at another they

Musée de la Marine

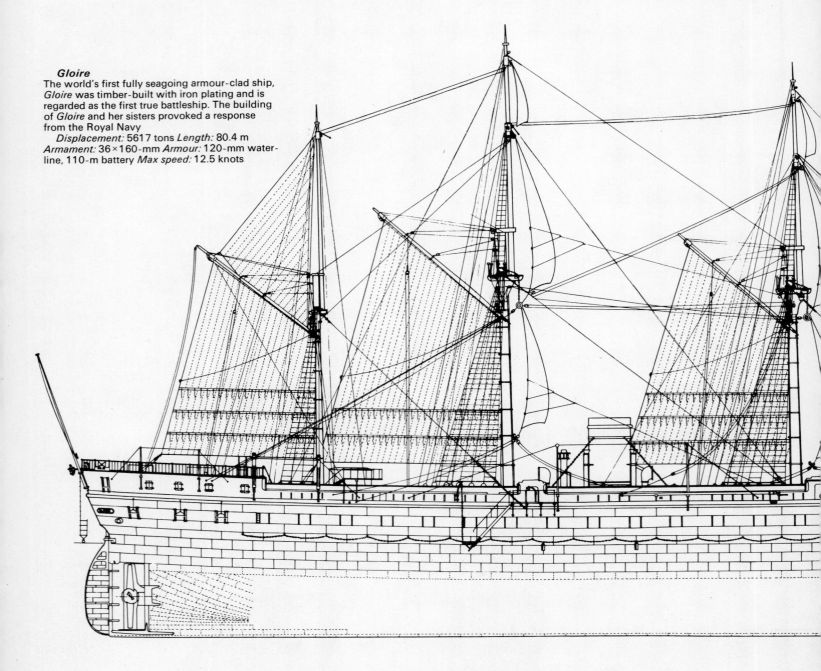

Gloire

The world's first fully seagoing armour-clad ship, *Gloire* was timber-built with iron plating and is regarded as the first true battleship. The building of *Gloire* and her sisters provoked a response from the Royal Navy

Displacement: 5617 tons *Length:* 80.4 m
Armament: 36×160-mm *Armour:* 120-mm water-line, 110-m battery *Max speed:* 12.5 knots

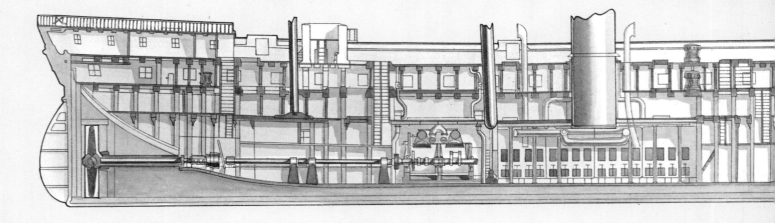

Gloire: Inboard Section

Note the relatively small space devoted to engines but the very large uptake required to provide draught for the inefficient rectangular boilers. The hull was mainly of wood with iron stiffening to compensate for the weight of armour

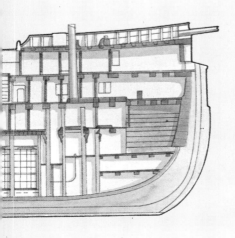

Solférino
A French armour-clad ship similar to the *Magenta,* and developed from the *Gloire* design, *Solférino* had its armament arranged on the broadside on two levels
  Displacement: 7000 tons *Length:* 92 m
Armament: 16×50-pdr, 34×30-pdr *Armour:* 100/120-mm *Max speed:* 12 knots

were credited with gunpower they could never have possessed. Yet a Parliamentary Committee recommended nothing more than an accelerated programme to convert the remaining wooden three-deckers to steam!

These were enormous ships, twice the tonnage of HMS *Victory,* armed with 131 8-in and 68-pdr shell-guns capable of firing at a range of 1200 yards. But they were expensive anachronisms, even before the building of ironclads, for the greater range and accuracy of guns meant that there was no longer any need for the massive concentration of fire from three decks. There was strong pressure from naval tacticians for the building of two-deckers or even single-decked frigates, which were smaller, handier and required smaller crews. The Americans had shown the way in 1854 when they laid down five big frigates, which included the *Roanoke* and *Merrimack* (of which more later), and the British had built six big frigates in 1856-58 as a reply. These ships relied on speed and long-range gunfire in place of armour, and they showed that a single-decked warship could carry sufficient armament to make her a threat to a capital ship.

The nervousness in England engendered by the building of ironclads in France was not allayed by the strong reaction in France to the Orsini conspiracy, an attempt on Napoléon III's life which had been plotted by exiles in England. French newspapers talked wildly of invasion to 'hunt down the assassins.' A visit by Queen Victoria and Prince Albert to Cherbourg in August 1858 simply underlined the fact that the French were feverishly expanding their navy, and the Admiralty plucked up courage to demand the immediate construction of ironclads to match the French programme.

The British were fortunate in one respect; when and if they decided to turn to iron for warship-building they had far better resources than the French. Not only had their shipbuilders more experience in building iron ships, but their iron foundries could produce far greater quantities of armour. In fact the British had built four floating batteries with iron hulls at the end of the Crimean War, and in William Scott Russell they had the leading designer of iron ships; all they needed was the will to act.

When that will finally manifested itself the results were dramatic. Throughout the summer of 1858 tests were carried out against the old ship-of-the-line *Alfred,* fitted out as a target with sample plates, and the floating batteries *Erebus* (iron-hulled) and *Meteor* (wooden-hulled). The Admiralty called for designs for ironclads from no fewer than 12 private firms as well as their own designers, some indication of the resources that could be called upon. In November 1858 the estimates for the following year included the sum of £252,000 for the building of two armoured frigates.

The first was laid down on the River Thames on 25 May, 1859 and launched as the *Warrior* on 29 December, 1869, shortly after the *Gloire* had successfully completed her trials; her sister *Black Prince* was launched on the Clyde in February 1861. HMS *Warrior* joined the Fleet in October 1861 and the *Black Prince* just 11 months later. They were the world's first iron-hull seagoing ironclads, as the French *Couronne,* although laid down in March 1858 with the *Gloire,* was not launched until March 1861.

The British choice of an all-iron hull resulted in two important advantages: watertight bulkheads could be provided to close the ends of the battery, and the gun-ports could be positioned further apart. This last was important, for having gun-ports close together as in the *Gloire* weakened the armour and increased the risk of several guns being disabled by a hit. Like the *Gloire,* the *Warrior* and *Black Prince* were frigates, ie with a single gun-deck, and their long, low profile resulted in the nickname 'the black snakes of the Channel'. Certainly their arrival in the Channel Fleet in 1861-62 led to a distinct improvement in Anglo-French relations.

Iron Ship-building
The *Black Prince* and *Warrior* were the *only* warships which ever merited the title 'invincible', even if they deserved it for little more than six months. When new they could outrun the *Gloire* (14.3 knots against 12.8) and stand up to any shell-guns afloat; the worst that could have happened would have been to run aground and be slowly pounded to pieces by a squadron of floating batteries.

What the French press had not borne in mind was the fact that France did not have anything like the industrial potential to sustain a massive programme of iron ship-building. The *Couronne,* far more successful than the original *Gloire* design by virtue of her iron hull, was followed by only two more by 1866, during which time the Royal Navy had completed an additional nine. Admittedly some of the British ironclads had timber hulls, in order to make use of the enormous supplies of seasoned timber which had been stored in the Royal Dockyards

HMS Minotaur's *full-length armour and broadside batteries made the ship long and unwieldy. The brief reign of the broadside ironclad ship was drawing to a close, inevitably dictating the frenzied period of experimentation in the 1870s to devise means of concentrating fire from barbettes and turrets*

Gloire and Warrior in Comparison

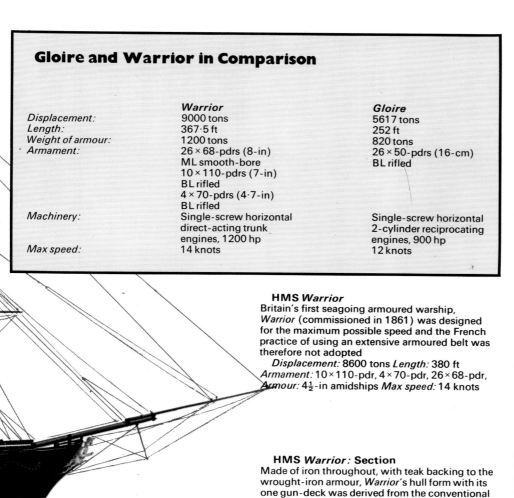

	Warrior	*Gloire*
Displacement:	9000 tons	5617 tons
Length:	367·5 ft	252 ft
Weight of armour:	1200 tons	820 tons
Armament:	26 × 68-pdrs (8-in) ML smooth-bore	26 × 50-pdrs (16-cm) BL rifled
	10 × 110-pdrs (7-in) BL rifled	
	4 × 70-pdrs (4·7-in) BL rifled	
Machinery:	Single-screw horizontal direct-acting trunk engines, 1200 hp	Single-screw horizontal 2-cylinder reciprocating engines, 900 hp
Max speed:	14 knots	12 knots

HMS *Warrior*
Britain's first seagoing armoured warship, *Warrior* (commissioned in 1861) was designed for the maximum possible speed and the French practice of using an extensive armoured belt was therefore not adopted
Displacement: 8600 tons *Length:* 380 ft
Armament: 10 × 110-pdr, 4 × 70-pdr, 26 × 68-pdr,
Armour: 4½-in amidships *Max speed:* 14 knots

HMS *Warrior*: Section
Made of iron throughout, with teak backing to the wrought-iron armour, *Warrior*'s hull form with its one gun-deck was derived from the conventional large frigate. *Warrior*'s hull still survives at Pembroke Dock, Wales, as an oil pontoon

since before the Crimean War, but it gradually dawned on the British that their shipbuilding industry's speed and facility was a safe enough insurance against the French threat. In any case, France's need to spend money on her large conscript army for continental defence meant that the momentum of the naval programme was soon lost.

But both countries had changed the course of ship design permanently. The term 'frigate' was obviously no longer adequate as an expression of fighting worth, and the ironclad was the cause of the abandonment of the old rating system of warship classification. It was absurd to pretend that a 1st Rate wooden 131-gun ship-of-the-line was superior to the 6th Rates *Gloire* and *Warrior*, and the distinctions were soon abandoned in favour of the term ironclad, and then line-of-battle ship, subsequently shortened to battleship.

The supremacy of the *Gloire* and *Warrior* did not last long. Within months a series of much larger broadside ironclads were under construction for the Royal Navy, such as the 380-ft *Achilles* and the 400-ft *Minotaur*. The length of these monsters and the lofty rig needed to move them under sail made it evident that the type could not develop much further. The answer was the turret, a revolving mounting capable of carrying one or two guns. A ship fitted with one or more turrets could bring guns to bear on a number of bearings, and this would do away with the need for a lengthy broadside of guns. The enormous armoured sides of the original ironclads demanded a great weight of iron, but a turret-ship could have a much shorter hull.

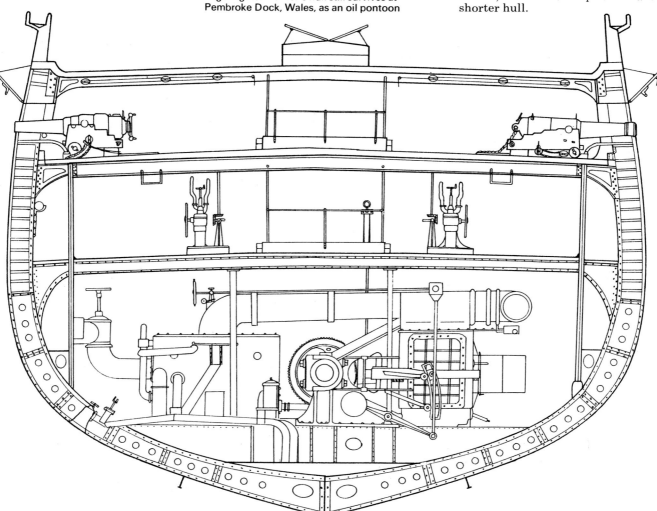

BROADSIDES AND BARBETTES

Federal sailors relax on the deck of Monitor *after her one action against the CSS* Virginia – *note the dent*

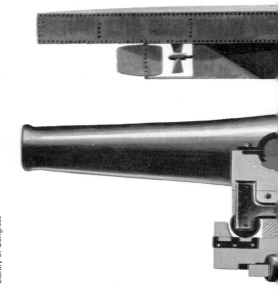

The turret or cupola mounting had been put forward in 1854 by the Swedish engineer John Ericsson and an English naval officer, Captain Henry Cowper Coles. Both men appear to have stumbled on the idea at the same time, an occurrence which is more common than people might think, but we do know that Coles designed an armoured raft after his experience with a wooden gun-raft in the Crimean War. By 1859 his ideas had

matured to the point where he could file patents, and in 1861 the first turret was mounted in the floating battery *Trusty* for trials. Although hit 33 times by heavy shells the turret was still in working order, and the Navy began to take Coles seriously.

The outbreak of the American Civil War in 1861 caught the United States Navy in a very poor state, with only 42 warships, none of them armoured. The Confederate

States Army's successes on land merely worsened the problem by over-running the main naval dockyard at Norfolk, Virginia, on 20 April, 1861. Among the debris was the brand-new wooden steam frigate USS *Merrimack*, which had been burned and scuttled to avoid capture. The waterlogged hulk was raised and found to be in good condition below the waterline, and so in June work started on rebuilding her as an armoured

CSS *Virginia*

An ironclad floating battery, with 68-pdr shell-guns contained in a sloping iron casemate. The *Virginia* was based on the wooden hull of the frigate USS *Merrimack,* captured when the South overran the Norfolk naval dockyard, with the addition of armour cladding built up from railway lines. The North responded by building the *Monitor* as a counter, and the two ships fought one inconclusive battle against each other
Displacement: 4500 tons *Length:* 275 ft
Armament: 6 × 9-in, 2 × 7-in, 2 × 6-in *Armour:* rails bolted in groups of three *Max speed:* 9 knots

A Dahlgren cannon points through the sloping casemate protecting the side of the CSS Virginia

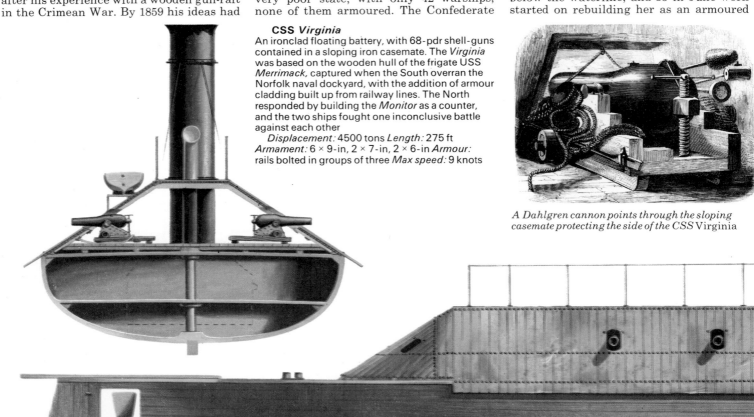

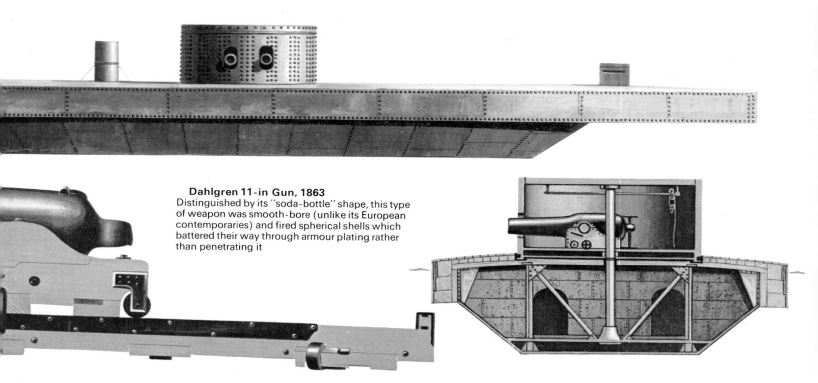

Dahlgren 11-in Gun, 1863
Distinguished by its "soda-bottle" shape, this type of weapon was smooth-bore (unlike its European contemporaries) and fired spherical shells which battered their way through armour plating rather than penetrating it

ship. Explosive shells from forts were as big a menace to ships as they had been in the Crimean War, and it was hoped that the new CSS *Virginia* would be able to withstand the Federal batteries and drive off the blockading warships.

The warship which resulted bore a likeness to the British and French floating batteries, apart from lacking masts and yards; she had a sloped iron casemate containing 68-pdr shell-guns and an iron ram. She was not a battleship, and her machinery was never reliable enough to allow her to venture far afield. Nor could the ingenuity of the South match the industrial might of the North. Knowledge of the new ironclad quickly reached Washington and in August 1861 Congress authorized the construction of iron armoured ships to match her.

Although other designs were started, the main effort was concentrated on a design put forward by John Ericsson, which alone promised to carry enough armour and armament to deal with the *Virginia*. The ship which resulted was the *Monitor*, a 172-ft armoured raft surmounted by a single turret carrying two 11-in smooth-bores.

Armoured Box
Speed of building was the essence of the *Monitor*'s design, and everything was subordinated to that end. The main feature was the raft-like top to the hull, an armoured box which was laid on top of the hull and overhung it all around. This served three purposes. First, it improved stability to provide a good gun-platform; secondly, the overhang provided good protection against

USS *Monitor*
An armoured raft carrying a single two-gun turret, *Monitor* was the North's response to the Confederate *Virginia*. The armoured box enclosing the hull improved stability, protected against ramming and deflected incoming shells. *Monitor* gave her name to a type of ironclad generally used as floating artillery
Displacement: 987 tons *Length:* 172 ft
Armament: 2 × 11-in *Armour:* 3¼-in waterline, 8-in turret, 1-in deck *Max speed:* 9 knots

ramming; and thirdly, the flat trajectory of the shells fired against the deck would tend to make them bounce off, leaving the turret as the main target. The deck was covered with 1-in iron plate but the turret had 8-in plates made up of 1-in laminated layers. British armour was rolled in mills as solid 4-in plates, but American foundries could only roll 1-in plates.

Despite the problems associated with her highly novel design, the little *Monitor* was launched just under four months after the signing of the contract, and she was commissioned on 25 February, 1862. She was just in time, for the *Virginia* (perversely known to history under her original name *Merrimack*) appeared on 8 March in Hampton Roads and destroyed the wooden frigates *Congress* and *Cumberland*. That night the little turret ship joined the Federal squadron and prepared for battle the next day.

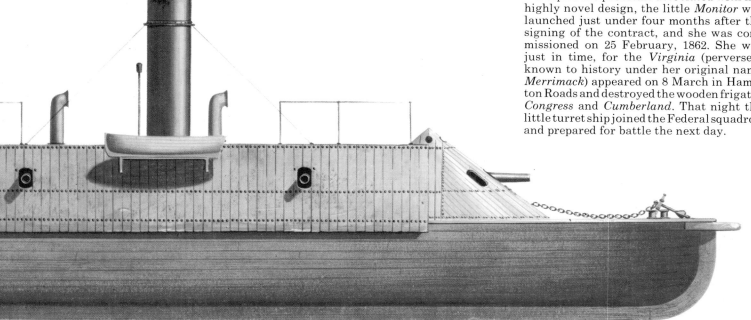

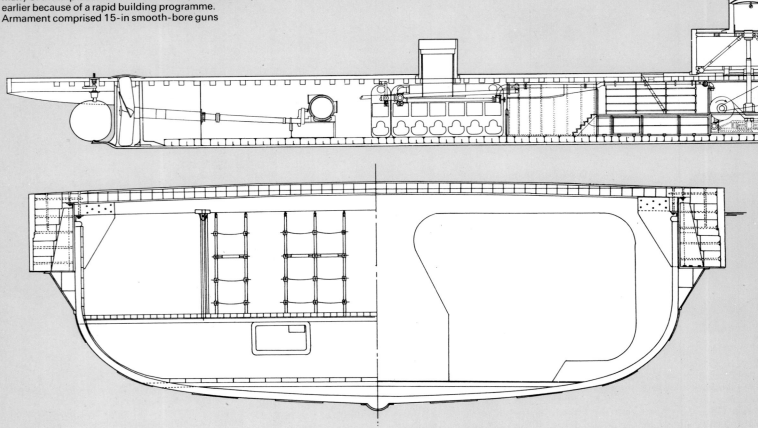

USS*Tecumseh*
One of the third group of monitors, incorporating many of the improvements which could not be used earlier because of a rapid building programme. Armament comprised 15-in smooth-bore guns

USS Tecumseh *sinking at the Battle of Mobile Bay*

HMS *Royal Sovereign*
A wooden ship of the line, *Royal Sovereign* was converted to a turret-ship during building and has been described as the ugliest battleship ever built, with three masts and a huge funnel. She was completed in 1864
 Displacement: 5080 tons *Armament:* 5×10.5-in in four turrets

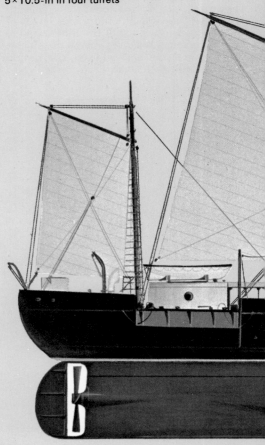

The confident Confederates in the *Merrimack* were surprised to see what they called a 'cheesebox on a raft', but they soon discovered that their shells could make no impression.

Unfortunately the *Monitor*'s guns made no impression either, for her captain had strict orders to use only single charges (15 lb) as his guns had not been proof-fired. Had the *Merrimack* fired solid shot and the *Monitor* fired 30-lb charges the world's first ironclad fight might have had some interesting results, but as it was the 'Battle of Hampton Roads' was a draw. Some idea of the state of naval gunnery in 1862 can be gained from the fact that the *Merrimack* fired a broadside every 15 minutes and the

Monitor replied with two shells every 7 minutes. Firing continued for about 3½ hours, with frequent attempts at ramming. Finally the contestants drew apart, never to meet again.

Although the battle had a profound impact on public opinion it had little effect on the design of battleships. In March 1862, some days *before* the Battle of Hampton Roads, the British Controller of the Admiralty announced plans for building two turret ships. One was to be built of iron and the other was to be converted from the incomplete hull of a three-decker wooden ship-of-the-line, to see if money could be saved by conversion of the now useless 1st and 2nd Rates. The first was the *Prince*

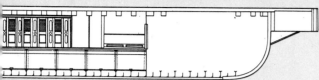

Albert and the second was the *Royal Sovereign*. Neither ship bore any resemblance to the *Monitor*, being seagoing vessels with four turrets and side armour. Both ships were quickly overshadowed by later developments, but they are outstanding as they enshrine basic features which did not reappear until 1903: multiple centreline turrets and a virtual absence of masts and yards. They were in fact the true ancestors of the twentieth-century battleships, rather than the original broadside type exemplified by the *Warrior* and *Gloire*.

As the Civil War progressed more 'monitors' were built, and so a new type of armoured ship came into being. But there were no more encounters like Hampton Roads, although the *Manhattan* helped to finish off the *Tennessee*, another Southern ironclad similar to the *Merrimack*. For a time the Northern press talked of taking on the Royal Navy, for feeling was running high over British sympathy for the Southern cause, but the miserable seakeeping of the monitors precluded them from fighting in the Atlantic, or indeed anywhere other than sheltered waters. In the words of a modern authority, they were nothing more than 'river-going rafts,' and their influence on proper battleship design must not be overemphasized.

Another battle was soon to take place, one which was much more important in the development of battleships for it involved two ocean-going fleets. This was the Battle of Lissa fought on 20 July, 1866 between the Austrians and the Italians. On paper the Italian fleet was impressive, with brandnew ironclads bought at a high price from England, France and the United States. The *Re d'Italia* and *Re di Portogallo* were 300-ft steam frigates, protected by 4.7-in armour belts and armed with a mixture of 100-pdr (6.3-in) Armstrong guns, 150-pdrs (7.8-in) and 300-pdrs (10-in). A further five ironclad frigates were backed up by the new English-built 'turret-ram' *Affondatore*, which had only just joined the fleet. She carried two single 10-in guns in Coles turrets at the extremities of the ship, and in addition to these she was 'armed' with a huge projecting spur underwater. During the American Civil War several ships had been sunk by ramming, one of the few ways of letting water into an ironclad hull if you lacked armour-piercing guns, and this revival from the days of galleys seemed likely to be useful.

Armour-piercing guns were just what the Austrian fleet lacked. The barque-rigged *Ferdinand Max* and *Hapsburg* resembled the *Gloire*, but their designed armament of rifled Krupp 21-cm guns had not been delivered (Austria was at war with Prussia as well as Italy) and so they mounted 48-pdr smooth-bore shell-guns. The smaller ironclad frigates had some rifled guns, but the Austrian Rear-Admiral Wilhelm Tegetthoff mustered only 74 rifled guns in all against

HMS Agincourt *of 1871, although fully rigged, was an intermediate design with a central battery. The development of turret ships for the Royal Navy had been checked by the loss of HMS* Captain *in 1870*

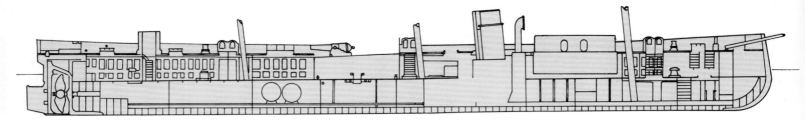

the 200 modern weapons of his opponent, Count Carlo Pellion di Persano. As a further disadvantage a large part of the Austrian fleet was composed of unarmoured wooden ships, the sort which could be destroyed in minutes. The largest of these was the screw two-decker *Kaiser*, armed with 90 30-pdr smooth-bores and two 24-pdr rifled guns.

Tegetthoff was not dismayed by these odds, and chose to remedy his material deficiences with leadership and imagination. He knew that the Italian Navy was a new creation, like the incomplete Italian state itself; it lacked training and confidence. Knowing that his guns were outranged he decided to come to close quarters – at short range some of his shells might have a chance of penetrating the Italian armour. He also chose to engage end-on, as Nelson had done at Trafalgar, to allow his ships to break into the Italian line, but as his fleet was so weak in gunpower he ordered it to sink by ramming. Like Nelson, Tegetthoff was prepared to accept the risk of damage during the initial phase, confident that superior training and morale would enable his men to survive long enough.

Clumsy Ironclads

With such determination on one side and lack of it on the other it is hardly surprising that Lissa was an overwhelming victory for the Austrians. It was a scrappy melée, reminiscent of the sea fights of the seventeenth century, and it proved singularly difficult for the clumsy ironclads to aim themselves with enough precision. For some time both sides charged about, colliding with one another or missing by a few feet; the *Affondatore* failed to ram the *Kaiser* but wrecked her upperworks with 300-pdr shells at point-blank range. The *Kaiser* then tried to ram the *Re di Portogallo* but lost her foremast figurehead and bowsprit and was set on fire.

Then came the unlucky moment in all battles. The *Re d'Italia* was hit in the rudder by a shell and became unmanoeuvrable; while her crew fought desperately to effect repairs she was spotted through the billowing clouds of powder smoke by Tegetthoff

in the *Ferdinand Max*. Inexorably the Austrian ship bore down at 11½ knots and her ram bow tore into the *Re d'Italia* full amidships, tearing an enormous hole below her waterline. As the *Ferdinand Max* backed off the stricken ship listed slowly to starboard, righted herself as the water poured in, and then rolled quickly over to port and disappeared. The corvette *Palestro* made a gallant attempt to divert the Austrian flagship from the *Re d'Italia* but she took a shell in the wardroom which set her ablaze, and she later blew up. The Italian fleet withdrew to lick its wounds, leaving the Austrians in possession of the Adriatic.

Lissa was in its way as indecisive and insignificant as Hampton Roads, but it had a disproportionate effect on ideas and tactics. For the next 30 years all navies were obsessed with ramming, and ships were even built for the sole purpose of ramming. Yet the weapon had proved singularly ineffective against moving ships. The lessons that were *not* learned from Lissa were the important ones: the slow rate of fire, the dense powder-smoke and the relative clumsiness of big ships made it very difficult to hit anything, either with rams or shells. Another point that was overlooked was the superior training and morale of Tegetthoff's fleet. Yet for many years naval designers continued to equip battleships with monster guns which promised the mythical 'knock-out blow', and apparently ignored the problem of achieving that hit.

Another effect of the Civil War actions and Lissa was an increased pace of development of guns and armour. Within five years of the building of the first ironclads armour thickness had increased from 4 inches to 6 inches, but in the same period gunmakers produced guns which pierced 9½ inches. This reinforced the arguments about doing away with a broadside armament and its full-

length armoured belt, to allow thicker armour to be fitted over a shorter length. The British designer Edward Reed (later Sir Edward Reed KCB) pioneered the 'box-battery' or 'central battery' ship, in which the guns were mounted in the central part of the hull, with the guns firing through two ports on either broadside and alternative angled ports to give some measure of fore-and-aft fire. Reed's prototype, the sloop *Research*, was only 195 ft long and displaced a mere 1743 tons, but was armoured with 4½-in plates similar to the *Warrior's*; her armament of four 100-pdr (7-in) guns was rated as equal to her original designed armament of 17 68-pdrs.

Oval Bore

Gun-design was in a state of flux in the early 1860s, making the naval architect's task even more difficult. Just before the Crimean War the British had introduced the rifled muzzle-loading Lancaster gun, which used an oval bore to impart a twist to the shell. The French followed in 1855 with their *système la Hitte*, using shells with zinc studs to fit three shallow spiral grooves. This was also known as 'shunt' rifling, for the shell was rammed into the gun base-first, when fired it 'shunted' into shallower grooves which gripped the studs. However crude this sounds, it imparted more accuracy to the shell than the old smooth-bore muzzle-loaders, but it still failed to solve the problem of 'windage', the gap between the shell and the bore of the gun which had to to be left to allow loading from the muzzle.

Naval guns had originally been breech-loaders, as far back as the sixteenth century, but muzzle-loading guns replaced them entirely, because a gun cast in one piece could eliminate virtually all weaknesses. But the need for more powerful charges and the novel forms of rifling adopted in the 1850s imposed new stresses which were too much for the old cast-iron guns, and they developed a distressing habit of bursting. The British gun-manufacturer William Armstrong started to experiment with strengthening barrels by shrinking hoops of iron around them, and found that these guns

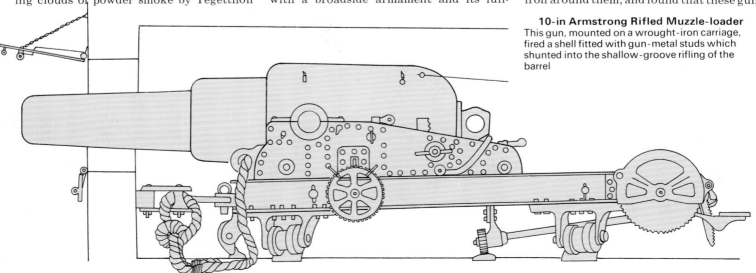

French gun-makers developed the interrupted screw, with part of the threads cut away so that the block could be screwed home with only one-third of a turn. This 270-mm weapon, mounted in the bow of the Redoutable, *was a Model 1881 built in 1884 and weighed 28,240 kg*

could withstand much greater pressures. From there he moved on to the problem of windage, and decided to adopt a 'wedge' system of breech-loading similar to the sliding block tried in Prussia by Krupp.

The French had come to much the same conclusions, but chose a different system, with a hinged threaded block. The time taken to screw the threads home made loading too slow, and so the French soon improved the system by cutting away every sixth part of the threads, making an 'interrupted screw' which needed only a sixth-turn to lock it in place. The Prussians clung to their sliding block, but Armstrong switched to another system, with a vent-piece dropped into a slot cut into the rear

part of the gun and a hollow screw plug. This system had features of both the Prussian and the French systems but lacked the virtues of either, but nevertheless the Royal Navy adopted it in 1859.

The Royal Navy took only four years to find out about the Armstrong gun's vices. In 1863 a squadron in action in Japan reported 28 accidents in 365 rounds and the larger types of Armstrong were thereafter abandoned. But the Armstrong principle of strengthening the barrel by shrinking hoops survived this fiasco, and it was used with a modified version of the French system.

Meanwhile the Americans had taken a different direction entirely. Under the aegis of Admiral Dahlgren a series of large-calibre

smooth-bores was developed, culminating in a 15-in monster used in the monitors. These 'soda bottle' guns were intended to batter a way through armour by firing a heavy low-velocity spherical shell, whereas European guns were now using elongated conical shells which could punch through a solid plate.

Guns grew very rapidly now that they could be made to take bigger charges. The smooth-bore jumped from the previous maximum of 10 inches at the time of the Crimean War to a monster 13-in 600-pdr developed by Armstrong, while the new rifled muzzle-loaders and breech-loaders grew from 6.3-in to 12.5-in calibre. Weights went up in proportion, from the 4-ton 110-pdr to the

Armstrong 110-pdr Gun
The British gun-manufacturer William Armstrong developed a method of strengthening barrels by shrinking iron hoops on to them. This 7-in 110-pdr of 1860 weighed just over four tons, and as bigger charges became practicable the size of Armstrong weapons grew rapidly to 600-pdrs weighing 22 tons

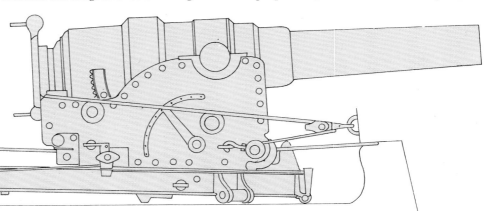

Musée de la Marine

Océan (1868) introduced guns mounted en barbette, *ie in circular armoured towers inside which the guns themselves revolved. Reduction in weight allowed such guns to be mounted higher and the high-freeboard battleship made its reappearance*

22-ton 600-pdr Armstrong guns. New mountings had to be designed to cope with this problem. For many years small warships had used a 'central pivot' mounting in which the gun was mounted on a slide instead of the traditional 'truck' mounting on four wooden wheels. This idea was developed into wooden and later wrought-iron slide mountings, with plate compressor systems for checking the recoil.

In France designers showed little sympathy for the turret, preferring the 'barbette' mounting. Taking its name from land fortifications, the barbette was a circular iron or steel tower, inside which the guns were carried on turntables. The main advantage was that it allowed the guns to be carried fairly high above the waterline, whereas the great weight of the turret limited the height at which it could be mounted if ship dimensions were not to grow inordinately. The *Ocean, Marengo* and *Suffren* of 1868 had four 14-ton guns in a high central battery of four barbettes.

The 1870s were the 'Dark Ages' not only for the Royal Navy but for others. The much-feared French Navy of the previous decade had been very slow to complete its ambitious programmes, and furthermore did little to justify its existence against the considerably inferior Prussian Navy during the Franco-Prussian War in 1870. In that year the Royal Navy's pride in its new ships suffered a tragic blow, when the new turret ship *Captain* turned turtle during a gale in the Bay of Biscay. What made the matter worse was that she took with her Captain Coles, the man who had invented the turret, and in addition had designed the ship. Ever since the ordering of the *Prince Albert* and *Royal Sovereign* and the vindication of that decision at Hampton Roads, Coles had pestered the Admiralty to build a seagoing turret ship. Nobody but the Americans believed in the seagoing properties of monitors, and it was necessary for a blue-water-navy to have ships which could cross the Atlantic.

Naval Architect

In 1866 the Admiralty ordered the world's first seagoing turret ship, the *Monarch*, but Coles was not satisfied with her. Making adroit use of support in the Press and in Parliament he orchestrated a campaign to be allowed to design his own ship, and finally the Admiralty bowed to the inevitable, however preposterous it sounds to modern ears. But Coles was a sick man, and furthermore he had a grossly inflated idea of his capabilities as a ship designer. What he and many officers did not realise was that the introduction of armour and steam machinery had totally altered the funda-

Brazil
Another solution to the weight problem was the box-battery concentrating guns and armour in a central armoured citadel. The ironclad corvette *Brazil* was built in France in the late 1860s

mentals of naval architecture; the days when a sea-officer had as good an idea of how to build a ship as most shipwrights were gone for ever. Needless to say, the dispute over the *Monarch* had alienated the Chief Constructor, Reed, who refused to have anything to do with the design of the *Captain*. Coles was anxious to have a ship with maximum endurance and so he insisted on the maximum scale of masting, three tripod masts and about 26,000 sq ft of canvas.

The *Captain* went to sea in January 1870, and was an immediate success, although she was overweight and drawing about $2\frac{1}{2}$ ft more than her designed draught. She joined the Channel Squadron, and on the night of 6 September in a full gale the *Captain* heeled over on her beam ends and then sank with the loss of 473 officers and men. Reed would not have been human if he had not drawn some satisfaction from the way in which the Admiralty and Parliament turned to him for an explanation, having previously allowed the unqualified Coles to impugn his ability. The court martial found that the ship was capsized by the 'pressure of sail assisted by the heave of the sea', something which should not have been possible in a fully stable ship. At the time the chief cause of instability was seen as excess weight which had been incorporated as a result of Admiralty inspectors not being allowed to weigh materials in the yard, but modern opinion is that the ship's unusual hurricane deck helped to act as a wind-trap.

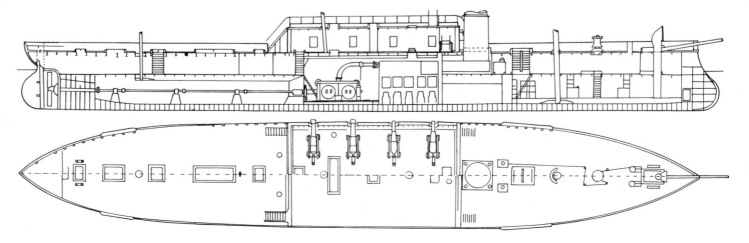

The First True Battleships
CAPITAL SHIPS

Fortunately the disaster had no effect on future battleships, apart from ensuring that no more fully rigged, low-freeboard ships were built. In the next class low-freeboard and turrets were retained but masts and yards were discarded. In their place was sufficient coal to allow them to steam nearly 5000 miles. The two ships, called *Devastation* and *Thunderer*, entered service under a cloud of pessimism and foreboding, and when the *Devastation* was commissioned an anonymous notice was fixed to the gangway, reading macabrely 'Letters for the *Captain* may be posted here.' In fact she proved remarkably steady, and amply justified her designer's faith in her. 'Steady as the old *Thunderer*' became a byword and they served for over 30 years.

Throughout the 1870s a variety of unusual ships were built, and it seemed as if the purity and simplicity of the *Devastation* design were unappreciated. The French continued to favour barbettes for ocean-going ships, and the French *Admiral Duperré* of 1879 had two single barbettes forward, side by side, and two aft on the centreline. Italy had recovered from Lissa, and in 1876 she launched the *Duilio*, the most provocative design of the decade.

Monster Guns
The talented designer Benedetto Brin was ordered to build a ship armed with four 38-ton 12.5-in guns with the thickest armour and the highest speed possible. Unfortunately the British firm of Armstrongs egged

the Italians on to upgun the ships with 50-ton 15-in guns, and then again with 100-ton 17.7-in, and the luckless Brin was forced to 'adjust' the design accordingly. The armour had to be increased in case any competitor introduced similar monster guns, and eventually he settled on a heavily armoured citadel less than a third of the length of the ship.

The hulls of the *Duilio* and her sister *Dandolo* would never have withstood the stress of firing the 100-tonners for any length of time (only one gun could fire at a time, to avoid structural damage), and the slow rate of fire made it unlikely that they would hit anything. Furthermore, Brin's theory of an underwater 'raft body', on which the ship would float if the unarmoured two-thirds of

Redoutable in a French channel port, forming part of the Défense Mobile, *the reserve fleet. She was a turreted development of the high-freeboard barbette ship developed from the* Océan. *'Lozenge' disposition of main armament remained a feature of French battleship design until the end of the century*

Musée de la Marine

21

the ship were flooded, was over-optimistic. In action progressive flooding would have caused the ship to founder, even if the watertight compartments had all remained watertight, which was rarely the case.

However, the *Duilio* and *Dandolo*'s drawbacks were ignored, and a wave of panic ensued. The Chief Constructor of the Royal Navy, Nathaniel Barnaby, was ordered to reply with something similar, and in 1874 the keel of the *Inflexible* was laid. This remarkable ship epitomizes the transitional stage of battleship design in the 1870s, with a preposterous brig rig, twin turrets *en*

echelon amidships, and a squat hull only four times as long as it was wide. She had not only the heaviest armour ever mounted in a battleship, 24-in compound (steel and iron), but the largest muzzle-loading guns ever used by the RN, four 80-ton 16-in. She would have carried 100-ton guns just like the *Duilios* but the Navy was only allowed to buy guns from the Government Arsenal at Woolwich, and Woolwich could only produce a 16-in gun.

The *Inflexible*'s guns were also transitional. Experience had shown that the new slow-burning gunpowders being deve-

Redoutable
In 1872, after the land war with Germany, France began battleship construction again in the form of *Redoutable*—the first armoured ship with steel frames. The bow did not contain a ram, despite its appearance, but was cut away to avoid damage from the bow-mounted chaser gun
Displacement: 9200 tons *Armament:* 4×108-mm *Armour:* 350-mm belt, 240-mm battery

loped were not suited to short-barrelled guns, as part of the powder remained unburnt when the shell left the gun. Increasing the length of barrel solved the problem, but of course it increased the difficulties of muzzle-loading. The Royal Navy was not alone among the front-rank navies in clinging to the muzzle-loader, but the *Inflexible*'s problems convinced even the doubters. To cope with the extra length of barrel the loading gear was put *outside* the turret and beneath the deck. The barrels were depressed until the muzzles were below a glacis or ramp, underneath which rammers pushed the charges and the shells up the bore.

Like the *Duilio*, the *Inflexible* relied on a raft body, with a buoyant unarmoured superstructure carried above the raft, on

HMS Devastation, *the first ocean-going battleship without sails. The weight formerly devoted to masts and full-rig could now be used for increased coal capacity to give far greater endurance. As such HMS* Devastation *was the progenitor of the modern battleship and as important as the* Dreadnought

Dandalo, with four turret-mounted 17-in guns, caused panic in rival navies in the mid-1870s

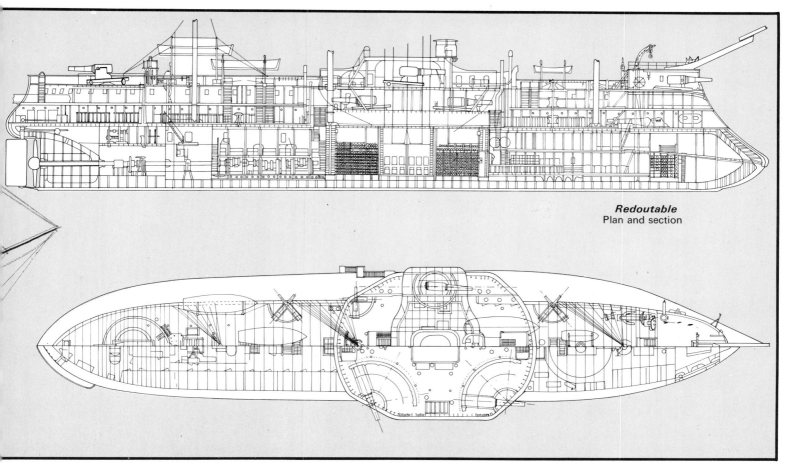

Redoutable
Plan and section

which the turrets were mounted. She was the first ship illuminated throughout by electric light, and also the first with anti-rolling tanks. But she was without doubt the most ungainly ship yet built for the Royal Navy, and the British would have done well to have ignored the *Duilio* for the freak that she was.

As the *Inflexible* was largely experimental she was full of complicated new machinery, and in addition her layout was far more involved than in any previous battleship. Her first captain was John Fisher, later to erupt in volcanic fashion as Sir John Fisher, the man who refashioned the Royal Navy. The new captain was dismayed to find that his ship's company were losing themselves in the 'iron labyrinth', and so he designed a series of colour-symbols for marking bulkheads, passage-ways and deck-levels. But all this zeal passed for nothing until Fisher, having worked his men up to fighting efficiency, then turned them to drilling aloft. And only when the most modern steam-powered battleship in the world could shift a topsail quicker than her squadron-mates was she judged to be efficient.

The *Inflexible* was commissioned in 1881, and a year later she fired her guns in anger at the Bombardment of Alexandria, when

the Mediterranean Fleet opened fire on the Egyptian forts in protest against a rebellion and massacre of Europeans. She fired 88 of her enormous shells and was hit by a 10-in shell, which did less damage than the concussion of her own guns. The glamour of her big guns and heavy protection soon wore off, and although she was followed by smaller editions she marked the end of the era of bizarre designs. Enormous techno-logical changes were on the way, and the emergence of the true battleship was close.

The Italians however could not resist one last attempt at out-doing the rest of the world. In 1876, the year in which the *Inflexible* was launched, they began the *Italia* and *Lepanto* as much improved

Duilios. They were armed with 103-ton 17-in breech-loaders, but in place of the armoured citadel Benedetto Brin gave them a heavily armoured redoubt around the guns and a raft body running the length of the ship below the waterline. For their time they represented a rare example of maximum offence and defence in one hull, among the masterpieces of warship design.

Unfortunately a new development pro-mised to discredit many of the ships of the 1870s and early 1880s. This was the quick-firing gun of 3- to 6-in calibre, which could deliver a large number of high-explosive shells against the large unarmoured parts of the hulls of such ships as the *Inflexible* and *Italia*, destroying the cellular com-

HMS Inflexible *was an overhasty reply to the Italian* Duilio, *adopting the same configuration, and carrying the largest muzzle-loading rifled guns ever mounted in the Royal Navy*

Duilio, as potent as her sister but again weakly armoured and only suitable for the Mediterranean

Museo Storico Navale

National Maritime Museum

partmentation which gave them additional buoyancy. Although the quick-firer shells would not sink a battleship by themselves they could cause fires and widespread destruction, sufficient to disable the largest battleships. It was like the shell-scare after Sinope, with some ludicrous claims about small cruisers vanquishing mighty battleships, but there was no doubt that a ship like the *Italia*, firing one shell every four or five minutes from her 17-in guns, might well be unable to prevent a fast and manoeuvrable ship from coming within range to smother her with 6-in shells. The quick-firer was simply a gun with an improved breech-mechanism, which automatically readied the firing mechanism as the breech was closed, thereby speeding up the rate of fire considerably, but it revolutionized tactics and ship-design.

Not only light guns were being improved. The British had dropped the breech-loader for good reasons in 1863 – not least because of inferior construction of the Armstrong gun. Although the French and German systems of breech-loading were retained they were by no means perfect, and accidents occurred through weaknesses at the breech. But in 1875 the Prussians produced at Meppen the so-called 'mantle-ring', a mantle or jacket shrunk over the breech end. This strengthened the body of the gun, and allowed much lighter construction for a given charge. The Royal Navy was not slow to hear of the progress at Meppen, particularly as there was a strong body of opinion within the Service in favour of a return to breech-loading. A bad explosion in one of the *Thunderer*'s turrets in January 1879 also helped to shake faith in the reliability of muzzle-loaders.

The *Thunderer* explosion not only illustrates how a gun could be double-loaded, but also gives some clue to what it was like to fire the great guns of a Victorian battleship. Both guns were being fired simultaneously, and apparently one 'hung fire'. But as the men in the turrets often put their fingers in their ears (no ear-plugs were issued until well after the First World War) and even shut their eyes just before the guns fired, they then immediately operated the run-in levers without noticing that one gun

HMS Benbow, *last of the 'Admirals' and in fact an individual design. Weight considerations allowed only two of the 16.25-in guns to be mounted, one in each main turret. The midships battery carried ten 6-in guns*

had not recoiled as far as the other. The 38-ton guns were run inside the turret and then depressed for loading, but this time one gun was loaded twice, and the indicator on the rammer simply jammed without being noticed by the loading number. Understandably the gun burst on being fired, wrecking the turret and killing two officers, nine ratings and wounding a further 30.

The French continued to build battleships with high freeboard and barbette-mounted heavy guns into the early 1880s, and it was in reply to the last of these, the *Formidable* and *Courbet* classes, that the British built what was to prove their best design since the *Devastation*. This was the handsome *Collingwood* class, the first fruits of the genius of William White, the naval architect who was to dominate warship design for 20 years.

The layout of the *Devastation* was revived, a return to simplicity and balance, but this time the guns were in French-style barbettes. The reason for this was to allow the guns to be carried at 22 ft above the waterline, as White had to restrict freeboard to save weight. There was a tacit understanding between the Admiralty and Parliament that displacement should not exceed 10,000 tons, despite the fact that this was only 10% more than the *Warrior*'s tonnage 20 years before. To stay within this unofficial limit White had no choice but to go for a short and heavy waterline armour belt, closed by a transverse bulkhead and protected additionally by coal bunkers. The ends were left completely unarmoured, and could be penetrated even by machine-gun bullets, but, although speed and stability might be diminished, this could not be avoided even if another 1000 tons of armour were added to protect the ends. So White plumped for an 'all or nothing' scheme some 30 years before it became widely accepted as the only method of armouring.

The armament of the *Collingwood* also reflected the revolution in naval architecture. In place of the giant muzzle-loaders familiar for so long she carried four 12-in breech-loaders, widely separated at either end of the superstructure. On each side of the superstructure at upper deck level there were three 6-in guns, with good arcs of fire before and abaft the beam. She was also an extremely handsome ship, in total contrast to the angular freaks which had been

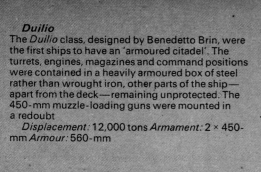

Duilio
The *Duilio* class, designed by Benedetto Brin, were the first ships to have an 'armoured citadel'. The turrets, engines, magazines and command positions were contained in a heavily armoured box of steel rather than wrought iron, other parts of the ship — apart from the deck — remaining unprotected. The 450-mm muzzle-loading guns were mounted in a redoubt
Displacement: 12,000 tons *Armament:* 2 × 450-mm *Armour:* 560-mm

common for many years. Her two tall funnels and single mast stamped her as a creation of William White, and began what was later regarded as a typically British 'look' for battleships.

Sir Edward Reed had resigned from the post of Chief Surveyor after the loss of HMS *Captain* in 1870, and from his position as a Member of Parliament he ceaselessly attacked all official Admiralty designs. The *Collingwood* gave him what he saw as a

chance to undermine confidence in the current administration, and to allow him to return to take charge. But this time Reed went too far, and his rancour was instrumental in persuading the Japanese and Spanish navies not to order new battleships from British yards. Although there were doubts about the *Collingwood*'s 'soft ends' it gradually dawned on her critics that Reed's fulminations were not based on precise knowledge of the design. Some idea

of the value of soft ends was gained some years later, at the Battle of the Yalu River in 1894, when the Chinese turret ships *Chen Yuen* and *Ting Yuen* were hit nearly 200 times each without sinking, and certainly without their soft ends being blown to pieces, as the *Collingwood*'s critics claimed would happen.

The French were not idle in the face of this challenge, and in 1880 they laid down the *Hoche, Magenta, Marceau* and *Neptune,*

HMS Collingwood, *William White's brilliant design of 1887. A development of the* Devastation, *she was the forerunner of the 'Admiral' class*

impressive ships armed with four guns: two in barbettes fore and aft, and two in barbettes on either side amidships, or 'lozenge' fashion. The French Navy had been expanding for some years, having built 22 battleships since 1874, as against 13 British, and although the French programme was not to continue after 1881 the Admiralty felt bound to reply to maintain the relative strength. The choice was far from easy, for not only were there a number of tempting freakish designs like the *Inflexible* and *Italia* to recommend themselves, but to complicate matters the RN was in the middle of its change-over from muzzle-loading guns to breech-loaders. Four types of large-calibre guns had been adopted in 1881, ranging from the 29-ton 10-in to the 110-ton 16.25-in.

The five ships built were improved versions of the *Collingwood*, and they became known as the 'Admiral' class: *Anson*, *Camperdown*, *Howe*, *Rodney* and *Benbow*. But in place of the 12-in guns four were armed with a new 30-cal 13.5-in gun weighing 30 tons, giving them a more massive look than the prototype. But the ship which caught the public eye was the fifth vessel, the *Benbow*, for she was armed with two of the 16.25-in monsters. Despite the fact that she could only fire a round every four or five minutes, and that the barrel-life was only 75 rounds, the public thought very highly of her. The 'Admirals' were much admired professionally too, and the Italian Navy built the *Sardegna* class along similar lines.

HMS *Victoria*

Designed for use in the Mediterranean, *Victoria* and her sister *Sanspareil* carried a main armament of only two guns but mounted weapons of eight calibres in all. *Victoria* was lost following a collision with the *Camperdown* during an exercise

Displacement: 10,470 tons *Length:* 340 ft *Armament:* 2×16.25-in, 1×9.2-in, 12×6-in, 12×6-pdr, 12×3-pdr, 8×mg *Armour:* 16/18-in belt, 18-in turret, 3-in deck *Max speed:* 17.5 knots

Sanspareil class

Name	Completed	Fate
Sanspareil	1889	
Victoria	1891	Sunk in collision 1893

It might be thought that the successful 'Admirals' might have been followed by a series of improved vessels, but this was not so. Instead a new series of freaks appeared. Obsessed by the 'lozenge' disposition of guns in French ships, the British opted for end-on fire, despite the fact that the *Hoche* class could only fire their forward guns over a 180° arc and their midship guns over 90°, because of the blast damage to their superstructure. It is an unchanging rule of naval architecture that foreign designers must be credited with special exemptions from the problems one's own team find intractable. The results of this particular aberration were the two turret ships *Sans Pareil* and *Victoria*, armed with two 16.25-in guns in a turret forward and a single 10-in on the after superstructure. They looked like giant slippers, with low freeboard forward, two funnels side-by-side and massive superstructure aft.

The voices of those who lent their support to this awkward-looking pair were remarkably silent when the *Victoria* sank after a collision with the *Camperdown* off Tripoli in the Levant. On 22 June, 1893 the Mediterranean Fleet, eight battleships and five cruisers under Vice-Admiral Sir George Tryon, was entering Tripoli Bay in two columns, with the Port Division headed by Rear-Admiral Markham in HMS *Camperdown* and the Starboard Division led by the flagship, HMS *Victoria*. One point must be made clear: Sir George Tryon was an unorthodox tactician, and was regarded as one of the Navy's ablest flag-officers. The two columns were steaming 6 cables (1200 yards) apart, and as the two leading battleships had turning circles of about 3½ cables (700 yards) Admiral Markham was not the only officer to be puzzled by a signal from Tryon ordering each division to turn inwards 180° 'preserving the order of the Fleet'. The normal distance for such a manoeuvre would be eight cables (1600 yards), but when Markham indicated that he did not understand the signal (by leaving the answering signal pendants 'at the dip') Tryon asked the *Camperdown* what she was waiting for.

As the two leading ships began their ponderous turns inward it became more and more clear to Markham that his ship was going to strike the *Victoria* on her starboard side. Tryon's flag-captain had already ordered the *Victoria*'s port propeller to be reversed to tighten her turning circle, but nothing could slow down the *Camperdown*; a 10,000-ton ship travelling at eight knots has no brakes, and even reversing both engines had little effect. With a terrible grinding of steel the *Camperdown*'s ram bow struck the *Victoria* on her starboard bow, penetrating about 9 ft, some 12 ft below the waterline. But this was not all, for the impact swung the *Victoria* nearly 70 ft to port and so the *Camperdown*'s ram enlarged the hole to an enormous gash over 100 sq ft in area.

Both ships had gone to 'collision stations' about a minute before the impact, but closing watertight doors and hatches took all of three minutes, and in addition many of the smaller drainage valves were either inaccessible or clogged with dirt and rust. Water flooded in as the *Victoria* headed slowly for shallow water in an attempt to beach herself, but 12 minutes after the collision she suddenly lurched to starboard and capsized. Only half of the 700 men on board were saved, partly because of the devotion of the ship's company who did not desert their posts until ordered to save themselves, and partly because the old-fashioned sailor rarely learned to swim. The *Camperdown* was also holed, and it was feared that she would sink too, but she was saved by the quick action of her carpenter, who built a wooden cofferdam across the main deck. In neither ship could basic design be blamed; the same lessons had to be relearned in 1914, that small openings and minor leakages will make nonsense of any

HMS Nile, *and her sister the* Trafalgar, *were updated versions of the* Devastation, *launched in 1886. The Financial Secretary to the Admiralty predicted that they would be the last battleships, made obsolete by the mine and torpedo*

The Italian Sardegna *class copied the best features of the British 'Admirals' but had splinter-proof shields over the two barbettes*

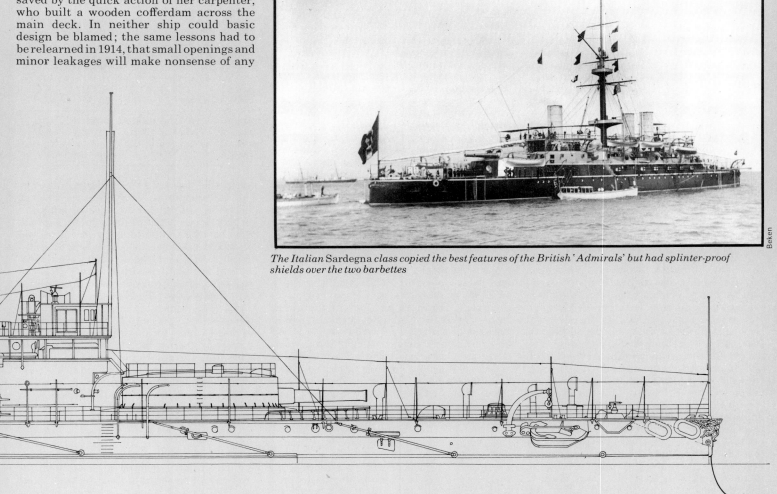

27

theoretically watertight system. Still, there was profound alarm at the rapid sinking of a modern battleship, and even more disquiet at the spectacle of two admirals colliding in broad daylight while attempting an apparently simple manoeuvre.

The discussion of Tryon's intentions continued long after the Royal Navy had quietly made several improvements to the drainage of its battleships and had studied the problems of rapid flooding. All hinged on the distance between the columns, for Tryon had either made a mistake or had been misunderstood. The likeliest explanation lies in the fact that the manoeuvre was unorthodox, and did not even appear in the signal book. Quarter-circle turns were made constantly, whereas half-circle turns (the ones ordered by Tryon) were very rare. It is possible that Tryon automatically allowed a safe distance (a minimum of four cables or 800 yards) for a quarter-circle turn, forgetting that he needed twice that distance for the turn he was making. Admiral Mark Kerr claimed that Tryon had made a similar mistake during the 1890 Manoeuvres, and that his attention had been drawn to it in time. If so, we must assume that this was a blind spot in Tryon's considerable tactical skill, and Admiral Kerr's anonymous informant went on to say that Tryon had admitted as much on the bridge of the *Victoria* as she went down.

Premature Obituary
The next ships to be built for the RN were far from ideal, as they were little more than up-to-date versions of the *Devastation*, but were nevertheless a considerable improvement over such flights from sanity as the *Victoria*. The *Nile* and *Trafalgar* at least had thick armour, a citadel which reached a maximum thickness of 20 inches of compound armour, because the Admiralty was allowed to increase displacement to nearly 12,000 tons. But the design was overshadowed by a new fear, the possibility of the torpedo boat making the battleship redundant. In the first of many premature obituaries for the battleship the financial secretary to the Admiralty said of the *Nile* and *Trafalgar* in 1886, 'these large ironclads will probably be the last of this type that will ever be built in this or any other country'.

Although the automobile or 'fish' torpedo dated back to 1868, when Robert Whitehead brought his device to England, little had been achieved in the way of making it a dominant weapon at sea. The British had shown more interest than anyone else, and had built large numbers of torpedo boats. Naturally the French were not going to be left behind and so they followed the British lead in ordering large numbers. In the only torpedo action of the 1870s, the fight between the British unarmoured ships *Amethyst* and *Shah* and an ex-Peruvian 'pirate' ship, the *Huascar* out-ran the *Shah*'s torpedo at a speed of about 9½ knots!

French enthusiasm for the torpedo was remarkably similar to the excitement caused first by the Paixhans shell and then by the introduction of armour. Here was another 'David' weapon which would offset the uncomfortable and inescapable fact that Great Britain could build 'Goliath' battleships faster. In 1874 the French Admiral Aube pointed out that Britain's seaborne trade was still her most vulnerable asset, and that a blockading fleet of battleships was no more an effective way of preventing

individual commerce-raiding ships from slipping out of French harbours than Nelson's three-deckers. Aube and his disciples, soon dubbed the New School or *Jeune Ecole*, went further in saying that France ought to devote more of her maritime resources to commerce destruction and much less to trying to equal the Royal Navy in battleships and cruisers.

None of this was particularly novel, but the Whitehead torpedo lent a great deal of point to these theories, for it could be launched by small, fast craft. Unlike the big gun, which needed a stable and well designed platform to function properly, the torpedo needed only a tube or launching cradle to eject it into the water, and the weight saved could be devoted to machinery for high speed. The limited range of the torpedo was not important; guns were slow-firing and inaccurate at long range, and so were unlikely to register annihilating hits on small, highly mobile targets.

The introduction of the quick-firing gun demolished much of the basis for the theories of the *Jeune Ecole*, for it was not likely that alert gunners would allow a torpedo boat to approach to within 400 yards of a battleship. And there were other defences, notably the anti-torpedo net, which could be extended on booms around a ship at anchor. But this restricted movement and although heavier nets allowed the ship to use them at low speeds, they were hardly ever used outside harbour. Machine guns were developed for use against torpedo boats, a .65-in Gatling which was later replaced by the more effective 1-in Nordenfelt, and searchlights were introduced to provide illumination at night. The *Jeune Ecole* arguments paid little attention to the improvements in ships' gunnery, for the quick-firing gun was regarded as a menace equal to that of the battleship. But the torpedo continued to inhibit designers and tacticians, and by the end of the 1880s all modern battleships were armed with numbers of light guns, searchlights and torpedo nets.

So far the story has been almost exclusively about British and French innovations; this is not surprising, for other navies had not shown the same inclination to experiment. The US Navy had suffered a relapse after the end of the Civil War, and no new construction in any category was sanctioned after 1874. The last big monitors had been laid up, as if somehow their inflated reputations would suffice as a deterrent. Monitors had caught the attention of the Swedes, one suspects partly because of Ericsson's Swedish origins, and they built four. France bought the double-turretted *Onondaga* from the US Navy after the Civil War and Chile bought two of the *Canonicus* class. Russia invested in no fewer than 14 Ericsson-type monitors, and for some years they were the only Russian armoured ships.

Although the British clearly regarded the seagoing ironclad as the only proper answer to the monitor they showed some interest in the type as a coast-defence ship, and were active in building them for other navies. Thus the *Rolf Krake* (1863) was built for Denmark, the *Huascar* for Peru and the *Buffel* and *Tijer* for the Netherlands. The navies of Argentina and Brazil also featured monitors, such as the French-built *Javary*. The US Navy was, however, unique in clinging to the idea of the big monitor long after every other major power had aban-

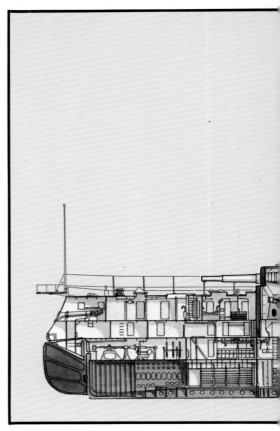

USS *Indiana*
The three battleships in this class were similar to the later *Royal Sovereigns* but had paired turrets, giving a low freeboard. Neither seakeeping ability nor top speed was impressive
Displacement: 10,200 tons *Armament:* 4×13-in, 8×8-in, 4×6-in *Max speed:* 16 knots

Indiana class

Name	Completed	Fate
Indiana	Nov 1895	Scrapped 1924
Massachusetts	Jun 1896	Sunk as target 1920
Oregon	1896	Scrapped 1956

doned the type as a front-line battle unit. The circumstances were unusual in that Congress would not allow new construction. In 1874, in a desperate attempt to provide some sort of shipbuilding programme, the US Navy resorted to the old eighteenth-century trick of a 'great repair'. An unsuspecting legislature voted money for the 'repair' of five Civil War monitors whose hulls had been attacked by dry rot.

The five ships, *Puritan*, *Amphitrite*, *Monadnock*, *Terror* and *Miantonomoh*, bore no resemblance to the original ships, apart from their low freeboard; they had breech-loaders and other refinements, and might more correctly be described as coast-defence battleships. The ships took 17 to 22 years to build, partly because it was necessary to allocate money in driblets to avoid alerting suspicious Congress watchdogs. To make matters worse the Navy's insistence on the right to build the monitors resulted in over-enthusiastic support from senior officers and the few navy-minded politicians. A further five were authorized between 1887 and 1898, and by a happy coincidence they turned out to be ideal submarine tenders because of their low freeboard. But seagoing ships they were not, as witness the conditions aboard the *Amphitrite*, which recorded a temperature of 205° in her boiler-room. During one Atlantic 'cruise' in 1895 so many of her stokers were prostrated by

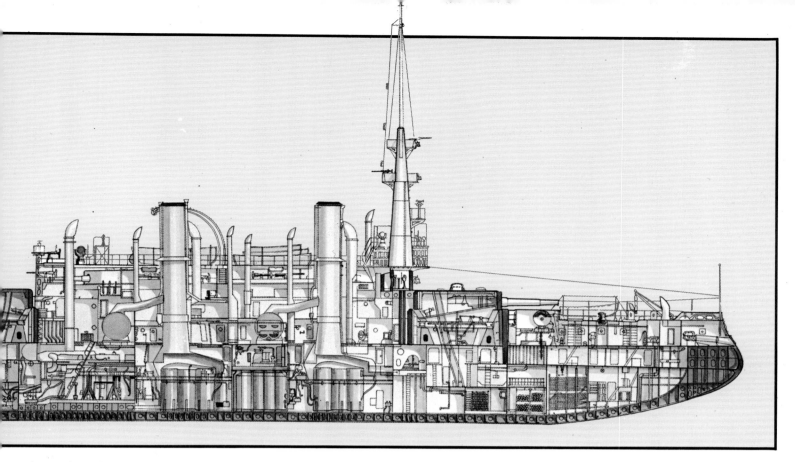

heat exhaustion that she lost steam pressure and had to anchor until the temperature had cooled.

From this nadir the US Navy could only make slow progress. For a start the domestic steel industry's capacity had to be built up. Battleships could only be built if the right industrial base existed, and so the first two ships ordered in 1886 were the 2nd Class battleship *Texas* and the armoured cruiser *Maine* (re-rated as a 2nd Class battleship during construction). Neither ship struck terror into her foes, for they were turret ships of small, obsolescent design, with turrets amidships. The *Maine*'s only memorable achievement was to be blown up in Havana in February 1898, thus providing the US Government with the excuse it wanted to go to war with Spain. With noteworthy zeal for truth and justice the US Government refused to allow an international committee of ordnance experts to examine the hull for proof of sabotage, but modern opinion inclines to the view that the *Maine* suffered an internal explosion from deteriorating powder rather than an external detonation caused by a time-bomb or mine.

Despite the slow start America soon discovered the extent of her industrial resources. In 1890 Congress authorized the building of three seagoing battleships. The designation 'seagoing' was insisted upon to stress that the ships were for coast defence, for Congress had no intention of allowing ambitious naval officers to agitate for bigger and better ships than the European navies. Despite this the *Indiana*, *Massachusetts* and *Oregon* compared favourably in gunpower and protection, with four 13-in guns, a heavy secondary battery of eight 8-in guns and an armour belt 18-in thick. The value of the four twin 8-in turrets at the corners of the superstructure was not as great as it looked on paper. Blast interference from them made the 13-in turrets unusable, as the sight-setters in

the sighting hoods were concussed when the 8-in guns fired overhead.

There was a much more serious fault in the design of the 13-in turrets: the positioning of the carriages of the guns too far forward. This had been done to avoid having too large a gunport, but its effect was to make the turret unbalanced. When the guns were trained on the beam the ship listed several degrees and submerged the armour belt. On one occasion the *Indiana*'s turrets broke loose from their stops and it took the efforts of 100 men to bring them

under control again. With so much armour and armament on a limited displacement there was no room for coal, and the normal load of 400 tons (theoretically a maximum of 1800 tons could be carried) would be good for about 700 miles' steaming at full speed (probably not more than 2000 miles at economical speed). A fourth ship, the *Iowa*, was ordered in 1892 to a similar design, but she was armed with four 12-in guns to allow for greater freeboard, as the 12-ft freeboard of the *Indianas* had proved inadequate.

USS Texas, *launched in 1892, was heavily influenced by both French and German ideas emphasising gunpower at the expense of speed. Poor sea-keeping and range reflected US emphasis on coast defence*

To maintain a high freeboard, French battleship designs of the late 1880s (above Masséna) adopted an exaggerated tumblehome, the maximum waterline width sloping to a narrower upper-deck. The snout bow was not a ram but a device to avoid excessive blast damage from the foremost turret

République

The two vessels in this class, along with those of the *Vérité* class, formed the backbone of the French battle fleet for many years. They continued the practice of mounting the secondary armament in turrets

Displacement: 14,865 tons full load *Length:* 135 m *Armament:* 4 × 305-mm, 18 × 165-mm, 13 × 65-mm, 10 × 47-mm, 5 × 450-mm torpedo tubes *Armour:* 180/280-mm belt, 320-mm main turrets, 60-mm main deck *Max speed:* 18 knots

République class

Name	Completed	Fate
République	1906	Scrapped 1921
Patrie	1906	Scrapped 1927

The French Navy's actual building rate contrasted dramatically with its predictions. The four ships which inspired the British to build the 'Admirals' were laid down in 1880-81 but not completed until 1890-92, whereas the British ships were commissioned two to three years sooner. The new *Directeur de Matériel*, Emile Bertin, produced a series of designs which marked him as a worthy successor to Dupuy de Lôme, but the slow pace of construction made them look somewhat dated by the time they appeared. In other respects, too, the French Navy seemed curiously reluctant to embrace progress. Having pioneered the barbette system they dropped it in favour of the turret, but kept turrets years after every other navy had dropped them. The obsession with the 'lozenge' disposition of guns meant that French battleships had to pay a heavy penalty.

Like the Chinese, the French believed that opponents should be frightened before the battle, and their ships had a 'fierce-face' appearance, with massive funnels and built-up masts. The hulls were given very high freeboard, which was of course a good feature as it allowed a high command for the guns, but this resulted in unacceptable topweight, which had to be reduced by

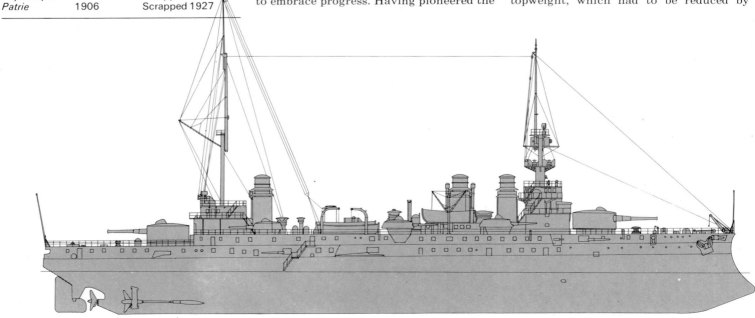

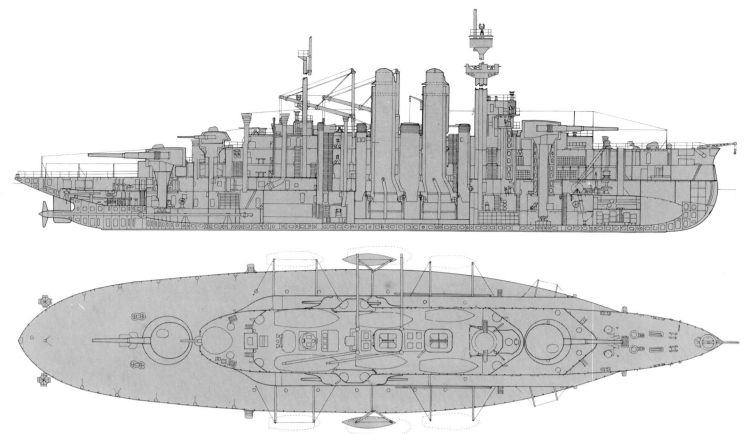

'tumblehome', the archaic term for sloping the sides to make the upper deck beam narrower than the waterline width. Again, this was quite logical, but it had to be exaggerated to allow the beam guns to fire end-on, at best a theoretical advantage. Armour was limited to a very narrow waterline belt running the length of the ship, a waterline deck and virtually nothing else apart from armour on the turrets. The worst feature of this system was that the ship lost stability at any moderate angle of heel; with only 4-in armour starting about $1\frac{1}{2}$ ft above the load waterline, the sides could be perforated and water would enter the ship above the armoured deck during a roll of only 9°.

At the end of the 1880s the British position was not nearly as bad as the critics had assumed. In 1886 the French Chamber of Deputies learned that only ten seagoing battleships were ready for sea. Only one of six ships laid down between 1878 and 1881 was near to completion, and one, the *Neptune*, was only 38% complete after five

Henri IV

Although intended only for coast defence *Henri IV* was guardship at Bizerta at the outbreak of the First World War and was later sent to the Dardanelles

Displacement: 8,800 tons *Length:* 108 m
Armament: 2 × 275-mm, 7 × 140-mm, 12 × 45-mm, 2 × mg, 2 × 355-mm or 450-mm torpedo tubes
Armour: 180/280-mm belt, 300-mm turrets, 76-mm deck *Max speed:* 17·2 knots

Name	Completed	Fate
Henri IV	1902	Scrapped 1921

years on the stocks. In contrast the Royal Navy had got rid of all but two of the old wooden-hulled ironclads and had virtually written off the old *Warrior*-type broadside ironclads. But there were a number of new technical developments in ship design, and it was felt in Parliament and in the Navy that the time had come for an overhaul of the system. What was needed was not a vast increase in the nominal strength of the Fleet but more efficient building.

The first step was to reorganize the Royal Dockyards, and this task was given to Sir William White, the gifted naval architect who had left the Navy in 1882 to work for a private firm. In 1885 he returned, and transformed the Dockyards from being grossly inefficient into the cheapest and fastest building yards in the world. Much was made of the building of HMS *Dreadnought* in just over a year, but the same dockyard built HMS *Majestic* in only 22 months. And these were the same yards which in 1884 had been officially considered to be capable only of repair work. White's reforms were made possible because of a virtual moratorium on battleship-building; until the reforms were completed only small cruisers and gunboats were ordered.

On the material side the old ironclad *Resistance* was used as a target to test various types of armouring and shells. Even torpedoes were fired at the ship, and from these experiments White and the newly formed Royal Corps of Naval Constructors were able to prepare revolutionary new de-

Charlemagne running trials without armament, emphasising the theoretical advantages of 'fierce-face' appearance with heavily built-up masts and superstructure, long a preoccupation of French warship design

St Louis, a sister of Charlemagne, seen in the later overall grey paint scheme. The shape of the ship and the pronounced tumblehome is much more recognisable, emphasising the camouflage properties of the peacetime scheme

USS Massachusetts, *the second unit of the* Indiana *class. Low freeboard prevented the use of the main battery in a seaway*

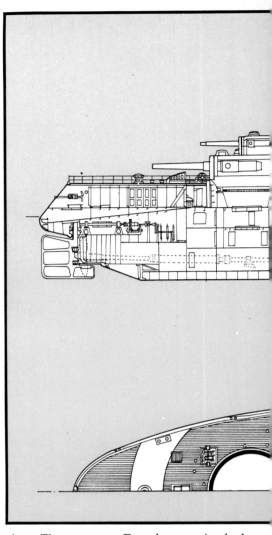

HMS Repulse *(seen in 1904) of the* Royal Sovereign *class broke new ground in combining the barbette system with high freeboard to produce a more effective sea-going battleship*

The design of SMS Baden, *launched in 1884, reflected the continuing emphasis put on the embryonic German Navy as a coast-defence force*

signs. The scare over French expansion had loosened the purse-strings, and so, when White proposed larger battleships than ever before, for the first time there was no political opposition.

In July 1886 the Conservatives under Lord Salisbury were returned to power, and Lord George Hamilton returned as First Lord of the Admiralty with hardly a break in policy, since the Liberal Government was only in power for six months. The public suddenly became very Navy-minded, having taken the Navy for granted since the Crimean War, and a powerful Press campaign helped the politicians to make up their minds. In March 1889 the Government introduced the Naval Defence Act, a special programme to modernize and strengthen the Fleet:

    8—1st Class battleships
    2—2nd Class battleships
    9—1st Class cruisers
   29—2nd Class cruisers
    4—3rd Class cruisers
  18—torpedo gunboats

These 70 ships were to cost £21.5 million, a staggering sum by the standards of the day, and construction was to be spread over five years.

Having achieved such a remarkable degree of political support William White responded by producing ships of exceptional military qualities. His 1st Class battleships, the *Royal Sovereign* class, were remarkable ships. With the 10,000-ton limit behind him he was able to take the best feature of his 'Admiral' class, the barbette-mounted gun armament, and combine it with proper freeboard. Not only was spray interference thus

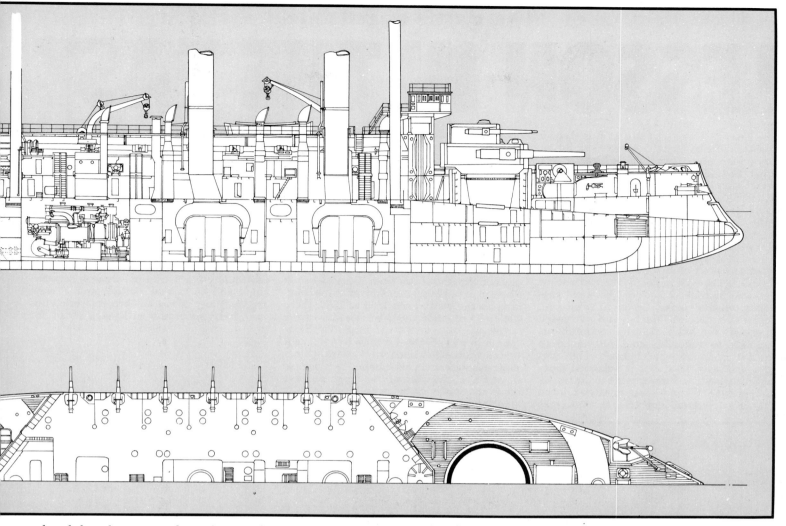

reduced, but the sea speed was increased. Tumblehome was used to avoid excessive topweight. The main armament was the same as in the 'Admirals', four 13.5-in, but the 6-in guns were mounted in two casemates or enclosed armoured boxes at main-deck level on each side, and three ordinary shielded mountings a deck higher. These secondary guns were quick-firers, and were the equivalent of about double the number of the older slow-firing breech-loaders.

The *Royal Sovereigns* were an outstanding success, and what is more they struck a new note in being handsome ships, with funnels side by side and a symmetrical silhouette. The odd man out was the eighth ship, the *Hood*. The First Sea Lord, Sir Arthur Hood, was adamant in his belief in the turret, despite all White's arguments about its great weight. In deference to the First Sea Lord's prejudices the last unit of the class was given two twin 13.5-in turrets, and if she did nothing else she clinched the argument for good. Because of the weight she had to have low freeboard and so was always·slower than the other seven ships. Also, when they were rearmed with additional 6-in casemates in 1902–04 the *Hood* was found to have insufficient stability to allow the alteration. She only redeemed herself by her valuable service in testing the first anti-torpedo 'bulges' in 1913, and was sunk as a blockship at Portland in 1914, where she can be seen to this day.

White was not content with one master-piece. There was one serious disadvantage in the *Royal Sovereign* design; the main armament was unprotected from shells bursting overhead, as the guns were mounted in barbettes. In 1893, with the Naval Defence Act building programme still under way, the Admiralty was pressing for a continuation of the drive for supremacy. Seven more battleships were authorized, and White took the chance to make several technical improvements, such as the provision of 'hoods' for the barbettes, adopting a lighter but more powerful 12-in gun and putting all the 6-in guns in casemates. The result was not only the ultimate nineteenth-century battleship design but also an even better looking ship than the *Royal Sovereign*, with a compact, balanced profile and two funnels set close together, side by side. The US Navy paid the most sincere compliment of all by building the *Alabama* class along almost identical lines.

After making such a strenuous effort the British settled down to build more battleships along very similar lines. With the completion of the last *Majestic* the Royal Navy had 16 new battleships of basically similar design, which could manoeuvre together and therefore be handled as one homogeneous force. To preserve this homogeneity the Royal Navy made few demands for detailed changes in succeeding classes for nearly ten years, and so a total of nearly 40 ships were built in quick succession. The speed with which British shipyards could turn out battleships is demonstrated by the fact that the *Majestic* was built by Portsmouth Dockyard in less than 22 months, a record which was only equalled by the *Dreadnought*'s 14 months from the same yard. But the *Dreadnought*'s record was achieved by using gun turrets earmarked for two other ships, whereas all nine

USS *Kearsage*
The battleships in this class employed the two-storey turret arrangement in an attempt to save weight so that the ships could operate more easily off the Mexican coast. The disadvantages outweighed the benefits, however
Displacement: 11,540 tons *Length:* 368 ft
Armament: 4×13-in, 4×8-in, 18×5-in, 2×3-in AA (from 1918), 4×6-pdr, 1×18-in torpedo tube
Armour: $9\frac{1}{4}$/$16\frac{1}{4}$-in belt, 15/17-in turrets *Max speed:* 16 knots

Majestics were built on time.

From this point the French Navy went into relative decline. The *Jeune Ecole* stressed the importance of numbers, and wanted to replace battleships with torpedo boats and submarines. But manoeuvres showed that however useful small torpedo boats and submarines might be in defence, they were not yet good enough to fight on the oceans. And even if French cruisers could harry British shipping around the world there was still the risk of the French coast being attacked by the British battle fleet, and so the battleship was still needed. But the latest French battleships were hardly a match for ships like the *Royal Sovereigns* and the *Majestics*. They carried less than 700 tons of coal, as against the 2000 tons specified for the *Majestic*, and carried their guns in single turrets. Although French designers favoured high freeboard they also liked complex superstructures, which raised the centre of gravity. Great expanses of their sides were unarmoured, and this factor combined with the exaggerated tumblehome made them potentially unstable if the hull was holed.

The Battle of Tsushima

LESSON IN THE EAST

The German Navy was still at this stage a coastal defence force committed to do no more than protect the Baltic shores. Not until the late 1890s did Admiral Tirpitz get permission to increase the size of new battleships. But once that decision was made, and given the authority of long-term policy in the form of Navy Laws modelled on the Naval Defence Act, the German Navy rose swiftly in power and reputation.

Paradoxically the French Navy, which reached a peak of new efficiency at the end of the 1890s, was suddenly turned into a political football. An ardent political supporter of the *Jeune Ecole*, M. Pelletan, became Minister of Marine and proceeded to cripple the battle fleet by such dubious methods as reducing coal allowance to restrict manoeuvres. Pelletan's reign was comparatively brief, but it achieved more lasting harm than anything since the Battle of Trafalgar. When he was finally replaced France's declining industrial strength was

not up to the effort needed to modernize her battle fleet. Nor was the political will present, for the *Entente* with Great Britain removed much of the exaggerated fear of a naval war in the Channel or the Mediterranean which had previously sustained the expansion of the navy.

Technical Advance

One of the problems facing naval architects at the turn of the century was the lack of practical experience. With no battle of any consequence later than Lissa and such a hectic pace of technical advance, particularly in the years from 1885 to 1900, there was little to guide the theorists apart from target practice against old ships. The Sino-Japanese war of 1896 did little to help, as it was an affair of fast, modern cruisers against slow, obsolescent coast-defence battleships. As at Lissa, the dash of the Japanese gave them an easy victory over the tactically inept Chinese at the Battle of the Yalu

River, but the result was interpreted by everybody to prove their chosen views. To the British the 'hail of fire' from medium- and light-calibre guns had been the clincher, whereas the French claimed that cruisers could now fight any battleship!

The Japanese provided the next object lesson, when they fought the Russians at Tsushima in 1904, but again the disparity between the two sides baffled and misled the naval theorists. The naval side of the Russo-Japanese War in general, and Tsushima in particular, was a trial of strength between ships and tactics of British and French origin. Many of the modern Russian ships were built according to French ideas, for

A Japanese battleship, one of two lost to Russian mines in May 1904, is seen about to meet its end (from a contemporary French print)

The Russian battleship Petropavlovsk, *flagship of Admiral Makarov, explodes after being lured into a Japanese minefield (also depicted in a French print)*

34

The 12,000-ton Petropavlovsk *was completed in 1894 and blew up outside Port Arthur ten years later after hitting a Japanese mine*

The Retvizan *was fitted with a 250-ft long steel belt to protect her against torpedoes, but was damaged by just such a weapon while at anchor*

Asahi *and her sister,* Shikishima, *breached the 15,000-ton barrier. Each carried five torpedo tubes, used to good effect against the Russian fleet*

Russian shipyards relied heavily on French investment, whereas the Japanese were ordering their ships from Britain, in most cases following the latest British innovations in weapons and equipment. Ironically the Japanese equipment was hardly exposed to severe testing, whereas the Russian ships were tested in every conceivable way. The Russian ships and the French ideas they represented failed lamentably, whereas British ideas were largely vindicated.

The most unusual feature about the Battle of Tsushima was the enormous range at which the Japanese opened fire, 7000 yards. The fact that they hit nothing, and

continued to hit nothing until they had closed the range to something more reasonable, was lost on the observers who reported on the battle. The British learned most; being the mentors of the Japanese they were allowed to examine the Russian ships salvaged at Port Arthur and those surrendered after Tsushima. Other countries had all sent observers, and opinion was unanimous that all future naval actions would be fought at long range.

This immediately created a new set of problems. Nobody had yet designed a battleship to fight at a range of more than about 4000 yards, which was little more than the extreme range of the guns at Trafalgar. This

was not, as has been claimed, because it never occurred to anyone to fire a gun at a greater range. For many years guns had been capable of much greater ranges, but the powders available produced irregular rates of burning, and at extreme range this resulted in a wide scatter of shots. Only after the introduction of large-grain, slow-burning powders in the 1890s was it possible to 'calibrate' a gun to land shots repeatedly on the same spot at ranges of more than 3000-4000 yards. And even when this became possible there was a delay before ships' gun-mountings could be given higher elevation. At 7000 yards or more the only thing visible was a plume of smoke from the target and the enormous 100-ft high splashes made by one's own shells. To complicate matters the slow rate of fire of a large gun like a 12-in (one shell every two-and-a-half minutes) meant that the target had time to move away (the 'rate of change') and might well be missed by the next salvo of shells. Even when a crude rangefinder was provided, this time-lag between salvoes was inescapable.

Even before Tsushima, gunnery experts were studying the problem, Cpt Percy

Potemkin

Having been taken over by her crew in 1905, *Potemkin* was renamed *Panteleimon*, served in the Black Sea during the First World War, resumed her original name and then became the *Boretz Za Svobodu* before being broken up in 1922—24

Displacement: 12,600 tons full load *Length:* 113 m *Armament:* 4×305-mm, 16×152-mm, 14×76-mm, 6×47-mm, 5×450-mm torpedo tubes *Armour:* 152/230-mm belt, 250-mm turrets, 63/75-mm decks *Max speed:* 16 knots

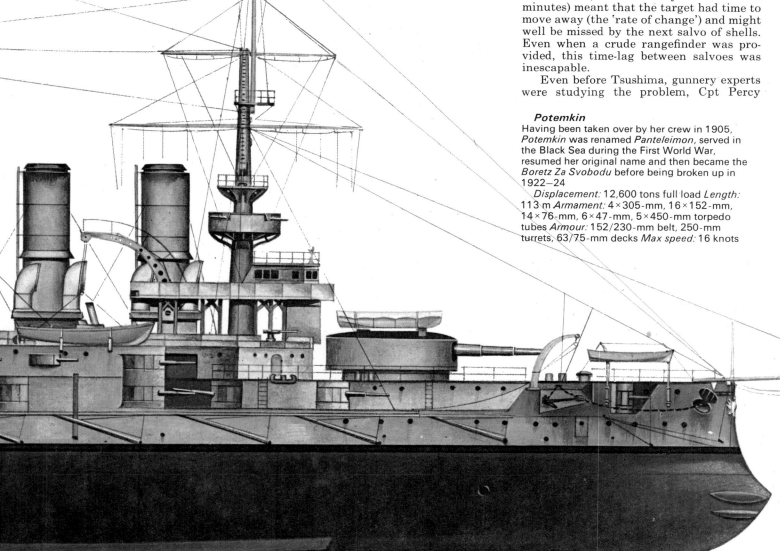

Fuji, *along with sister-ship* Yashima, *was built to counter the Chinese Navy's pair of German-constructed battleships. The 1892 Sino-Japanese war was over by the time they were completed, however, and* Fuji's *first action was against the Russians in 1904. She sank the Russian battleship* Borodino *at Tsushima*

Scott in the Royal Navy and Captain William Sims in the United States Navy. But the Japanese experience proved that battleships would have to fight at a greater range than before. Sims and his British and Japanese contemporaries knew that the one way to improve shooting at long range was to fire larger numbers of shells, dividing them into two salvoes to provide a smaller gap between firing. The Americans had for many years insisted on a heavy secondary battery of 8-in guns in their battleships, the Germans had 6.7-in guns and the Italians had also produced ships with 8-in batteries.

The British finally followed the trend in the *King Edward VII* class of 1901, the last battleships of the William White era. These handsome ships had four single 9.2-in guns at the corners of the superstructure, with 6-in guns in a battery a deck lower, and in theory both 9.2-in and 12-in shells could penetrate the heaviest armour afloat at 7000 yards. The Japanese copied the *King Edward VII* class in the *Kashima* and *Katori*, giving them 10-in guns instead of 9.2-in, but neither ship was ready in time for the war. The British quickly followed with the *Lord Nelson* and *Agamemnon*, armed with a secondary battery of ten 9.2-in guns in a mixture of twin and single turrets on the beam, and again the Japanese ordered something similar, with four 12-in and 12 10-in guns.

The race to produce a bigger secondary battery might have gone on unchecked had a practical objection not suddenly raised its head. At 7000 yards or more shell-splashes from 8-in, 9.2-in or 10-in shells looked very like 12-in shell-splashes. This meant that the gun layers could not distinguish the fall of shot of individual guns, and so could not correct their aim. The only way to minimize this difficulty was to arm ships with a uniform armament of a single calibre, devoting the weight saved on smaller guns to a larger number of 12-in guns. The logic of this was inescapable, and the Americans took the plunge first in 1903 when they designed the *Michigan* and *South Carolina* with four 12-in turrets, two forward and two aft. Even more significant was the fact that the intermediate guns were replaced entirely by 3-in guns, suitable only for

defence against torpedo boats. The Japanese came to the same conclusion during the war against Russia, and drew up plans for two ships armed with 12 12-in guns. The British might have been left standing by these developments, but they turned the tables by using their vastly superior shipbuilding resources. In secret they produced a design for a new, fast ship with five twin 12-in gun turrets to outmatch anything afloat.

12-in Gun Turret, 1899
The British battleships *Albion* and *Glory* introduced a new type of hydraulic turret mounting 12-in guns. They had all-round loading, speeding up the rate of fire. With only minor refinements this design of turret was retained until 1945

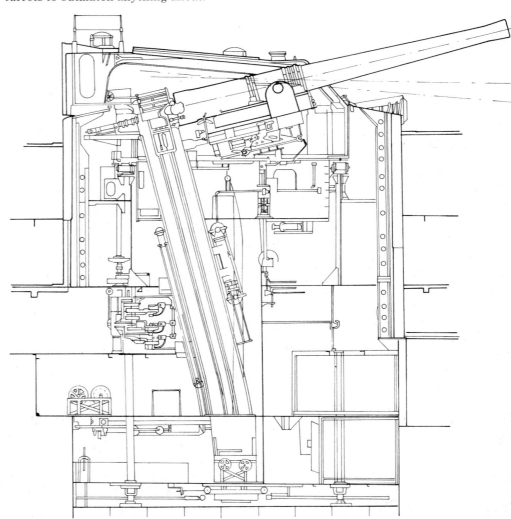

DREADNOUGHT

The new First Sea Lord, Sir John Fisher, immediately grasped the potential of the design, to be called HMS *Dreadnought*, but his motives for doing so were different from the intentions of her designers. Fisher had very little grasp of such matters as long-range gunnery, and his main concern was to modernize and enlarge the Royal Navy to meet what he saw as the threat from the rapidly expanding German Fleet. To achieve this overhaul of *matériel* Fisher knew that he had to make great economies in some directions, for the British taxpayer was in no mood to sanction vast expenditure on the Navy.

What attracted Fisher about the *Dreadnought*'s design was simply economy. Her four-shaft Parsons steam turbines, the first to be installed in a major warship, were cheaper to run and easier to maintain. They also dispensed with secondary and tertiary batteries, thereby saving the problem of maintaining the armament. The fact that the gunnery branch also valued the arrangement of heavy guns for long-range gunnery does not appear to have entered into

Fisher's head, and he valued her simply on the basis that 30 *Dreadnoughts* could be run at the same annual cost of 29 of the preceding *Lord Nelson* Class.

Fisher's demonic energy was harnessed to the building of this monster, for he wanted to astound the world and give Britain a lead over her rivals: the French, Russians, Germans and Americans. The major delay would be caused by the lack of gun turrets, which took at least 2½ years to assemble. Fisher immediately sanctioned the diversion of the four turrets already earmarked for the *Lord Nelson* and *Agamemnon*, and by such shortcuts Portsmouth Dockyard was able to beat its own record set up when the *Majestic* was built in 22 months. On 2 October, 1905 the keel was laid, and with much material already stockpiled it was only four months later, on 10 February, 1906, that she slid down the launching way. To the consternation of Britain's rivals HMS *Dreadnought*'s completion was announced on 3 October, 1906, 366 days after her keel-laying. In fact this was a typical piece of Fisher bombast; the ship

moved for the first time on that day, but was in no sense complete for another two months. Nevertheless, the building of the *Dreadnought* in only 14 months is a record which has never been beaten.

The *Dreadnought* gave her name to a whole generation of battleships, and today the term is still used loosely to describe any big battleship. She was a complete break with previous ships in every way, with her starkly simple superstructure, massive tripod mast between two funnels, and hull devoid of small guns. But even more remarkable was the vindication of the decision to engine her with Parsons turbines. Not only was she three knots faster than her contemporaries, but her turbines gave virtually no trouble. Gone were the days when the engine-room of a battleship was a 'cross between an inferno and a snipe-marsh', with massive pistons and connecting rods and a shroud of leaking steam. There was little or no mercantile experience to guide the Royal Navy's Engineer-in-Chief in this audacious experiment, for the first large turbine-driven passenger liner was not

Although the advent of the Dreadnought *rendered the vast predominance of the Royal Navy's battleship strength obsolete at a stroke, British shipyards were in a commanding position to compete in the new naval race. The next three battleships were virtually repeats of* Dreadnought. *The Hercules class (below) were, however, the first to break away from the original disposition of turrets, with the midships armament staggered to give a big-gun broadside*

HMS Invincible, *prototype of the battle-cruiser idea. The combination of speed and heavy armament was bought at the expense of armour, and in action the battle-cruiser concept was to prove very vulnerable*

completed until 1907, and any one of a number of minor faults could have condemned the *Dreadnought* to failure. Another point in her favour was that she achieved her massive increase in speed without any sacrifice of armour; her 11-in belt of armour was equal to that of any of her contemporaries.

The drawback to the *Dreadnought* was her cost, but Fisher solved this problem by reducing the enormous number of old ships of all sizes which had swollen the Navy List, partly because of the reassuring effect that numbers had on Parliament and the press when the time came to prepare returns of numerical strength. Fisher condemned hundreds of ships to be scrapped, on the grounds that they were 'too weak to fight and too slow to run away', but he also tried to get rid of cruisers, because he convinced himself that the future lay with the destroyer, the submarine and the fast battleship. Undoubtedly there were too many obsolescent small warships around the world, and Fisher's reorganization of the Reserve Fleet produced a smaller, cheaper and much more effective battle fleet, but it was not long before the Navy found itself desperately short of minor warships, and had to reprieve some of Fisher's victims. But Fisher reinforced the public's tendency

HMS Dreadnought, *the ship which gave her name to a whole new kind of warship*

to see naval strength as a matter of numbers only, a fault which was dutifully copied by the politicians and the press. Henceforth all naval issues tended to boil down to numbers of 'dreadnoughts', with the older ships dismissed as useless.

Fisher disliked cruisers, as we have seen, and just after the *Dreadnought* was laid down he ordered a '*Dreadnought* armoured cruiser' to render the existing large cruiser obsolete. This was a ship of approximately the same tonnage as the *Dreadnought* but designed to steam at $25\frac{1}{2}$ knots, with thinner armour and only four twin 12-in turrets to allow the horsepower to be doubled. Known later as the 'battleship cruiser' and then the battle-cruiser, the new *Invincible* proved even more successful than the *Dreadnought*. Her purpose was to hunt down armoured cruisers on the trade routes and to replace them as scouting units for the main battle fleet. The idea was that they could shoulder aside the cruisers which tried to bar their way, and as they were armed with 12-in guns they could only be safely chased away by battleships. Like other creations of the fertile Fisher brain the idea had not been worked out to its logical conclusion. The battle-cruiser idea was quite reasonable so long as the enemy fleet did not possess its own battle-cruisers.

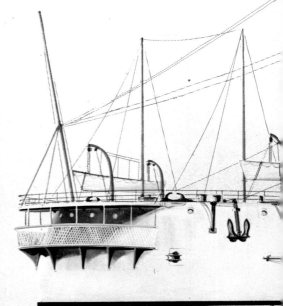

At the high tide of the Royal Navy's world-wide command of the seas, Admiral Sir John Fisher portrayed in the sea-cabin on board HMS Renown, in 1899. Already the Germans were stirring, beginning to challenge British supremacy at sea

Brazil's second battleship, São Paulo, *on trials in 1910. Unlike* Dreadnought, *she had superimposed end turrets*

São Paulo

This ship and her sister, closely resembling the *Dreadnought* but more heavily armed, ensured Brazilian naval supremacy over neighbouring Chile and Argentina

Displacement: 21,200 tons full load *Length:* 530 ft *Armament:* 12 × 12-in, 22 × 4·7-in, 8 × 3-pdr *Armour:* 4/9-in belt, 8/12-in turrets, 2¼-in deck *Max speed:* 21 knots

Minas Geraes class

Name	Completed	Fate
Minas Geraes	Jan 1910	Scrapped 1954
São Paulo	Jul 1910	Sank in North Atlantic 1951

Petty Officer's cap badge, Imperial German Navy

BIRTH OF THE HIGH SEAS FLEET

If Fisher hoped to frighten the Germans out of naval rivalry he was badly mistaken. The advent of the *Dreadnought* and particularly the rapidity of her building did take the German Navy by surprise, and all battleship construction was suspended to give the *Marineamt* a chance to work out its reply. The Kiel Canal would have to be deepened and locks widened if similar ships were to be built, and this vast programme was immediately sanctioned; the German Navy relied on the canal to move squadrons from the Baltic to the North Sea, and regarded it in much the same way as the American Navy does the Panama Canal. The *Nassau* class was not started until the summer of 1907, by which time six improved *Dreadnoughts* had been started in England. The *Nassaus* were inferior to the *Dreadnought* in many ways; they did not have turbines for the simple reason that the only firm capable of making turbines was building a set for the first German battle-cruiser, and although they had a cumbersome arrangement of six twin 11-in guns they could only fire four of them on the beam, giving them less gunpower than the British ship. However, in one respect the *Nassaus*

Admiral von Tirpitz, force behind the German Navy

were better: their armour was better distributed and their underwater protection against torpedoes was superior.

The German prototype battle-cruiser *Von der Tann* was a worthy opponent of the *Invincible*, with eight 11-in guns, slightly less speed but heavier armour. As soon as she appeared the rationale of the battle-cruiser idea disappeared, but Fisher was not easily persuaded that his toys had been superseded, and three more were ordered, two to be paid for by Australia and New Zealand. Now the dreadnought race was on between Germany and Great Britain, and each year more ships were laid down. Whenever the diplomats of both countries tried to negotiate a reduction of the tempo they were answered by arguments about national survival. Germany feared British 'encirclement', but above all the Navy Laws were an obstacle to any political understanding. Tirpitz had asked for long-term legislation to prevent any future government from cancelling or trimming his programmes, but this had a disastrous political side-effect; any suggestion from the Wilhelmstrasse about reductions of naval armaments was rejected on the

SMS Von der Tann, *the German reply to the British* Invincible *class battle-cruisers. Fisher's bluff had been called and the German ships had lighter armament, devoting the weight saved to a heavier scheme of protection. At Jutland the British battle-cruisers proved fatally vulnerable*

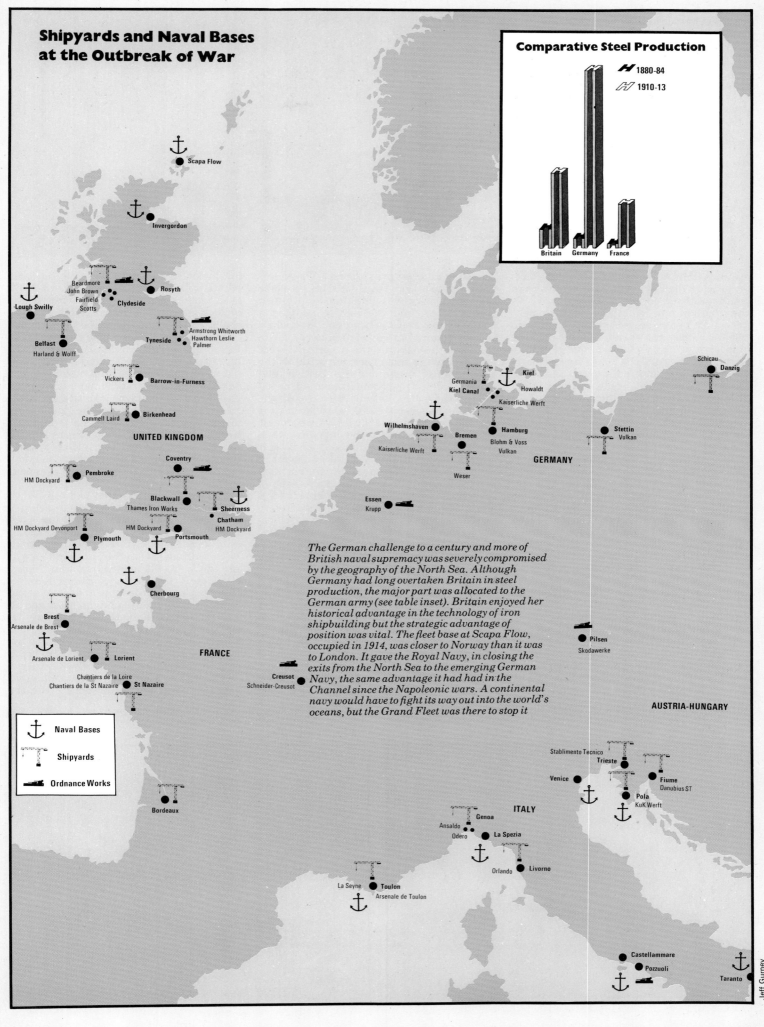

Shipyards and Naval Bases at the Outbreak of War

Comparative Steel Production

- 1880-84
- 1910-13

Britain Germany France

Scapa Flow

Invergordon

Beardmore
John Brown
Fairfield
Scotts
Clydeside
Rosyth

Lough Swilly

Belfast
Harland & Wolff

Armstrong Whitworth
Hawthorn Leslie
Palmer
Tyneside

Vickers
Barrow-in-Furness

Cammell Laird
Birkenhead

UNITED KINGDOM

Coventry

HM Dockyard
Pembroke

Blackwall
Thames Iron Works
Sheerness
Chatham
HM Dockyard

HM Dockyard Devonport
HM Dockyard
Portsmouth

Plymouth

Cherbourg

Brest
Arsenale de Brest

Arsenale de Lorient
Lorient

FRANCE

Chantiers de la Loire
Chantiers de la St Nazaire
St Nazaire

Creusot
Schneider-Creusot

Bordeaux

La Seyne
Toulon
Arsenale de Toulon

Kiel
Germania
Kiel Canal
Howaldt
Kaiserliche Werft

Wilhelmshaven
Bremen
Hamburg
Kaiserliche Werft
Blohm & Voss
Vulkan
GERMANY
Weser

Essen
Krupp

Schicau
Danzig

Stettin
Vulkan

Pilsen
Skodawerke

AUSTRIA-HUNGARY

Stablimento Tecnico
Trieste
Venice
Fiume
Danubius ST
Pola
KuK Werft

ITALY

Ansaldo
Genoa
Odero
La Spezia

Orlando
Livorno

Castellammare
Pozzuoli

Taranto

The German challenge to a century and more of British naval supremacy was severely compromised by the geography of the North Sea. Although Germany had long overtaken Britain in steel production, the major part was allocated to the German army (see table inset). Britain enjoyed her historical advantage in the technology of iron shipbuilding but the strategic advantage of position was vital. The fleet base at Scapa Flow, occupied in 1914, was closer to Norway than it was to London. It gave the Royal Navy, in closing the exits from the North Sea to the emerging German Navy, the same advantage it had had in the Channel since the Napoleonic wars. A continental navy would have to fight its way out into the world's oceans, but the Grand Fleet was there to stop it

Legend:
- ⚓ Naval Bases
- Shipyards
- Ordnance Works

Jeff Gurney

Andrei Pervozvanni
This battleship and her sister were the pride of
Russia's Baltic Fleet in 1914, but the only action
they saw was in the Civil War. Armour was
used over the complete hull as a result of
experience in the Battle of Tsushima
Displacement: 18,580 tons full load *Length:*
138 m *Armament:* 4 × 305-mm, 14 × 203-mm,
12 × 120-mm, 4 × 47-mm, 8 × mg, 3 × 450-mm
torpedo tubes *Armour:* 90/215-mm belt, 200-mm
main turrets, 32/57-mm decks *Max speed:* 18 knots

Imperator Pavel I class

Name	Completed	Fate
Imperator Pavel I	Sep 1910	Scrapped 1922
Andrei Pervozvanni	Aug 1910	Scrapped 1922

grounds that the size and building programme of the navy was fixed by law, and
could not therefore be set aside. From 1906
the British had a Liberal Government
dedicated to retrenchment on defence to
release money for social reform, and the
climate was ripe for some sort of Anglo-
German understanding, but again and again
the diplomats and politicians failed to
reach a compromise. The world was going
through an extraordinary upsurge of violent
nationalism, and the German and British
newspapers echoed jingoistic demands for
stronger armaments. Dreadnought battleships were the visible embodiment of sea
power, and as they also provided employment in shipyards there was an understandable reluctance to make the first cut.

The turning point came in 1908, when
Tirpitz used a loophole in the Navy Law to
increase the strength of the German Fleet.
The original law had allowed for the building of eight *Grosse Kreuzer*, the original
armoured cruisers now made redundant by
the battle-cruiser, and Tirpitz simply referred to his future battle-cruisers as 'large
cruisers' and added them to the programme.
The battle-cruiser, although she was still
known as a dreadnought armoured cruiser,
was widely regarded as the equivalent of a
battleship, and Tirpitz had in effect added
eight battleships to the future strength of
his fleet. The British saw this as chicanery,
and even the Liberal Government had to
bow to pressure for an expansion of the

British building programme. Thereafter
until August 1914 there was no pretence
that each navy was building for its own
requirements, and the British adopted a
policy of 'two keels to one', doubling whatever figure the Germans announced.

Across the Atlantic the Americans were
also expanding their fleet, but without the
same frantic haste as the British and
Germans. The French and Russians dropped
out of the race, largely because of the
enormous expense involved, and did not start
to build dreadnoughts until 1911. Economic
reality caught up with the Japanese when
the post-war boom collapsed, and their
dreadnought-building was slowed down. The
Americans had considerable trouble with
turbines, and took the remarkable step of
reverting to reciprocating machinery for a
while in order to force the machinery
suppliers to accept General Board specifications. In 1911 the battleships *Nevada* and
Oklahoma were designed to radically new
principles, making them the most revolutionary since the *Dreadnought*.

Zone of Immunity

Unfettered by the need to match a rival
programme, the Americans sat down to
work out theoretically the best way to
protect battleships against long-range gunfire. They discarded the medium armour
used in contemporaries against lighter
shells, and concentrated on keeping out
large shells at 10,000 yards or more. This

led them to the discovery of the 'zone of
immunity', ranges between which heavy
shell cannot penetrate either side armour
or deck armour. As the range increases the
shells tend to plunge more and so the number
of hits on deck armour tends to rise. What
had been learned at Tsushima was that
light armour tended to burst shells, with
the result that splinters did nearly as much
damage; on the other hand, unarmoured
structures were unlikely to trigger off the
relatively insensitive fuze of an armour-
piercing shell, and so shells would pass
through without bursting. From this the
US Navy formulated the 'all or nothing'
theory of armouring, that armour should be
put on the deck or on the side, at maximum
thickness or not at all.

The ship which resulted had some of the
classic simplicity of the *Dreadnought* or
even the old *Devastation*, with her single
massive funnel, minimal superstructure and
lofty 'cage' masts, all in a balanced profile.
With twin and triple 14-in turrets forward
and aft and 13½-in armour, the *Nevada*
class were the most powerful warships in
the world when designed, and had they
appeared sooner they might have had the
reputation that they deserve. Part of their
success was due to the adoption of oil fuel,
which saved a great deal of weight, and part
was due to the reduction of weight by
concentrating ten guns in only four turrets.

As British and German dreadnoughts
appeared each year it became clear that

The Austro-Hungarian battleship Radetzky *and her two sisters were
completed in 1910–11. They had a heavy secondary battery, typical of the later
intermediate dreadnoughts*

Had the USS Michigan *(below) and her sister the* South Carolina *been
completed earlier they would have beaten* Dreadnought *into service as the
first all big-gun ships*

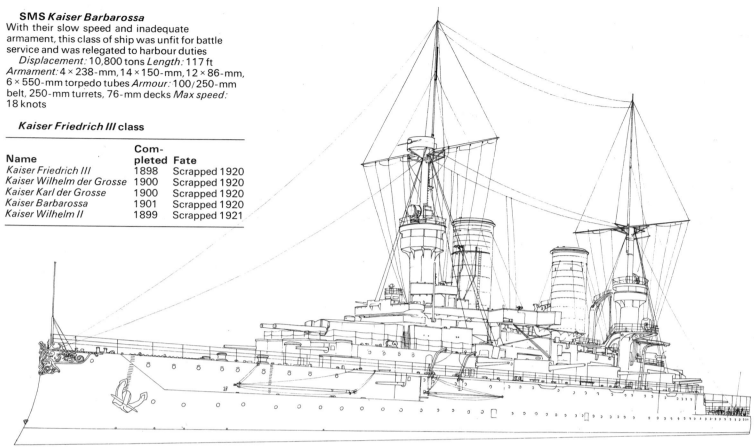

British and German designers were pursuing different objectives. The Germans
emphasized protection, preferring to retain
the 11-in gun for as long as possible to
save weight for armour, whereas British
designers emphasized gunpower at the
expense of armour. Thus the 12-in gun gave
way in 1910 to the 13.5-in gun in HMS *Orion*,
whereas the Germans only reluctantly
adopted a 12-in gun in the *Helgoland* class
in 1909. This divergence was much criticised
by British observers, and has been blamed
on Fisher's unhappy influence over design,
but looked at dispassionately it can be seen
as the logical outcome of British strategic
aims. The British wanted a quick decisive
victory over the German Fleet if war should
come, a clear-cut victory along the lines of
Tsushima or even Trafalgar, whereas the
Germans, whatever their propagandists
might boast, intended to survive by avoiding
just that sort of battle. Their strategy was
to use torpedo craft, submarines and mines
to whittle down the British margin of
superiority, and use the surface fleet only
to cut off and destroy isolated portions of
the British fleet. Therefore the British had
to emphasize speed and gunpower, to bring
the enemy to battle and to sink him, while
the Germans had to concentrate on defensive characteristics if they were to survive
the heavier shells likely to be fired at their

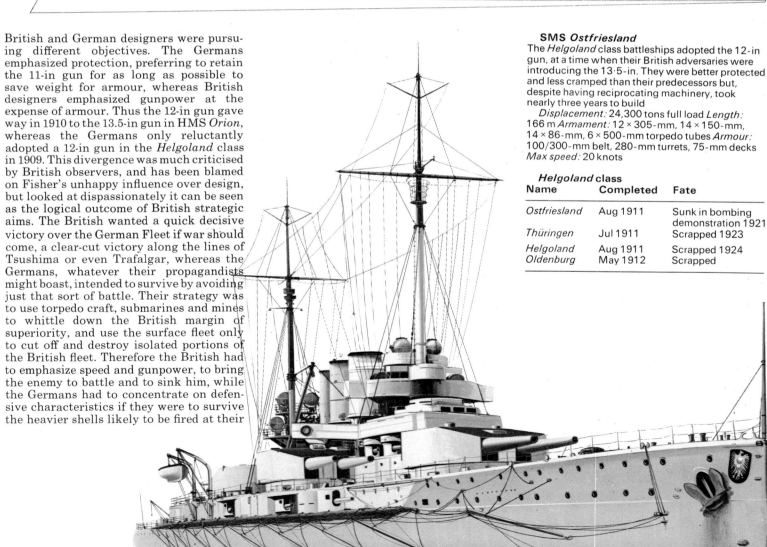

ships. For this reason a straight comparison between British and German designs is not easy, and a mere comparison of dimensions and armour thicknesses is misleading. Other factors are also important; for example, German battleships tended to cost more and used less standard equipment.

When Fisher left the Admiralty in 1911 he took many of his obscurantist opinions about ship design with him, and British battleships improved noticeably in consequence. In 1912 work started on a class which more than wiped out the disparity between British and German designs. This was the famous *Queen Elizabeth* class, which were the first British battleships to adopt all-oil fuel, for the same reason as the American *Nevadas*. But there was more to the *Queen Elizabeths*. Alarmed by news about the Americans and the Japanese arming new ships with 14-in guns, the Admiralty decided to give itself a comfortable margin for some years by making a big jump from the fairly new 13.5-in gun to a 15-in 42-calibre weapon. What sounds like a small increase in shell diameter resulted in a very large increase in shell weight: whereas the 12-in shell weighed 850 lb, the 13.5-in weighed 1400 lb and the 15-in jumped to 1920 lb. Another virtue of the new gun was its low muzzle velocity. The British were the first to appreciate that too much muzzle velocity was actually detrimental to long-range gunnery; although the shell travelled further it 'wobbled' more in flight. The 13.5-in shell had been increased from 1250 lb to 1400 lb and was greatly improved as a result, and this characteristic was built into the 15-in as well. Another reason for the phenomenal accuracy of the 15-in was

the phenomenal accuracy of the 15-in was that improved manufacture of steel produced bigger forgings, which gave greater rigidity to the barrel. To make everybody even happier lower muzzle velocities produced less wear on the barrel-liner.

Fast Division
The greatly increased power of the 15-in gun made another innovation possible. Tacticians were hankering after a breakaway from rigid line-of-battle tactics, and the idea of a 'Fast Division' of battleships was mooted. This was in complete contrast to the battle-cruiser concept, and called for ships with a four-knot advantage over existing ships, but with full armour protection. The fundamental weakness of the battle-cruiser, as the more perceptive observers could see, was that it really dared not spend too long in action against a battleship. There were those who might be called the 'whizz-kids' of naval tactics, like Fisher and some of the less cautious admirals, who convinced themselves that speed was protection in itself and that battle-cruisers could be used as fast battleships. But the fact that the Fast Division was proposed as early as 1911 shows that someone in the Admiralty had spotted the flaws in their

France
The last ship in the *Courbet* class, which were the first French Dreadnoughts. The long building time, three years, resulted in the ships being outclassed by the time they entered service
Displacement: 25,850 tons full load *Length:* 165 m *Armament:* 12 × 305-mm, 22 × 138-mm, 4 × 47-mm, 4 × 450-mm torpedo tubes
Armour: 270-mm, 230-mm turrets, 70-mm main deck *Max speed:* 21 knots

Courbet class

Name	Completed	Fate
Jean Bart	Jun 1913	Scrapped 1945
Courbet	Sep 1913	Used as breakwater, Normandy, June 1944
Paris	Aug 1914	Scrapped 1956
France	Jul 1914	Sank in Quiberon Bay, 1922

argument. The introduction of the 15-in gun made a true fast battleship feasible for the first time, for by dropping the fifth turret room could be found for double the horsepower. As in the *Nevada* design the use of oil fuel meant that the weight formerly taken up by coal could be devoted to armour, and space could be saved on stokers' messdecks, etc. Also the greater thermal efficiency of oil meant that the higher horsepower could be achieved economically.

To change the whole of the British Battle Fleet from coal to oil was, in Churchill's words, 'to take arms against a sea of troubles'. Coal of the highest quality was available in the British Isles, whereas oil had to be imported from far-off countries. But in the tactical field there could be no doubt of the advantages: ships could refuel in a quarter of the time and so be ready for action faster, and full speed could be maintained for a longer time. Tactical considerations triumphed and the Admiralty immediately bought a large shareholding in Iranian oilfields to ensure a plentiful supply of crude oil. There were many critics of the change to oil, but the main objection, that coal provided a defence against torpedoes, was invalid, since the equivalent weight of coal could be easily spared for armour which would do more good.

The 15-in was ordered in great secrecy as the '14-in Experimental' in 1912, and at first there were grave doubts about the wisdom of ordering a whole class of ships before their armament had been proved. Should the new ships not be armed with 13.5-in guns in case the 15-in was a failure? The Admiralty Board and the Director of Naval Ordnance were assured by the manufacturers, Armstrong, Whitworth of Elswick, Newcastle-on-Tyne, that they had such faith in the new gun and its mounting that they would guarantee that it would meet its specification. To insure against accidents and to reassure the Admiralty one gun was to be advanced and put through a series of tests, but in due course Armstrongs' confidence was completely justified. The *Queen Elizabeth* was ready just after the outbreak of war in August 1914, and a total of nine other 15-in-gunned ships were under construction or completing at the same time.

When war broke out between Germany and her allies and Great Britain, Russia and France the line-up showed how rapidly the major nations had been building battleships. (See tables pp 45, 46, 47.)

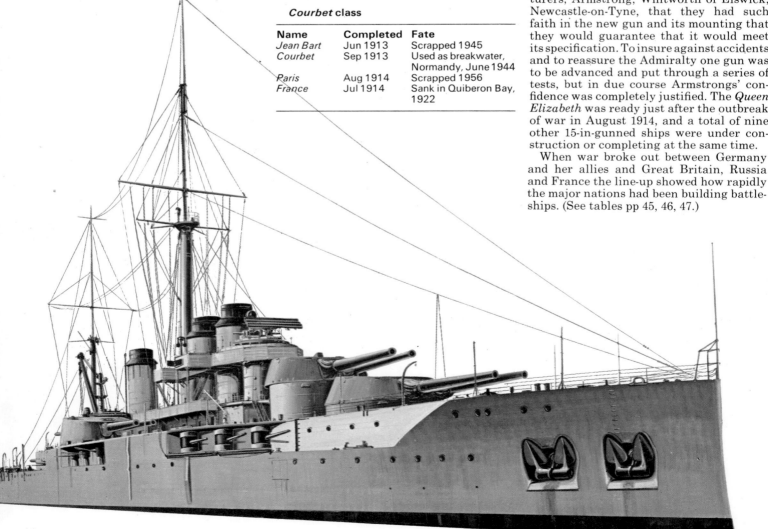

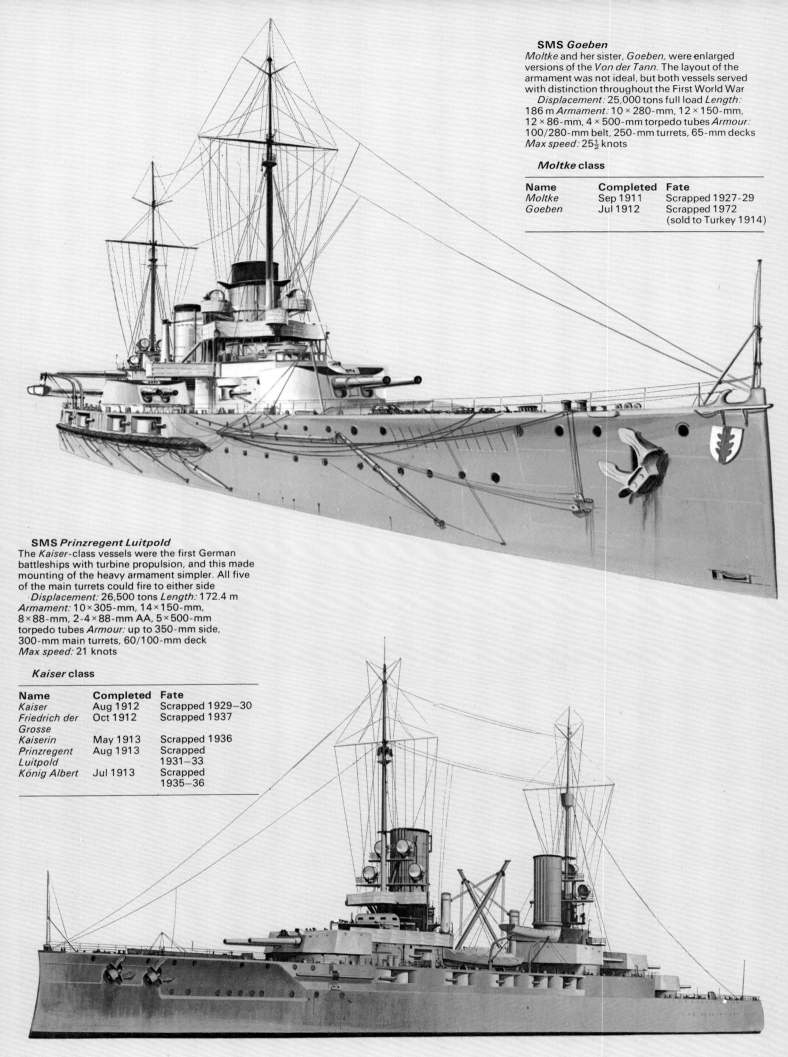

SMS Goeben
Moltke and her sister, *Goeben,* were enlarged versions of the *Von der Tann.* The layout of the armament was not ideal, but both vessels served with distinction throughout the First World War
    Displacement: 25,000 tons full load *Length:* 186 m *Armament:* 10 × 280-mm, 12 × 150-mm, 12 × 86-mm, 4 × 500-mm torpedo tubes *Armour:* 100/280-mm belt, 250-mm turrets, 65-mm decks
Max speed: 25½ knots

Moltke class

Name	Completed	Fate
Moltke	Sep 1911	Scrapped 1927-29
Goeben	Jul 1912	Scrapped 1972 (sold to Turkey 1914)

SMS *Prinzregent Luitpold*
The *Kaiser*-class vessels were the first German battleships with turbine propulsion, and this made mounting of the heavy armament simpler. All five of the main turrets could fire to either side
    Displacement: 26,500 tons *Length:* 172.4 m *Armament:* 10×305-mm, 14×150-mm, 8×88-mm, 2-4×88-mm AA, 5×500-mm torpedo tubes *Armour:* up to 350-mm side, 300-mm main turrets, 60/100-mm deck
Max speed: 21 knots

Kaiser class

Name	Completed	Fate
Kaiser	Aug 1912	Scrapped 1929–30
Friedrich der Grosse	Oct 1912	Scrapped 1937
Kaiserin	May 1913	Scrapped 1936
Prinzregent Luitpold	Aug 1913	Scrapped 1931–33
König Albert	Jul 1913	Scrapped 1935–36

The battleship had changed beyond recognition since the turn of the century. Average displacement had jumped from 15,000 tons to 28,000 tons, and speed from 18 knots to 28. As we have seen, gunpower was not overwhelming, with armaments of eight to twelve guns, and gunnery practices at 10,000 yards were normal. Both British and Germans regarded this as the range at which future battles would be fought; attempts at firing at greater ranges produced such poor results that the idea of ultra-long-range gunnery was dismissed as a mere waste of ammunition. The British, under the direction of Percy Scott, introduced a new system known as director-firing for controlling fire at long range. This meant in essence that a single master-sight mounted as high up in the ship as possible (usually on a masthead platform) calculated the range and bearing, and from there the guns were fired electrically. In 1912 HMS *Thunderer* was fitted with the first director, and beat the previous top gunnery ship of the Home Fleet. The Germans preferred the 'follow-the-pointer' system, in which individual gunlayers still fired their guns according to range and bearing information shown on a pointer in the turret, relayed from a master-sight abaft the forebridge.

Although the German fire-control system was generally inferior to the British it was greatly superior in one important respect. In place of the 9-ft incidence-type range-finder used in British dreadnoughts, German ships were given 20-ft or 27-ft Zeiss stereoscopic range-finders. The British range-finders were capable of producing reliable ranges at 10,000 yards or under, but they took time to find longer ranges, whereas the longer-base Zeiss instruments picked up all ranges quickly. The British became aware of the limitations of their range-finders but only the new *Queen Elizabeth* class had a better 15-ft model suitable for longer ranges. On the other hand the British range-finders performed well under stress, whereas the Zeiss range-finders were hard to operate when the range-taker was put off by such distractions as damage to his own ship, gun-blast, etc, and so British shooting tended to get better in battle, while German shooting started well but fell in action.

The German dreadnought SMS Friedrich der Grosse *entering Copenhagen in 1913. Completed in 1912, she was commissioned immediately as the flagship of the High Seas Fleet which she remained until March 1917. The guard of honour is presenting arms on the quarterdeck, sailors raise their caps in salute, and the fore and after bridges are lined with saluting officers*

Battleships and Battle-cruisers in Service: 1914

Germany

Great Britain

8 coast defence ships completed 1890-96

23 pre-dreadnoughts completed 1893-1908*

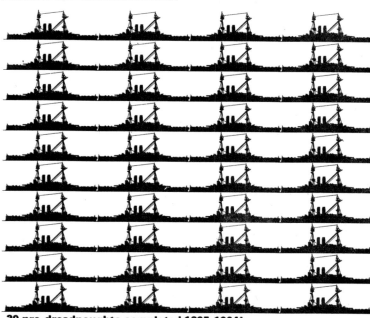

30 pre-dreadnoughts completed 1895-1904*
10 'intermediate dreadnoughts' completed 1902-08

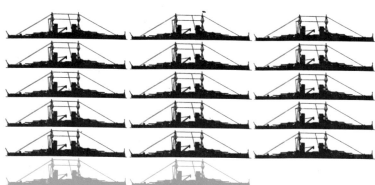

4 dreadnoughts armed with 11-in guns, completed 1909-10
11 dreadnoughts armed with 12-in guns, completed 1911-14†

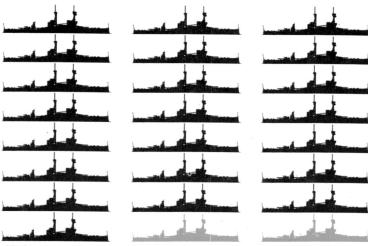

10 dreadnoughts armed with 12-in guns, completed 1906-11
12 dreadnoughts armed with 13·5-in guns, completed 1912-14

4 battle-cruisers armed with 11-in guns, completed 1910-13

*Two ships sold to Turkey 1911
†Two more ships nearing completion, and the
 battle-cruiser SMS *Derfflinger* (12-in guns)

Completed

Under Construction

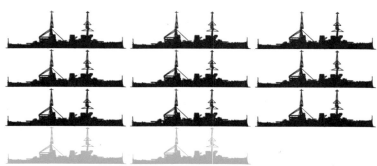

6 battle-cruisers armed with 12-in guns, completed 1908-12
3 battle-cruisers armed with 13·5-in guns, completed 1912-13†

*HMS *Montagu* lost 1906, two bought from Chile 1904
†A fourth ship, HMS *Tiger* was nearly complete. Additional ships were HMS
 Queen Elizabeth (15-in guns) nearly complete and two Turkish dreadnoughts
 which were seized after the declaration of war: HMS *Erin* (13·5-in guns) and
 HMS *Agincourt* (12-in guns)

Jeff Gurney

47

THE BATTLESHIPS' GREAT WAR

By a stroke of luck the entire Royal Navy in home waters had been mobilized in July 1914 for a giant fleet manoeuvre to test the mobilization plans. Thus when the news from Sarajevo set Europe on the road to war the Admiralty was able to delay the de-mobilization and ensure that the Fleet was at its war station before the ultimatum to Germany expired at midnight on 4 August. The dominant fear had been of a surprise attack by German torpedo craft, but in fact the German High Seas Fleet had not planned such an operation and indeed was not fully mobilized for some weeks. The British fleet, now known as the Grand Fleet in honour of the name given to the fleet gathered to fight the Spanish Armada in 1588, steamed in majestic lines out of Spithead and simply vanished from sight. Its chosen base was top secret: the desolate anchorage of Scapa Flow in the Orkney Islands. From here the Fleet was well placed to block the exit routes from the North Sea to the Atlantic, for Scapa Flow is nearer to Norway than to London. The old battleships were stationed in the Channel in case the High Seas Fleet should try to attack the shipping carrying troops to France.

The Germans, too, mustered their battle-ships at Kiel and Wilhelmshaven. Like the British, they expected action within hours, but apart from skirmishes between light forces the North Sea remained quiet. It was the battle-cruisers which saw action, first at the Battle of the Heligoland Bight on 28 August, when the British sent three battle-cruisers into the Bight to rescue their light forces from defeat. The risks were higher, but the gamble paid off and three German cruisers were sunk by the guns of HMS *Lion* and her sisters. What the Germans had banked on was a close blockade by the Grand Fleet, with dreadnoughts lying off German ports to enforce the blockade, just as the British Fleet had done against the French a hundred years before. But the British had dropped all ideas of a close blockade by 1913 and were content to guard the exits to the North Sea and leave the business of day-to-day contesting of the North Sea and Channel waters to light cruisers and destroyers.

In the Mediterranean the French Fleet was following a similar policy of penning the Austro-Hungarian battle fleet in the Adriatic, but there had been one bad mis-calculation. The British allowed the only German capital ship on an overseas station, the battle-cruiser *Goeben*, to escape from them. She offered herself for internment in Turkey, which promptly 'purchased' the ship and her entire crew, and joined the Central Alliance. The result was that the British and French could no longer hope to use the Dardanelles to get supplies to their Russian allies in the Black Sea without first forcing the Straits. It was a triumph of German diplomacy which was to cause untold suffering before long.

Battle-cruisers showed their qualities again in December. When the news came through in November 1914 that a squadron of German cruisers had annihilated a British cruiser squadron off Coronel on the coast of Chile, Lord Fisher sent two battle-cruisers to the South Atlantic to avenge them. The *Invincible* and *Inflexible* arrived at the Falkland Islands just 24 hours before the German cruisers under Admiral Spee arrived to capture the coaling station. This was the battle the *Invincibles* had been designed to fight, and they did it magnificently, running down their quarry in a long stern-chase and sinking them with relative impunity at a range of about 12,500 yards. Only one small German cruiser escaped the slaughter, to be hunted down later, and the battle-cruisers' victory was no less welcome because it wiped out the bitter memory of the disaster at Coronel and cleared the oceans of the last German commerce raiders.

The German battle-cruisers under Admiral Hipper were used in a series of raids on the east coast of England, firing shells at what were believed to be fortified towns, such as Scarborough. The purpose was to distract the Grand Fleet from its watch, and to lure a small part of it into battle on favourable terms. There were several near-misses, and on one occasion the High Seas Fleet nearly ran into a single squadron of four battleships, but the only practical result of the raids was that public alarm forced the Admiralty to move the battle-cruiser force south from Scapa Flow to Rosyth, on the Firth of Forth. From here they were better placed to intercept raids, although poorly placed to stop a break-out into the Atlantic. The new disposition paid off on 24 January, 1915 when Admiral Beatty, with five battle-cruisers under his command, met the German First Scouting Group under Admiral Hipper, comprising three battle-cruisers and a large cruiser.

The Battle of the Dogger Bank was dis-appointing for the British, for, although they had the advantage of numbers, speed and gunpower over the Germans, and although they managed to sink the slow armoured cruiser *Blücher*, a series of signalling errors allowed Hipper to escape virtually unscathed. The battle showed

The Iron Duke *arrives at Scapa Flow on the outbreak of war. This desolate anchorage in the Orkneys had been designated as fleet base some years before but had been kept secret*

Battleships and Battle-cruisers: 1914

France

2 coast defence ships armed with 10·8-in guns, completed 1885-1902

17 pre-dreadnoughts armed with 12-in guns, completed 1896-1911*

4 dreadnoughts armed with 12-in guns, completed 1913-14
*Two ships lost by explosion 1906-11

United States

8 pre-dreadnoughts armed with 13-in guns, completed 1895-1901
15 pre-dreadnoughts armed with 12-in guns, completed 1897-1908*

8 dreadnoughts armed with 12-in guns, completed 1910-12
2 dreadnoughts armed with 14-in guns, completed 1914
*Two ships sold to Greece 1914

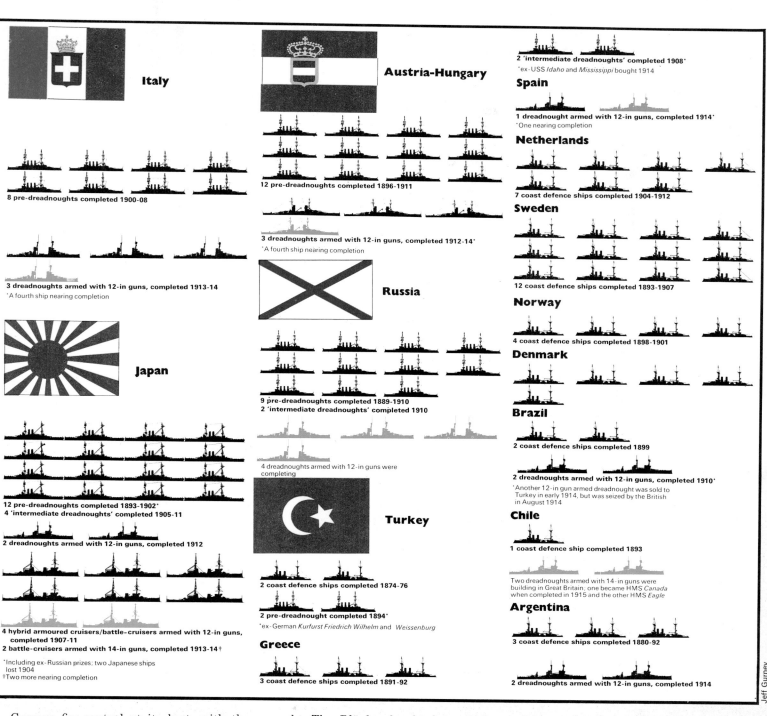

German fire-control at its best, with the British flagship HMS *Lion* hit by two shells from the *Derfflinger* and crippled by flooding; by comparison the British shooting was patchy, the *Tiger* not scoring a single hit. But British shells caused a disastrous fire in the after turrets of the *Seydlitz*, and burning killed nearly 200 men. Then a series of imprecise signals from Beatty was misinterpreted, and the remaining British battle-cruisers turned away from the fleeing Germans and concentrated on the slowest ship, the *Blücher*. By the time the mistake was sorted out (Beatty had been forced to shift his flag to a destroyer in a frantic attempt to catch up with his squadron) Hipper's ships were too far away to be caught. The *Blücher* fought doggedly but could not hope to survive the rain of hits, and capsized.

For the Germans the Dogger Bank had some disquieting lessons. The fire which burnt out the after turrets of the *Seydlitz* showed that too many cordite charges had been stored in the turrets for safety, but it did prove that German cordite was extremely stable. The British, whose cordite was less stable due to a relatively minor fault in the manufacturing process, knew nothing of the near-escape of the *Seydlitz*, and remained happily unaware of the fact that their own cordite might flash off instead of merely burning, as it was meant to do.

The Grand Fleet led by HMS Iron Duke *on manoeuvres just before the outbreak of war*

JUTLAND

Kaiser *class battleship fires her full broadside armament of eight 12-in guns*

The appointment of *Vizeadmiral* Scheer to the command of the High Seas Fleet in February 1916 brought a new offensive spirit to German fleet operations. For the next sortie he planned to use Hipper's battle-cruisers boldly to lure part of the Grand Fleet into a trap. He first sent out U-Boats to mine the routes likely to be followed by the British battle squadrons coming out of Scapa Flow and Rosyth, and then on 30 May took the entire High Seas Fleet to sea from the Jade River. Only one flaw marred the plan. Since 1914 the Admiralty had been reading a large number of German naval messages, and it was correctly deduced in London that the High Seas Fleet was putting to sea. The British followed Scheer's plan in essence, sending the battle-cruisers out from Rosyth separately to scout off the Skagerrak, where they would eventually be joined by the Grand Fleet coming south from Scapa Flow. Purely by chance the C-in-C Grand Fleet, Admiral Sir John Jellicoe, had chosen the

area in which Hipper's battle-cruisers would be operating, and the long-awaited main fleet action was imminent. Beatty's battle-cruisers by chance included four of the fast *Queen Elizabeth* class battleships, as three 12-in gunned battle-cruisers had been detached to Scapa Flow to practise their gunnery.

Even though fate had put the two rival battle-cruiser groups in the same area they

still met by chance on 31 May, when both sides' light forces turned to investigate a Danish steamer. The big ships sighted one another at a range of 14 miles (over 24,000 yards) and eagerly closed the range, each admiral confident that he was leading his opponent into a trap. The Germans had only five battle-cruisers, the British six, so Beatty did not hesitate to pursue them to the south, leaving the four battleships to

HMS *Agincourt*

Designed to meet a Brazilian requirement, sold to Turkey before completion and finally taken over by the Royal Navy, *Agincourt* was very heavily armed but generally under-armoured
  Displacement: 30,250 tons full load *Length:* 632 ft *Armament:* 14 × 12-in, 20 × 6-in, 10 × 3-in, 2 × 3-in AA, 3 × 21-in torpedo tubes *Armour:* 4/9-in belt, 8/12-in turrets, 1/2½-in decks *Max speed:* 22 knots

Name	Completed	Fate
Agincourt	Aug 1914	Sold for breaking 1922

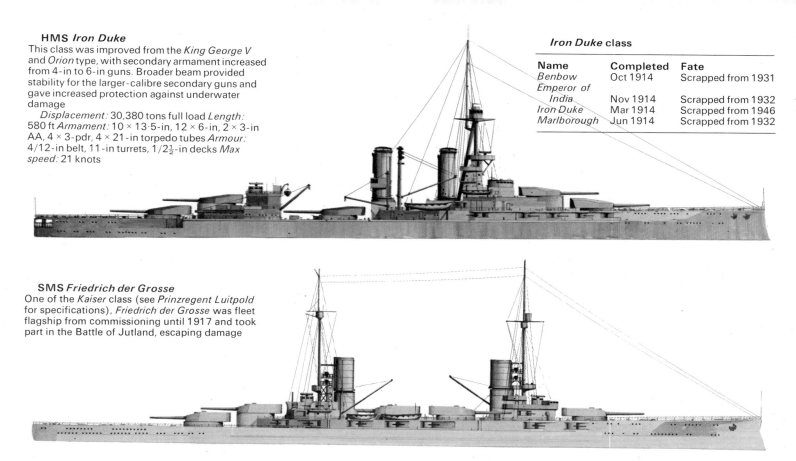

HMS *Iron Duke*
This class was improved from the *King George V* and *Orion* type, with secondary armament increased from 4-in to 6-in guns. Broader beam provided stability for the larger-calibre secondary guns and gave increased protection against underwater damage
   Displacement: 30,380 tons full load *Length:* 580 ft *Armament:* 10 × 13·5-in, 12 × 6-in, 2 × 3-in AA, 4 × 3-pdr, 4 × 21-in torpedo tubes *Armour:* 4/12-in belt, 11-in turrets, 1/2½-in decks *Max speed:* 21 knots

Iron Duke class

Name	Completed	Fate
Benbow	Oct 1914	Scrapped from 1931
Emperor of India	Nov 1914	Scrapped from 1932
Iron Duke	Mar 1914	Scrapped from 1946
Marlborough	Jun 1914	Scrapped from 1932

SMS *Friedrich der Grosse*
One of the *Kaiser* class (see *Prinzregent Luitpold* for specifications), *Friedrich der Grosse* was fleet flagship from commissioning until 1917 and took part in the Battle of Jutland, escaping damage

catch up. The *Queen Elizabeths* with their distinctive silhouettes had been stationed some miles astern so as not to tempt Hipper to avoid action, and above all it was essential to bring the Germans to action. It was already early afternoon, and, although the weather was calm, visibility was hazy; there was a distinct possibility that the Grand Fleet might not arrive in time to clinch the matter.

Both admirals reacted instinctively, Beatty swinging east to put his squadrons between Hipper and the German bases and Hipper turning south-east to draw the British towards the High Seas Fleet, now only 50 miles away. The *Lion* was in the lead, followed by the *Princess Royal*, *Queen Mary*, *Tiger*, *New Zealand* and *Indefatigable*, while Hipper was also leading his line in the *Lützow*, followed by the *Derfflinger*, *Seydlitz*, *Moltke* and *Von der Tann*.

At 1546 the duel began, fire gongs rang and ships shuddered as their guns belched flame and cordite smoke. The advantage lay with Hipper, for he had the sun behind him to illuminate the British, and his own ships were hard to see against the mist haze; to make matters worse, in a few minutes rolling clouds of coal smoke and cordite fumes reduced visibility even further. There was little Beatty could do about the light, but an error by his signals staff (reminiscent of the mix-up at the Dogger Bank) caused two of his ships to fire at the same German ship, and as a result the *Princess Royal* and *Lion* fired at the same ship and HMS *Indefatigable*, the last in the line and the weakest battle-cruiser, was left shooting

against the *von der Tann*. The German shooting was good, particularly the *Moltke*'s, and she soon scored two hits on the *Tiger*. Then the *Derfflinger* found the range of the *Princess Royal* and the *Lützow* began to score hits on the *Lion* and a hit on 'Q' turret amidships knocked out both guns. But the *Queen Mary* was hitting back with full broadsides, fired with 'fabulous rapidity' according to a German observer, and a range which came down to 14,000 yards.

At the rear of the line the *Von der Tann* registered three 11-in shell hits on the *Indefatigable* right aft. The stricken ship hauled out of line with smoke billowing from her stern, but before she could give any indication of the extent of her damage another shell hit near her forward 12-in gun turret and another hit the turret itself. For some seconds she seemed unhurt but then she blew up violently in a cloud of brown cordite smoke and sheets of orange flame. As debris hurtled into the air the hull turned over and sank, leaving only a handful of survivors out of her complement of nearly 1000 men. The time was 1603 and it had taken Hipper only twenty minutes to reduce the odds against him. But worse was to follow; at 1625 the *Derfflinger* shifted fire from the *Lion* to her sister *Queen Mary*, lying third in the line, and straddled her. Once again a vivid red flame shot up from

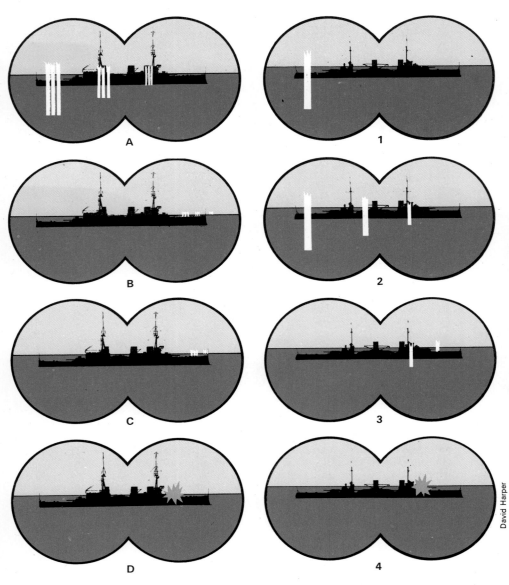

David Harper

Gunnery Fire Control: German System
- **A :** Main armament ladder, short
- **B :** Main armament ladder, over
- **C :** Down ladder, range found
- **D :** Main armament, rapid fire

Gunnery Fire Control: British System
- **1 :** Ranging shot, short
- **2 :** Ranging shots, approaching target
- **3 :** Ranging shots, straddle
- **4 :** Main armament, rapid fire

At the battle of Jutland the opponents used two different systems of fire-control. At ranges of 10,000 yards or more, as at Jutland, the only means of correcting the fire of heavy guns was by spotting the 200-ft shell splashes. The speed at which accurate full armament fire could be brought to bear on a target was crucial to the outcome of the battle, and in their system the Germans had an advantage. The German ladder system fired at maximum rate, increasing range by fixed distances or ladders. The British system relied on one or two guns actually estimating the range, trying to get a bracket, then going into rapid fire. Although the bracket system appeared to be more reliable, in practice the ladder system for finding the range was more successful and was adopted by the British after 1916

Opponents at Jutland: Admiral Sir John Jellicoe, Commander-in-Chief of the Royal Navy's Grand Fleet (left), and Vizeadmiral Reinhard Scheer, his German counterpart

Imperial War Museum

the forepart of the British ship, followed immediately by a tremendous explosion. The ship astern, HMS *Tiger*, had to alter course to dodge the clouds of debris, and horrified watchers testified later that the ship had 'opened out like a puffball'. The *New Zealand* reported seeing the stern sticking out of the water with men scrambling out of the after gun turret, but only nine officers and men out of 1285 survived. Beatty was now in trouble, with only four ships left to face five apparently undamaged Germans, but help was on its way. The slower battleships of the 5th Battle Squadron, the *Barham*, *Valiant*, *Warspite* and *Malaya*, were catching up by cutting corners wherever they could, and with their 15-in guns and vastly superior fire-control they were able to open fire at the astounding range of 19,000 yards. Within six minutes the *Barham* was hitting the *Von der Tann* and the *Valiant* was taking on the *Moltke*. At this range the Germans could not reply, and all they could do was to alter course slightly in an attempt to throw off the British range-takers. To gain time and to

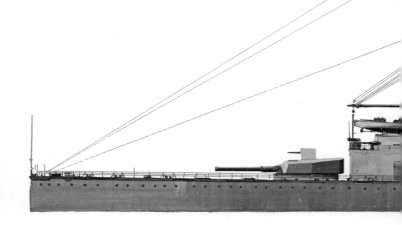

further harass the Germans Beatty ordered his destroyers to attack with torpedoes, and this forced Hipper to turn away. The *Seydlitz* was hit by a 21-in torpedo which tore a hole 13 ft × 39 ft in her side up forward, but despite heavy flooding which cut her speed the German battle-cruiser kept her station in the line.

Suddenly the 2nd Light Cruiser Squadron signalled to Beatty that battleships had been sighted, and two minutes later the High Seas Fleet was visible at a distance of 12 miles. Now it was Beatty who turned about, pretending to avoid action to tempt the German Fleet to follow him into the arms of the Grand Fleet. The British battle-cruisers made their 16° turn without difficulty, but once again sloppy signalling on the bridge of the *Lion* left the 5th Battle Squadron to its own devices. By the time its commander, Rear-Admiral Evan-Thomas, realized that the rest of the British force

was retreating in the opposite direction, his ships were nearly within range of the High Seas Fleet. The next few minutes were crowded and hectic as the four British battleships were exposed to the firepower of what seemed to them like the whole German Fleet. Battleships took time to turn, and the four *Queen Elizabeth*s were exposed to concentrated fire as they slowly hauled around. The *Barham* and *Malaya* were hit and suffered casualties, but all four continued to fire and scored hits on the *Grosser Kurfürst* and *Markgraf* as well as the battle-cruisers.

The Grand Fleet had been pushing southwards at maximum speed since 1555, and the Commander-in-Chief, Admiral Jellicoe, detached three *Invincible* class battle-cruisers under Rear-Admiral Hood to reinforce Beatty. These three ships arrived on the scene just as Beatty's ships had stopped their 'run to the north' to re-engage Hipper

Queen Elizabeth-class battleships practise their shooting. The Royal Navy's accuracy tended to improve as an action progressed, but the long-base Zeiss rangefinders in German ships were difficult to use accurately in battle, so the High Seas Fleet's gunnery started well but deteriorated. Inset: HMS Queen Elizabeth *takes aboard cordite in containers and a one-ton 15-in shell. Magazine design was to prove crucial in battle*

in an effort to stop him from sighting and reporting the Grand Fleet. This movement to the east across Hipper's bows began at 1726 and this time the advantage of the light lay with the British. Beatty manoeuvred his ships across the van of the battle-cruiser line, forcing it to turn away. The *Lützow* was hit badly, the *Derfflinger* began to take in water from bow damage, the *Seydlitz* was ablaze and the *Von der Tann* had all her 11-in guns out of action. In desperation Hipper ordered his destroyers to attack the British battle line, but just as the German light forces began to deploy at 1735 Hood's three battle-cruisers erupted on the scene and chased them away.

HMS *Inflexible*

The controversial *Invincible* class battle-cruisers combined the heavy guns of a battleship with the speed of a cruiser. They inevitably came off second-best when used as dreadnoughts
Displacement: 17,250 tons *Length:* 530 ft *Armament:* 8 × 12-in, 16 × 4-in, 3 × 4-in AA, 1 × 3-in, 7 × mg, 5 × 18-in torpedo tubes *Armour:* 6-in belt, 7-in turrets, 10-in conning tower, 2½/1-in decks *Max speed:* 25 knots

Invincible class

Name	Completed	Fate
Indomitable	Jun 1908	Sold 1922
Inflexible	Oct 1908	Sold 1922
Invincible	Mar 1908	Blew up at Jutland

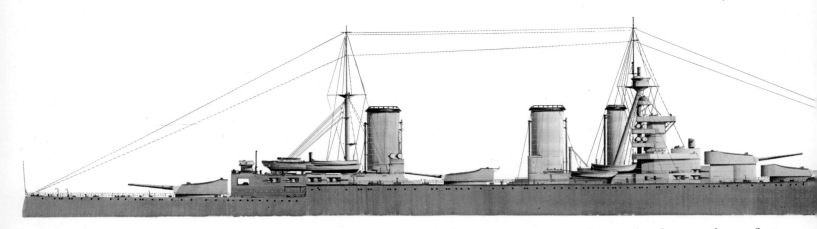

HMS *Lion*
This class of battle-cruiser was fast, powerful and heavily armed, but the main turrets were arranged in an inefficient way and the armour was inadequate. Other drawbacks necessitated extensive modifications
Displacement: 29,680 tons full load *Length:* 660 ft *Armament:* 8×13.5-in, 16×4-in, 1×4-in AA, 4×3-pdr, 2×21-in torpedo tubes *Armour:* 4/9-in belt, 4/9-in turrets, 1/2½-in decks *Max speed:* 27 knots

Lion class

Name	Completed	Fate
Lion	May 1912	Scrapped 1924
Princess Royal	Nov 1912	Scrapped 1926
Queen Mary	Sep 1915	Blew up at Jutland

To Jellicoe in the Fleet Flagship HMS *Iron Duke* the tactical situation must have been baffling. Visibility was dropping as the early spring twilight closed in, and he had only a series of estimates of the last known position, bearing and speed of the High Seas Fleet. He could see only seven miles from the flag-deck of the *Iron Duke*, which was much less than maximum gun-range, and it was essential that his fleet should be properly deployed in line, with all guns pointing in the right direction, ready to open fire as soon as a target presented itself. Anything less than that would forfeit the tactical advantage to the Germans and would expose the Grand Fleet to the risk of serious damage before it could reply. But Jellicoe was the ablest ship-handler and tactician in the Royal Navy, and possibly the best in the world. He studied the plot for no more than ten seconds, then ordered a deployment from the box-shaped cruising formation into a single line nine miles long, using the port column as the head of the line. This had the effect of simultaneously putting the Grand Fleet between the High Seas Fleet and its bases, avoiding complex

SMS *Seydlitz*
Developed from the *Moltke* class, with a raised forecastle to improve seakeeping and a longer, narrower hull to give a higher speed. She was hit more times at Jutland than any other German ship which survived the battle yet was able to return safely to the Jade River
Displacement: 25,150 tons full load *Length:* 200·6 m *Armament:* 10 × 280-mm, 12 × 150-mm, 12 × 88-mm, 2 × 88-mm AA, 4 × 500-mm torpedo tubes *Armour:* 100/300-mm side, 250-mm main turrets, 30/80-mm deck *Max speed:* 26½ knots

Seydlitz class

Name	Completed	Fate
Seydlitz	May 1913	Scrapped from 1928

wheeling and 'marking time', and putting the most modern and powerful battleships into action first. Few tacticians faced by an able opponent have had the good fortune to achieve such perfection, and although controversy raged over the deployment for years after Jutland, no serious historian today questions that Jellicoe achieved all that an admiral could ask:

The British battle-cruisers now effected the junction with the main fleet for which they had worked so hard, and indeed for which they had been built. But one more tragedy was to darken their achievement. Admiral Hood's flagship, the battle-cruiser

HMS Lion, *Beatty's flagship, making full speed during the battle. Shortly afterwards she was nearly blown up by a hit on 'Q' turret*

Invincible, was hit at 9000 yards, caught by a sudden improvement in visibility which left her clearly outlined against the setting sun – it was an opportunity which the *Derfflinger* and *König's* gunlayers could not waste. A salvo fell on the *Invincible's* midships turrets, and within seconds she collapsed in a huge cloud of smoke and coal dust. Because the battle was taking place over the shallow Jutland Bank off the coast of Denmark the two halves of the 567-ft ship rested on the bottom, standing up 'like gravestones to her 1026 dead'. Ironically, the officers and men of the Grand Fleet assumed that she was the remains of a German ship sunk, and cheers rang out as each battleship swept past at 20 knots.

The third phase of Jutland now began, a series of gun-actions between the two fleets. Admiral Scheer suddenly found his 'T' crossed by the fully deployed British line, the one thing that he and his predecessors had tried to avoid since the war began. From eight points of the compass a line of battleships, whose extremities vanished into the mist, poured shells into his van. The *Lützow* was completely disabled and the other battle-cruisers suffered heavily. Scheer was in a trap, and he had only one way out – a complete 180° turn by each ship, the so-called 'battle turnaway' which had been assiduously practised. This achieved its aim and contact was lost as the German battleships headed on a reciprocal course under cover of a smokescreen laid by destroyers.

Jellicoe swung the Grand Fleet round to the south-east at 1844 and again to the south at 1856 to keep himself between Scheer and his escape route. At 1908 the High Seas Fleet blundered into the Grand Fleet a second time while trying to feel its way around the flank. Once again Scheer's 'T' was crossed, and the British battle fleet opened fire from one end to the other at ranges of 9000 to 12,000 yards. But this time the German position was worse, with the British closer and their own line bent. Scheer was desperate, and threw his destroyers into an attack. To his battle-cruisers he said, 'Charge the enemy. Ram. Ships denoted are to attack without regard to consequences'. This 'death ride' of the battle-cruisers was led by the *Derfflinger*, which soon had two turrets destroyed by exploding ammunition, and lost her fire-control. The *Lützow* was burning fiercely, and her fighting days were over, but Hipper's 1st Scouting Group saved the day for his Commander-in-Chief. Amid the encircling gloom and the pall of smoke from gunfire, burning ships and funnels, the British could not see the second battle turnaway; although they did not know it, they had

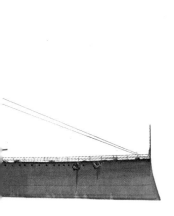

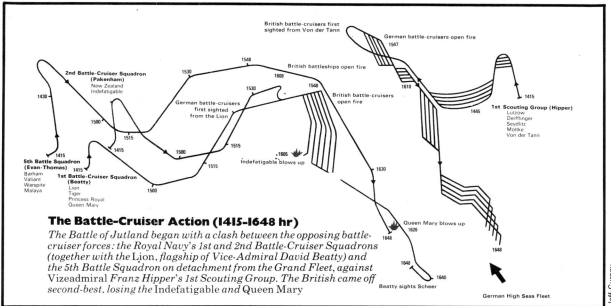

The Battle-Cruiser Action (1415-1648 hr)

The Battle of Jutland began with a clash between the opposing battle-cruiser forces: the Royal Navy's 1st and 2nd Battle-Cruiser Squadrons (together with the Lion, flagship of Vice-Admiral David Beatty) and the 5th Battle Squadron on detachment from the Grand Fleet, against Vizeadmiral Franz Hipper's 1st Scouting Group. The British came off second-best, losing the Indefatigable and Queen Mary

Jeff Gurney

seen the last of Germany's High Seas Fleet.

The only damage suffered by the Grand Fleet during this phase were two shell hits on the *Colossus* and a torpedo hit on the *Marlborough*, but neither ship was put out of action. Although the rival battle-cruisers exchanged a few more shots, the firing finally died away and by 2035 the fleet action was over. In the night action which followed British capital ships played no part, but German battleships engaged cruisers and destroyers when they forced their way through the British light forces stationed to the rear of the Grand Fleet. Jellicoe did not want to risk a night action, with all its fearful possibilities of mistaken identity and collision, but Scheer dared not wait for daylight and so he had to fight his way through at night. Also, his ships were equipped for night-fighting, so that he could take a calculated risk. This paid off handsomely, and Scheer got back to harbour safely, but minus the pre-dreadnought battleship *Pommern* which blew up with the loss of all hands when hit by a British destroyer's torpedo, and the *Lützow*, which had to be sunk by her destroyers when she could no longer steam.

The figures make it clear that, in terms of ships sunk, Jutland was more or less a

Vice-Admiral Sir David Beatty, commander of the Royal Navy's battle-cruisers at Jutland

drawn battle. In tactical terms there was no doubt that the Germans had sunk more valuable ships – three capital ships and three armoured cruisers as against one capital ship and one obsolescent battleship. But victories are not decided simply by numbers. The British were clearly in possession of the battlefield on the morning of 1 June, whereas the Germans were thankfully negotiating the swept channels outside Wilhelmshaven, and it could even be claimed that they lost another battle-cruiser, since the *Seydlitz* came to rest on the bottom of the North Sea *outside* her home port, and had to be salvaged. There is no doubt that the *Seydlitz* and the *Derfflinger* could not have faced a long voyage across the North Sea, whereas the entire Grand Fleet arrived safely in its harbours, docked its lame ducks, coaled and was ready for sea within 24 hours. But in a broader sense, Jutland, if not a defeat for the British, was a strategic stalemate. Millions of pounds had been lavished on the dreadnought battle fleet in the hope that it would provide a quick, decisive victory over Germany, but when the moment came nothing had happened and the slaughter in the trenches was still going on.

The inquisition began immediately after

Seydlitz was the most heavily damaged German warship to survive Jutland. Thanks to her captain's careful nursing she escaped the fate of the Lützow *but still sank outside Wilhelmshaven, having shipped 2000 tons of water and being completely burnt out*

Jeff Gurney

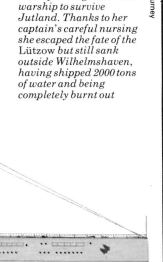

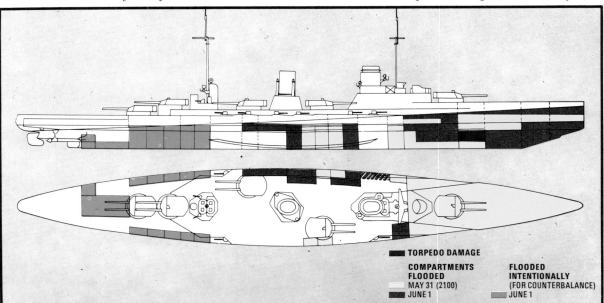

■ **TORPEDO DAMAGE**

COMPARTMENTS FLOODED
MAY 31 (2100)
JUNE 1

FLOODED INTENTIONALLY (FOR COUNTERBALANCE)
JUNE 1

Jutland. Jellicoe, true to his character, refused to issue a statement on the battle until all his crippled ships had been accounted for, so an anxious Admiralty caved in to pressure from the press and, incredibly, published the German communiqué. Naturally this made little of the fearful pounding taken by the High Seas Fleet and Scheer's two turns away from Jellicoe, and made much of the loss of three British battle-cruisers and three armoured cruisers. From this moment on British opinion divided into two camps, pro-Beatty and pro-Jellicoe, with a third lobby claiming that both admirals had been let down by inferior material.

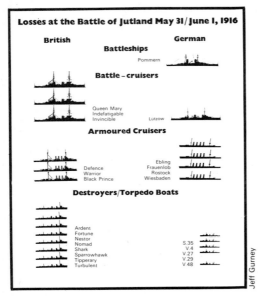

SMS König *seen running trials just before the war*

The truth, as so often happens, lies somewhere between the two extremes. Beatty had handled his battle-cruisers well; although this staffwork left a lot to be desired he had been acutely aware that time was essential, and he had delivered Scheer into Jellicoe's grasp. Jellicoe, on the other hand, had produced a masterly deployment with very little information to hand, and had positioned his fleet so well that twice he had achieved tactical perfection in crossing Scheer's 'T'. On the German side, Hipper had also handled his battle-cruisers well and had followed a difficult set of orders dutifully and had made much more out of the situation than anyone had dared hope. Of Scheer's tactics the less said the better. It has been claimed by a recent English commentator that British tactics were inferior to German in not having a 'battle turnaway', but 200 years of British naval history had demonstrated that naval victories were not to be won by a 180° turn in the face of the enemy. If the Royal Navy did not practise such a manoeuvre it was because they felt that it did little to bring a reluctant enemy to battle.

Many years later an earnest student asked Scheer what grand strategic design he had been pursuing at the time of his second encounter with the Grand Fleet; with more candour than regard for reputation Scheer replied, 'I don't know. As the virgin said when told she was pregnant, "It just happened".'

On the *matériel* side Jutland raised far more puzzling questions. Why had three modern British ships been blown up, but no German ships? The loss of the *Invincible* and *Indefatigable* could be explained away

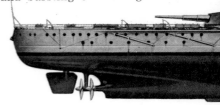

by the fact that they had only a 6-in armour belt, but the *Queen Mary* was protected by 9-in armour, and evidence from her two sisters showed that only two shells had penetrated British armour of that thickness. Disturbing reports also filtered through from neutral sources that British shells had failed to burst, and it was clear that something had gone wrong.

With only a handful of survivors from all three battle-cruisers there was little direct evidence as to the cause of the losses. But the *Lion* had suffered a nearly disastrous fire in 'Q' turret during the early stages of the action. According to Beatty's flag captain the shell hit the front plate at its joint with the roof plate, blowing half the roof into the air and bursting over the guns. The blast of the shell killed or wounded every man in the turret and severed the hydraulic pipes. Several cordite cartridges caught fire, and the left-hand gun tilted upwards from the weight of the breech-mechanism, causing the cordite charges in the breech to fall into the fire already burning below. But the unfortunate and disturbing fact about this fire was that although the ship's fire parties ran hoses into the turret and doused the fire, half an hour later the still-smouldering charges burst into flame, and ignited eight more charges jammed in the hoist. A tongue of flame leapt down the ammunition hoist, killing the 70 men of the magazine and shell-room crews, but fortunately the Royal Marine officer in charge of the turret, Major Marvey RMLI, had earlier given the order to flood 'Q' magazine, and so the ship did not blow up.

Examination of the *Lion* showed that her cordite charges were extremely unstable, whereas it had hitherto been assumed that they would merely burn rather than flash off if ignited. The Germans, on the other hand, had no such trouble. Their charges were encased in metal covers as against silk bags, but the matter went deeper than that. British cordite manufacturers still used a

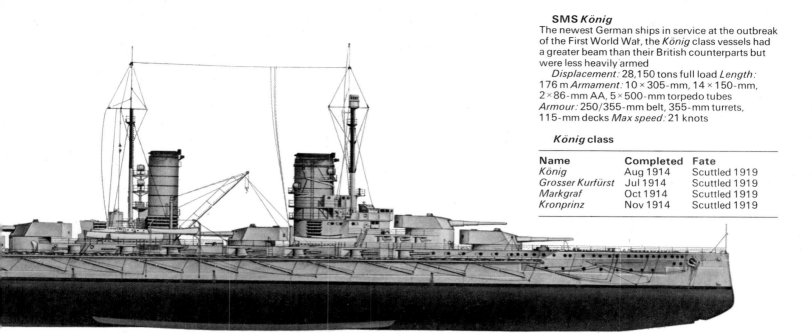

vaseline-based solvent to stabilize the propellant, whereas the Germans had moved on to solventless cordite. Tests showed that the so-called stabilizer actually reduced the stability of cordite, making it all the more likely to flash off. No German ship using solventless propellant blew up in the First World War, whereas the three navies using British-pattern cordite – British, Japanese and Italian – all suffered from magazine explosions:

British – *Bulwark* (1914), *Vanguard* (1917)
Italian – *Benedetto Brin* (1915), *Leonardo da Vinci* (1916)
Japanese – *Tsukuba* (1917), *Kawachi* (1918)

The British were worried by reports that many of their armour-piercing shells had failed to detonate properly. On investigation this was found to be true, and to its chagrin the Royal Navy realized that many German ships had reached harbour safely when they should have been sunk. Again, the problem was one of quality control rather than design. The nose-caps of the armour-piercing shell were too brittle and the Lyddite burster was too sensitive, so that when a shell hit armour it broke up or detonated prematurely. British ships scored a number of hits on German ships at Jutland, and had the shells detonated properly, *after* the intended delay to allow them to pass through the armour, they would have

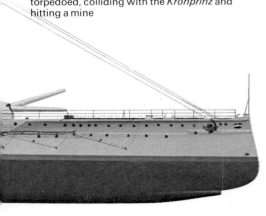

SMS *Grosser Kurfürst*

One of the *König* class (see that ship for specifications), *Grosser Kurfürst* had an eventful war which included action at Jutland, being torpedoed, colliding with the *Kronprinz* and hitting a mine

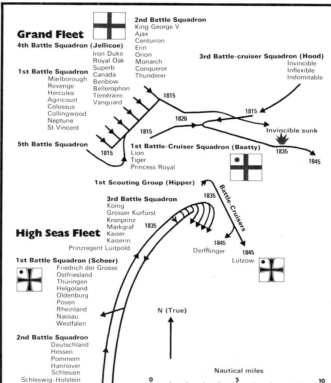

Grand Fleet

4th Battle Squadron (Jellicoe)
Iron Duke
Royal Oak
Superb

1st Battle Squadron
Marlborough
Revenge
Hercules
Agincourt
Colossus
Collingwood
Neptune
St Vincent

5th Battle Squadron

2nd Battle Squadron
King George V
Ajax
Centurion
Erin
Orion
Monarch
Conqueror
Thunderer

Canada
Benbow
Bellerophon
Téméraire
Vanguard

3rd Battle-cruiser Squadron (Hood)
Invincible
Inflexible
Indomitable

Invincible sunk

1st Battle-Cruiser Squadron (Beatty)
Lion
Tiger
Princess Royal

1st Scouting Group (Hipper)

3rd Battle Squadron
König
Grosser Kurfürst
Kronprinz
Markgraf
Kaiser
Kaiserin
Prinzregent Luitpold

High Seas Fleet

Battle-Cruisers

Derfflinger

Lützow

1st Battle Squadron (Scheer)
Friedrich der Grosse
Ostfriesland
Thuringen
Helgoland
Oldenburg
Posen
Rheinland
Nassau
Westfalen

2nd Battle Squadron
Deutschland
Hessen
Pommern
Hannover
Schlesien
Schleswig-Holstein

N (True)

Nautical miles

0   5   10

Note: times apply to the lead ship in a formation

The Fleets Collide :1

The long-awaited first clash between the Royal Navy's Grand Fleet and the German High Seas Fleet followed on the heels of the initial battle-cruiser action. Admiral Jellicoe in the *Iron Duke* ordered the 1st, 2nd and 4th Battle Squadrons to deploy from their cruising formation of six columns into a single line nine miles long, with the 5th Battle Squadron rejoining them.

This enabled Jellicoe's force to 'cross the T' of Vice-Admiral Scheer's 1st, 2nd and 3rd Battle Squadrons, which were steaming in line ahead. Scheer, in the *Friedrich der Grosse*, had little choice but to order a battle turnaway to starboard, turning each ship through 180° and reversing its order in the line.

Meanwhile Beatty's 1st Battle-Cruiser Squadron, minus the sunken *Queen Mary*, was joined by the 3rd Battle-Cruiser Squadron under Hood. This force steamed parallel with the battleship line, between those ships and the enemy. It was to suffer another setback, however; at 1835, after being pounded by the *König* and *Derfflinger*, the *Invincible* exploded.

But Hipper's 1st Scouting Group did not escape unscathed. The *Lützow* was disabled and her sisters were damaged, although the High Seas Fleet was intact.

Just over half an hour later the fleets clashed again. Scheer, finding his 'T' crossed for a second time, ordered his battle-cruisers to attack the enemy while his battleships carried out their second battle turnaway. A smoke screen laid by the accompanying torpedo-boats added to the gloom, and the High Seas Fleet yet again emerged intact.

The Fleets Collide :2

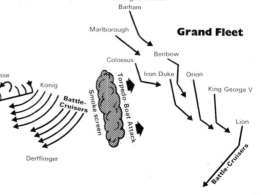

High Seas Fleet

N (True)

Friedrich der Grosse
König
Battle-Cruisers
Deutschland
Schleswig Holstein
Derfflinger

Smoke screen
Torpedo-Boat Attack

Grand Fleet

Barham
Marlborough
Benbow
Colossus
Iron Duke
Orion
King George V
Lion
Battle-Cruisers

Nautical miles

0   5

Note: all tracks start at 1918 hours and end at 1926

Jeff Gurney

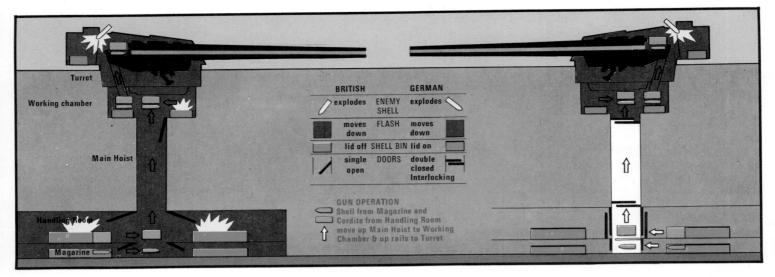

caused more serious damage. This is not to suggest that all German ships escaped without serious damage, as several battle-cruisers were badly damaged, and the common or high-explosive shell used by British ships was extremely destructive. However, the stable nature of German cordite meant that cordite fires were less of a hazard.

The British took energetic steps to remedy the faults in their ships; the armour-piercing shell was completely redesigned with a TNT burster, and all ships of the

Diagrammatic explanation of the way in which British battle-cruisers blew up at Jutland. The German practice of encasing cordite in brass saved them from fatal magazine explosions

Grand Fleet were given extra deck armour around the turrets and new flash-tight scuttles in the ammunition supply system. But the opportunity to settle the outcome of the war had been lost. There was to be no second chance, as the two fleets were not to meet again, apart from a brief sortie by the High Seas Fleet in 1917, which was cancelled as soon as reconnoitring Zeppe-

lins revealed that the Grand Fleet was heading southwards. In November 1917 a small battle-cruiser force tried to push into the Heligoland Bight, but after a brief skirmish with German outposts the fear of minefields proved too much and the British withdrew. Life for the two fleets became monotonous as the battleships swung at their anchors. In the end it was the High Seas Fleet's morale which cracked; the British had a much less hospitable base at Scapa but they were at least able to keep themselves busy by going to sea.

Adversaries in the Adriatic
The Naval Race between Britain and Germany was duplicated in the Mediterranean before the war as Austria-Hungary and Italy built up their fleets

Duilio

Similar to the ships of the *Cavour* class, but having greater power and with secondary armament upgraded in order to keep pace with foreign battleships. The secondary armament was exposed to spray interference

Displacement: 24,730 tons full load *Length:* 176 m *Armament:* 13 × 305-mm, 16 × 152-mm, 13 × 76-mm, 6 × 76-mm AA, 3 × 450-mm torpedo tubes *Armour:* 250-mm belt, 240-mm turrets, 40-mm deck *Max speed:* 21 knots.

Andrea Doria class

Name	Completed	Fate
Andrea Doria	Mar 1916	Scrapped 1958
Duilio	May 1915	Scrapped 1958

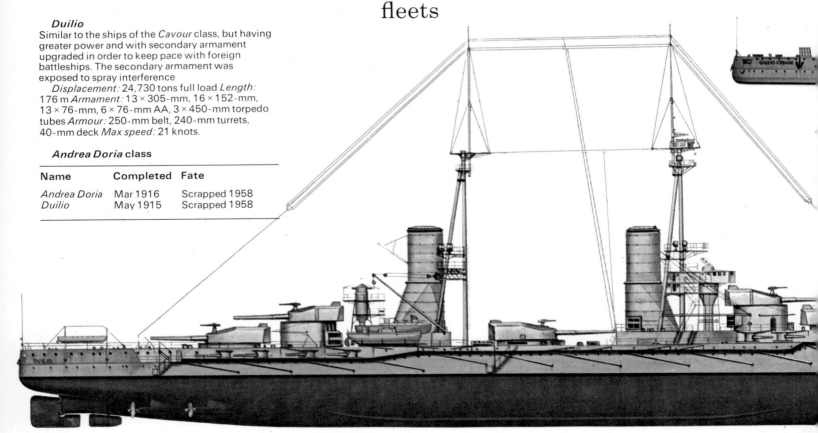

Viribus Unitis

Construction of this class of Austro-Hungarian battleships was prompted by the building of similar vessels in Italy. *Viribus Unitis* herself was fleet flagship from 1914 to 1918

Displacement: 22,500 tons *Length:* 161 m *Armament:* 12×305-mm, 12×150-mm, 18×70-mm, 2×75-mm AA (from 1918), 4×533-mm torpedo tubes *Armour:* 150/280-mm side, 305-mm main turrets, 48-mm deck *Max speed:* 20 knots

Viribus Unitis class

Name	Completed	Fate
Viribus Unitis	Oct 1912	Mined 1918
Tegetthoff	Jul 1913	Scrapped 1924—25
Prinz Eugen	Jul 1914	Sunk as target 1922
Szent Istvan	Nov 1915	Torpedoed 1918

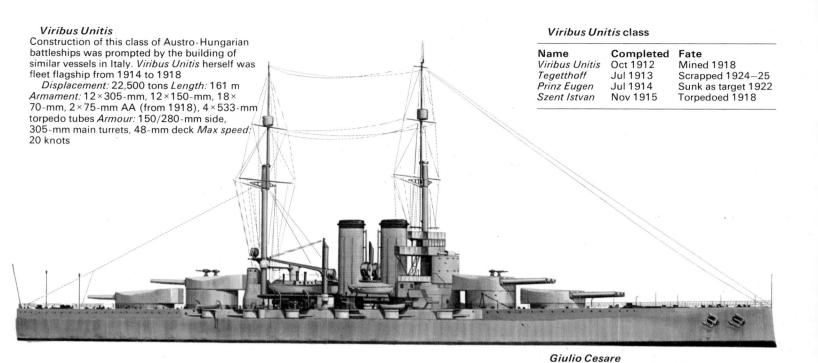

Giulio Cesare

Intended to match Austria's *Viribus Unitis* class, the three battleships of the *Conte di Cavour* class were fast and heavily armed but never met their adversaries

Displacement: 24,300 tons full load *Length:* 169 m *Armament:* 13×305-mm, 18×120-mm, 13×76-mm, 3×450-mm torpedo tubes *Armour:* 250-mm belt, 250-mm turrets, 40-mm decks *Max speed:* 22½ knots

Conte di Cavour class

Name	Completed	Fate
Conte di Cavour	Apr 1915	Torpedoed at Taranto 1940, broken up 1947-52
Giulio Cesare	May 1914	Transferred to Russia 1948, mined? in Black Sea 1955
Leonardo da Vinci	May 1914	Blew up 1916

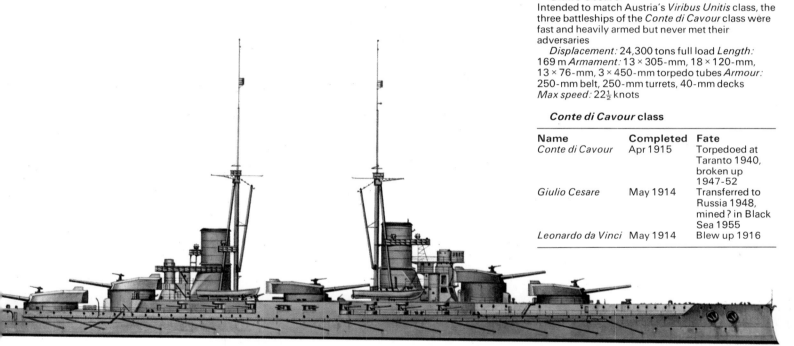

Giulio Cesare *at Taranto after the armistice, one of six Italian dreadnoughts. Unfortunately British pattern cordite was responsible for the loss of her sister, the* Leonardo da Vinci

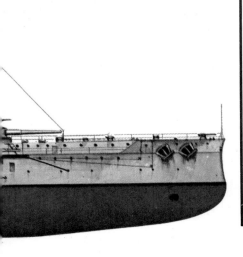

Imperial War Museum

THE OLD SHIPS FIGHT BACK

Paradoxically the pre-dreadnoughts, which had been written off by all the naval pundits as useless, had a much more exciting war. The old battleship *Canopus* was sent to South America in a vain attempt to reinforce Admiral Cradock against von Spee's squadron, but she did manage to put herself on the mud at the Falkland Islands to act as a fixed battery in defence. When the German armies reached the Belgian coast late in 1914 their right flank was vulnerable to bombardment from the sea, and so the Royal Navy mustered a scratch force of elderly ships to harass them. The *Venerable* was used for a time, and then someone remembered that the old *Revenge*, which had been struck off the Navy List in 1911, had not yet been scrapped. Her 13.5-in guns had already been relined to convert them to 12-in calibre when she was serving as a gunnery training ship, and as she also had a relatively modern outfit of fire-control she was eminently suited to the job. All that remained to be done was to fit her with the first primitive anti-torpedo 'bulges' and a few anti-Zeppelin guns on high-angle mountings, and she was ready. Apart from having to take the name *Redoubtable* in February 1915 to release her name for a new *Royal Sovereign* class battleship, she led an uneventful life. To increase the range of her guns she was often heeled over, but eventually she was replaced by specially built monitors in October 1915.

Only two British dreadnought battleships were sunk during the entire war, the *Vanguard* by ammunition explosion and the *Audacious* by a mine off Northern Ireland. The pre-dreadnoughts, on the other hand, soon showed that they were more vulnerable. In November 1914 HMS *Bulwark* blew up while loading ammunition at Sheerness, and in January 1915 the *Formidable* was torpedoed in the English Channel.

To the Dardanelles

When the Allies decided to attack the Dardanelles they sent all the old battleships they could spare, and it was even hoped that some could act as 'mine-bumpers' to clear the minefields. Seventeen pre-dreadnoughts were mustered for the attack on the Narrows on 18 March, 1915, backed up by a British battle-cruiser and the brand-new *Queen Elizabeth*. It was fondly hoped that the new battleship would be able to calibrate her 15-in guns against the Turkish forts, but it should have been realized earlier that ships had very little effect against forts. On 3 November, 1914, the battle-cruisers *Indefatigable* and *Indomitable* and the French battleships *Verité* and *Suffren* had fired at Seddulbahir (Sedd-el-Bahr) and Kum Kale forts; despite a lucky hit in a magazine, neither fort was destroyed. Vice-Admiral Carden, the British admiral commanding in the Aegean, asked for 12 battleships, two battle-cruisers and smaller warships such as cruisers, destroyers and minesweepers. In view of what happened later it is worth noting that he also forecast a heavy expenditure of 12-in shells. What he was finally given was:

The old battleship HMS Revenge *bombards the coast of German-occupied Belgium, listing to increase the range of her guns*

Allied Battleships at the Dardanelles

1 modern battleship (*Queen Elizabeth,* 15-in guns).
1 battle-cruiser (*Inflexible,* 12-in guns).
2 modern pre-dreadnoughts (*Lord Nelson, Agamemnon,* 12-in and 9·2-in guns).
10 old pre-dreadnoughts (*Ocean, Albion, Vengeance, Majestic, Prince George, Canopus, Irresistible, Cornwallis, Swiftsure* and *Triumph,* 12-in and 10-in guns).
4 French pre-dreadnoughts (*Suffren, Charlemagne, St Louis* and *Gaulois,* 12-in and 10·8-in guns).

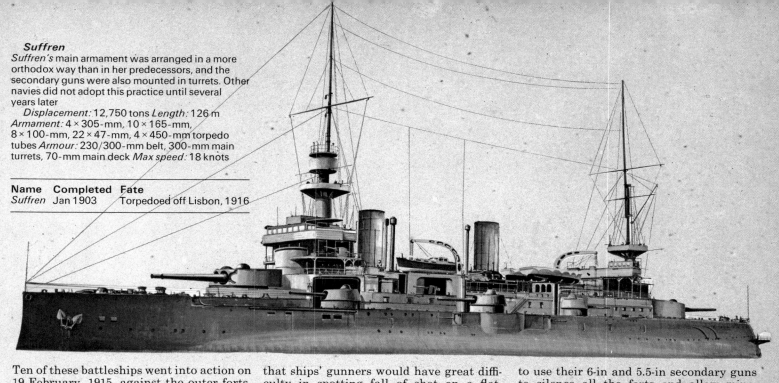

Suffren

Suffren's main armament was arranged in a more orthodox way than in her predecessors, and the secondary guns were also mounted in turrets. Other navies did not adopt this practice until several years later

Displacement: 12,750 tons *Length:* 126 m
Armament: 4 × 305-mm, 10 × 165-mm, 8 × 100-mm, 22 × 47-mm, 4 × 450-mm torpedo tubes *Armour:* 230/300-mm belt, 300-mm main turrets, 70-mm main deck *Max speed:* 18 knots

Name	Completed	Fate
Suffren	Jan 1903	Torpedoed off Lisbon, 1916

Ten of these battleships went into action on 19 February, 1915, against the outer forts. The *Cornwallis* opened fire at about 12,000 yards and the others joined in at about 8000 yards, but it was soon obvious that the ships would not be able to hit anything until they anchored. What had not been foreseen was

that ships' gunners would have great difficulty in spotting fall of shot on a flat, featureless landscape. Each gun position ashore needed a direct hit to disable it, and nothing short of a direct hit on a magazine could knock out a fort. To make matters worse the ships fired 139 12-in shells from 42 guns, an average of only 3.3 rounds per gun over a period of nearly eight hours.

A further bombardment the next day was cancelled because of bad weather, but on 25 February the battleships went in again in much the same formation as before. This time the ships did better because other battleships had been stationed on the flanks to spot the fall of shot (known in naval parlance as 'flank marking'). The *Queen Elizabeth* did much better this time, taking only 18 rounds to find the range and disable both the modern 9.4-in guns at Cape Helles. Even the older ships did well, the *Irresistible*, for example, knocking out the guns at Orkanie with 35 rounds. As the afternoon wore on the ships moved in closer to be able

HMS *Prince Rupert*
Old battleships drew too much water for shore bombardment and were vulnerable, so they were replaced by specially built monitors. The *Prince Rupert* and her sisters used 12-in guns and turrets removed from four old *Majestic* class battleships

to use their 6-in and 5.5-in secondary guns to silence all the forts and allow minesweepers to clear the dense minefields. Landing parties were able to demolish 50 guns with little loss from the demoralized Turkish troops.

The inner forts proved much harder to deal with. The Straits widen out above Seddulbahir, and so the gun batteries were too far away for accurate firing. There was no short-wave radio, and even the seaplanes present were too primitive to be of much use. Three more bombardments between 2 and 8 March achieved little, although the *Queen Elizabeth* again showed off by firing *over* the Gallipoli Peninsula at the Nagara forts on the European side. The methods indicate the crudity of long-range gunnery; the *Queen Elizabeth* used three pre-dreadnoughts as flank-markers, seaplanes and a cairn on a hilltop as an aiming mark, but it still took four hours at 14,000 yards. Once again the expenditure of ammunition was laughable, 33 rounds of 'common' (high-explosive) shell, one round per gun per hour.

Next day the *Queen Elizabeth* was involved in a dangerous and unique action. While she was firing at Fort Chemenlik on the Asiatic side of the Straits, the Turks brought up the old pre-dreadnought *Hairredin Barbarossa* (formerly the German *Kurfürst Friedrich*

Wilhelm built in 1894) in an attempt to interfere with her fire. The old battleship had one advantage in that her old 11-in (28-cm) guns had 25° elevation, and she was able to drop three shells near her giant adversary. The *Queen Elizabeth* at first assumed that the shells came from a mobile field-howitzer battery, and she moved out about a thousand yards, pausing only to demolish the German ship's spotting position on shore. But the Germans were not finished yet, and as soon as the spotting party was established in a new position the *Hairredin Barbarossa* found the range again in three rounds, this time hitting the *Queen Elizabeth* three times on her armour below the waterline. No battleship of that era was designed to withstand plunging fire, and the old Turkish battleship might well have crippled or even sunk the pride of the Royal Navy if she had scored a hit on the deck.

Although the *Queen Elizabeth* was not damaged in this bizarre action she was too valuable to be risked in this sort of work, and in any case the Admiralty was reluctant to ship too many 15-in shells out to the Dardanelles until stocks had been built up at home. Sending her out had been foolhardy and one of the 13.5-in-gunned *Orion* class would have been more useful, and now the Admiralty insisted that she be recalled as soon as Carden could get the major assault on the Narrows over, to force his way past the minefields. The problem was quite simple now: the mines prevented the ships from dealing effectively with the guns, and the guns prevented the minesweepers from sweeping the mines. To finish once and for all the Allies planned a massive sweep with all 18 battleships. Although Carden had a nervous breakdown his second-in-command, Vice-Admiral de Robeck, was able to take over with virtually no delay, and the attack was launched on 18 March, 1915.

The day began in brilliant sunshine and de Robeck's fleet looked magnificent as it advanced up the Narrows. First to open fire was the *Queen Elizabeth* followed by the other three ships, and by 1130 the whole of Line 'A' was in action, with the Turkish artillery firing back. All the ships were hit but not seriously. Things seemed to be going well, and de Robeck ordered the French Admiral Guepratte to bring up Line 'B'. Guepratte responded with great verve, taking his ships between the first line as if carrying out a drill manoeuvre, and soon both lines were firing at the forts. The Turkish guns were beginning to score more

hits now; the *Inflexible*'s bridge was set on fire, the *Gaulois* was holed below the line, and the *Agamemnon* was hit 12 times within half an hour. But even pre-dreadnoughts were built to take this sort of punishment, and casualties remained low, fewer than 40 killed and wounded. The Turkish gunners were beginning to run low in ammunition and fire slackened; de Robeck judged that the time had come to bring up his reserve line of ships to take the pressure off the elderly French battleships in Line 'B' which had been taking a fair amount of punishment.

Just after 1400 hours the *Suffren* began a wide turn to starboard into Erenkoy Bay, at the start of her turn towards Kum Kale and the open sea. Her three consorts followed her in a huge arc, but then, suddenly, the second ship *Bouvet* lurched as a huge explosion stopped her in a cloud of steam and smoke. In a matter of seconds she capsized and sank, taking nearly 600 men down with her. The unfortunate ship had already been hit by several heavy projectiles, and as she was turning under fire it was assumed that she had been hit in the magazine by a lucky shell. The bombardment continued, but two hours later the *Inflexible*, also manoeuvring in Erenkoy Bay, struck a mine and began to take in water fast. This time the cause was clearly understood, and three minutes later the *Irresistible* also reported that she had been mined. Admiral de Robeck had little choice but to cancel the bombardment until the extent of the danger was known.

The most obvious explanation was that the Turks had released drifting mines above the Narrows, but de Robeck feared that torpedoes might have been fired from fixed tubes ashore. Nobody suspected Erenkoy Bay, for the area had been swept repeatedly. In fact the sweepers had found three mines earlier but had not suspected that they formed part of a larger line, and the Allies had placed too much faith in the ability of seaplanes to spot mines. What they had missed was possibly the most effective minefield in the history of naval warfare.

On the night of 8 March a small Turkish minelayer, the *Nousret* under the command of Lieutenant-Colonel Geehl, had slipped down through the Narrows to lay 20 mines

in Erenkoy Bay. Geehl was a mine-warfare expert and had seen how the battleships used the bay for turning, and so he decided

to lay a trap. His gamble was more successful than he could have imagined, for a third battleship was to be claimed by the small minefield. The *Ocean* chose to ignore a request from Commodore Keyes to take the stricken *Irresistible* in tow (her captain would not take orders from a mere temporary commodore), and she steamed backwards and forwards at maximum speed, firing her 12-in guns at nothing in particular. This comic sideshow was brought to an end by one of the *Nousret*'s mines, and the *Ocean* drifted off up the Straits turning helpless circles. Neither she nor the *Irresistible* were seen again. Keyes made an eerie trip after dark to try to find the two battleships, with everything dark and silent, and only the searchlights probing the darkness.

The losses were made good, for both the French and British had plenty of obsolescent battleships, but the catastrophe unnerved the leaders of the expedition and their masters at home. The irony of it all was that those old battleships had been sent out as expendable units, but as soon as three were sunk the admirals began to talk about unbearable losses. Only the *Queen Elizabeth* and the *Inflexible* could be regarded as strategically important ships, and they should not have been there anyway. The alternative was the bloody attempt to take the Gallipoli Peninsula by means of amphibious landings, and when thinking of the colossal casualties incurred by British, French and ANZAC troops in trying to gain a foothold on that barren spur it is hard to avoid the thought that more attention to the problems of shore bombardment and a few more pre-dreadnought battleships sunk by mines would have been a cheaper price to pay. And if the Allies had been able to get reinforcements and supplies to Russia through the Black Sea, might the Revolu-

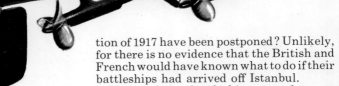

tion of 1917 have been postponed? Unlikely, for there is no evidence that the British and French would have known what to do if their battleships had arrived off Istanbul.

Many of the battleships stayed on at Mudros, for they were needed to provide covering fire for the landings. This they did very well, and the hard-pressed troops were encouraged by the sight of battleships

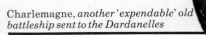

Charlemagne, another 'expendable' old battleship sent to the Dardanelles

Marius Bar

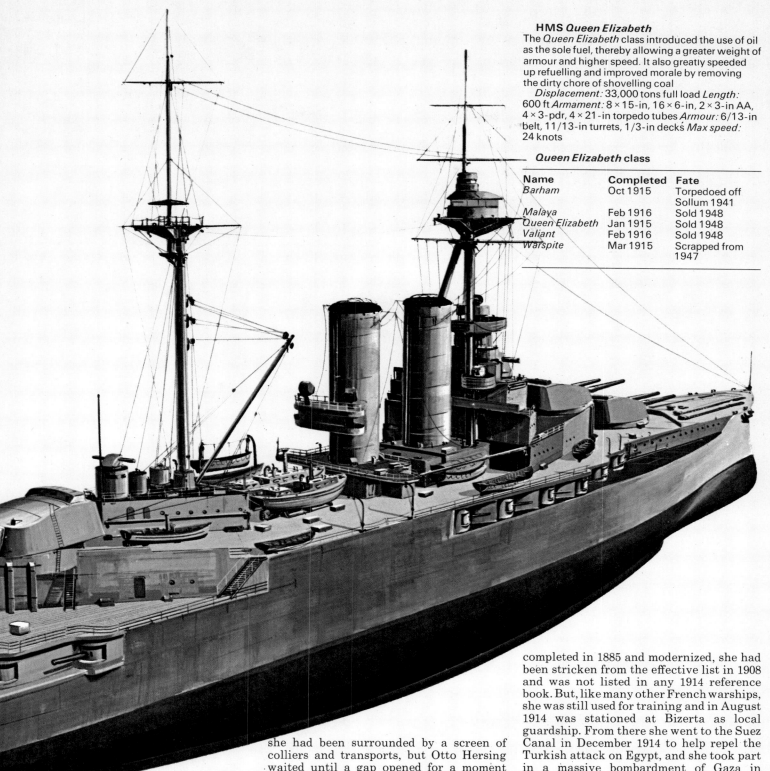

HMS *Queen Elizabeth*
The *Queen Elizabeth* class introduced the use of oil as the sole fuel, thereby allowing a greater weight of armour and higher speed. It also greatly speeded up refuelling and improved morale by removing the dirty chore of shovelling coal
Displacement: 33,000 tons full load *Length:* 600 ft *Armament:* 8 × 15-in, 16 × 6-in, 2 × 3-in AA, 4 × 3-pdr, 4 × 21-in torpedo tubes *Armour:* 6/13-in belt, 11/13-in turrets, 1/3-in decks *Max speed:* 24 knots

***Queen Elizabeth* class**

Name	Completed	Fate
Barham	Oct 1915	Torpedoed off Sollum 1941
Malaya	Feb 1916	Sold 1948
Queen Elizabeth	Jan 1915	Sold 1948
Valiant	Feb 1916	Sold 1948
Warspite	Mar 1915	Scrapped from 1947

pouring shells into the Turkish trenches. Under these circumstances the old battleships could fire much more accurately, for the troops ashore could spot and report the fall of shot, so that corrections could be made. But this happy state of affairs did not last. On the night of 13 May a Turkish torpedo boat crept down the Straits and torpedoed the *Goliath*, which was lying off the beaches. Then, on May 25, 1915, the German submarine *U-21* arrived after a long voyage from Germany via Austria, and torpedoed the *Triumph* off Gaba Tepe. Two days later *U-21* returned to find the old *Majestic*, once the pride of the Channel Fleet and newly appointed as a flagship, anchored with her torpedo nets out. In a desperate attempt to protect the battleship

she had been surrounded by a screen of colliers and transports, but Otto Hersing waited until a gap opened for a moment between two ships, and fired a single torpedo. The net-cutter did its work, the torpedo went straight through the nets, and within seven minutes the old ship capsized in only 50 ft of water.

The loss of three battleships off the beaches meant that it was no longer possible to give heavy fire-support and the battleships were withdrawn. The French ships went to Corfu and four British pre-dreadnoughts were sent to Taranto to strengthen the already-strong Italian Navy in its task of coping with the Austro-Hungarian Fleet in the Adriatic. The old ships saw a lot of activity in the Mediterranean but very little action, apart from bombardments carried out by Italian ships in northern Italy from 1916 onwards. The most curious career of all the old ships is that of the little French coast-defence ship *Requin*. Laid down in 1879,

completed in 1885 and modernized, she had been stricken from the effective list in 1908 and was not listed in any 1914 reference book. But, like many other French warships, she was still used for training and in August 1914 was stationed at Bizerta as local guardship. From there she went to the Suez Canal in December 1914 to help repel the Turkish attack on Egypt, and she took part in a massive bombardment of Gaza in November 1917.

Odd uses were also found for the old *Majestic* class. Early in 1915 the *Hannibal*, *Magnificent*, *Mars* and *Victorious* were disarmed to provide 12-in gun turrets for a new class of eight 'monitors'. These were shallow-draught ships designed to bombard the coast of Belgium, now under what promised to be long-term occupation by the right flank of the German Army. They bore little resemblance to the monitors of the 1860s, but they had the shallow draught and single gun turret so characteristic of Ericsson's creations. The four disarmed battleships were then used as troop transports and sent out to the Dardanelles. The *Jupiter* was sent to Archangel in North Russia at the end of 1914 to clear a path through the ice, and she created a record by being the first ship ever to dock in that port as early as February. Like the *Caesar*, she had an active career and did not return to the United Kingdom until 1918, the oldest British battleships still in commission.

Several ships were altered in various ways, usually to improve their fire-control, but the *London* was unique. In January 1918 she emerged from a year-long conversion to a large minelayer. Her 12-in guns were removed and a continuous mine deck was installed at main deck level. Most other navies made use of their old ships for patrol work and shore bombardment, but the German Navy paid off many of its old coast-defence ships and pre-dreadnoughts in 1915-16. The Germans lacked the manpower to keep too many useless ships in commission, and as they were virtually confined to the Baltic and North Sea they had no need for ships on distant stations.

This busy life led by the older battleships took its toll in casualties from mines and submarine torpedoes. In contrast the dreadnoughts led such sheltered lives that comparatively few were lost. The nature of the conflict in the North Sea meant that virtually all British and German dreadnoughts were committed to watching each other, apart from the few British ships despatched to the Falklands and the Dardanelles and the German ships involved against the Russians in 1916-17. The significant exception to this was the battle-cruiser *Goeben*, the only German capital ship on a foreign station at the outbreak of war. She escaped from British battle-cruisers just before the expiry of the Anglo-French ultimatum and reached Turkey, where she was first interned and then purchased. Renamed the *Yavuz Sultan Selim* she embroiled Turkey in the war by attacking the Russians at Sevastopol. She was in action with the Russian Black Sea Fleet more than once, fired on the *Queen Elizabeth* in April 1915, was mined and bombed. On January 20, 1918, she and a light cruiser sallied out of the Dardanelles and sank two British monitors off Imbros. Despite being mined twice and running aground immediately afterwards and being bombed by British aircraft, she was towed off by the old battleship *Torgud Res* (sister of the *Hairredin Barbarossa* mentioned earlier) and was finally scrapped in 1971 after 60 years of service.

FROM JUTLAND TO SCAPA FLOW

SMS *Baden*
Designed to counter the firepower of the Royal Navy's *Queen Elizabeth* class, the German ships were slower and intended to fight only in the comparatively sheltered conditions of the North Sea
Displacement: 28,000 tons *Length:* 170 m
Amament: 8 × 380-mm, 16 × 150-mm, 8 × 88-mm, 5 × 600-mm torpedo tubes *Max speed:* $22\frac{1}{4}$ knots

Bayern class

Name	Completed	Fate
Baden	Oct 1916	Sunk as target 1921
Bayern	Mar 1916	Scrapped 1935

The leading navies virtually stopped building any new capital ships at the outbreak of the war, although ships under construction were nearly all accelerated. The Germans were badly hit by the Army's overriding claims to heavy guns and steel, and the third ship of the *Derfflinger* class, the *Hindenburg*, was not completed until mid-1917. Only two of the four *Bayern* class were completed by mid-1916; the *Bayern* was still working up in the Baltic at the time of the Battle of Jutland, when her 15-in guns might have been useful. Seven battle-cruisers laid down in 1915-1916 were never completed.

The British completed five of their eight *Royal Sovereign* class ships in 1916-17; the remaining three were replaced by two battle-cruisers, *Renown* and *Repulse*, but unfortunately the design of this pair was approved by Lord Fisher, who had returned in triumph as First Sea Lord late in 1914. Although armed with 15-in guns and capable of 32 knots they had no more armour than the old *Invincible* class of 1908. When *Repulse* arrived at Scapa Flow in August 1916 a horrified Admiral Jellicoe sent her straight back into dock to have some extra magazine protection added. Three other Fisher-inspired freaks are worth

Displacement: 32,000 tons *Length:* 624 ft *Armament:* 12 × 14-in, 14 × 5-in, 4 × 3-in, 2 × 21-in torpedo tubes *Armour:* 14-in belt, 9/18-in turrets *Max speed:* 21 knots

New Mexico class

Name	Completed	Fate
New Mexico	May 1918	Scrapped from 1947
Mississippi	Dec 1917	Scrapped from 1956
Idaho	Mar 1919	Scrapped from 1947

HMS Glorious
Widely regarded as grotesque failures, the *Courageous* and *Glorious* later found fame after their conversion to aircraft carriers. In their original form they mounted extremely heavy armament on a light cruiser hull with very little armour protection
Displacement: 22,700 tons full load *Length:* 735 ft *Armament:* 8 × 15-in, 18 × 4-in, 2 × 3-in AA, 2 × 21-in torpedo tubes *Armour:* 2/3-in belt, 9-in turrets, $\frac{3}{4}$/1-in decks *Max speed:* 31 knots

Courageous class

Name	Completed	Fate
Courageous	Jan 1917	Torpedoed 1939
Glorious	Jan 1917	Sunk 1940

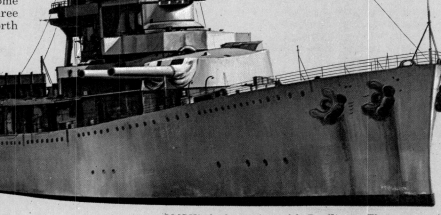

SMS Hindenburg, *sister of the* Derfflinger. *They were possibly the best capital ships of the First World War, with a very battleworthy combination of gunpower, armour and speed*

Imperial War Museum

mentioning: the 15-in-gunned 'large cruisers' *Glorious* and *Courageous* and their 18-in gunned half-sister *Furious*. With only 3-in armour they embodied the Fisher ideals of speed and gunpower without armour pushed beyond the bounds of logic, and by no stretch of the imagination could they be rated as capital ships. On the only occasion the *Glorious* and *Courageous* were in action, off Heligoland in November 1917, they suffered more damage from German light cruisers than they were able to inflict themselves.

The British had not intended to build any more capital ships, on the basis that the war would be over by Christmas. The Cabinet had only given approval to build the *Repulse* and *Renown* on the strength of the battle-cruisers' showing at the Battle of the Falklands, but in 1915 news leaked out that the Germans were building 15-in-gunned battle-cruisers, and so a new super-*Queen Elizabeth* design was prepared. This was the *Hood* class, drastically re-cast after Jutland from 36,300-ton battle-cruisers with 9-in armour belts to 41,200-ton fast battle-ships with 12-in belts. In other respects they were merely enlarged *Queen Elizabeth*s with another five or six knots' speed. Work did not start until just before Jutland, and when news of the slow progress in German shipyards filtered through three were slowed

down in 1917, leaving only the *Hood* to be launched in August 1918. For those who are superstitious it might have seemed unwise to have the ship christened by Lady Hood, the widow of the admiral who lost his life so tragically in HMS *Invincible* at Jutland.

Battleship design improved little during the war, apart from the British invention of anti-torpedo 'bulges', which were fitted to new ships in 1916-17. But equipment and particularly fire-control improved radically. Ships were fitted with more searchlights to improve night-fighting, range-clocks to concentrate fire, enlarged bridges to improve efficiency and accommodation for personnel, etc. Torpedo nets disappeared completely, the Germans being the last to discard them after Jutland. The biggest single change was the British introduction of aircraft platforms in 1917 to allow fighters and reconnaissance biplanes to be flown off at sea. The fighters were needed to curb the German Navy's Zeppelins, which repeatedly gave away the position of British warships, and by the end of the war the Grand Fleet had a large number of its battleships and battle-cruisers equipped with two aircraft apiece.

When the Armistice came on 11 November, 1918, it brought to an end the era of battle-ship supremacy. In little more than 20 years

it had grown enormously in fighting power and size, and had come to dominate the naval scene in a remarkable way, but its days were numbered. The enormous fleets which had been existing in 1914 solely to do battle with one another had been severely restricted throughout the war by the threat of mines and torpedoes, and far more had been lost to these methods than to the guns of other battleships. In November 1918 the Royal Navy had 60 battleships on the Effective List, but 18 of those were pre-dreadnoughts and 14 were 12-in-gunned dreadnoughts, most of them with thin armour, leaving only 28 ships armed with 13.5-in, 14-in or 15-in guns. There would be further battleships, much bigger and better armed, but never again would the battleship dominate the oceans and be the sole arbiter of sea power.

Symbolically, the battle fleet which had started the race towards war, the German High Seas Fleet, surrendered to the British off the Firth of Forth ten days after the Armistice. Fourteen dreadnought battle-ships and battle-cruisers steamed across to surrender, and passed between long lines of British, American and French warships before proceeding to Scapa Flow. There they rotted until 21 June, 1919, when the entire fleet was scuttled.

Battleship Losses 1914-18

Audacious (GB) — mined off Northern Ireland 27 October 1914
Bulwark (GB) — blew up at Sheerness 26 November 1914
Mussddieh (Turkey) — torpedoed in Dardanelles by Br. submarine 13 December 1914
Formidable (GB) — torpedoed by U-Boat in Channel 1 January 1915
Bouvet (FR) — mined at Dardanelles 18 March 1915
Irresistible (GB) — mined at Dardanelles 18 March 1915
Ocean (GB) — mined at Dardanelles 18 March 1915
Goliath (GB) — torpedoed by Turkish TB at Dardanelles 13 May 1915
Triumph (GB) — torpedoed by U-Boat at Dardanelles 25 May 1915
Majestic (GB) — torpedoed by U-Boat at Dardanelles 27 May 1915
Hairredin Barbarossa (Turkey) — torpedoed by Br. submarine 8 August 1915
Benedetto Brin (It) — blew up at Brindisi 28 September 1915
King Edward VII (GB) — mined off Cape Wrath 6 January 1916
Russell (GB) — mined off Malta 27 April 1916
Invincible (GB) — blew up at Battle of Jutland 31 May 1916
Indefatigable (GB) — blew up at Battle of Jutland 31 May 1916
Queen Mary (GB) — blew up at Battle of Jutland 31 May 1916
Pommern (Ger) — torpedoed at Battle of Jutland 1 June 1916
Lutzow (Ger) — scuttled after heavy damage at Jutland 1 June 1916
Leonardo da Vinci (It) — blew up at Taranto 2 August 1916
Impertritsa Maria (Russ) — blew up at Sevastopol 20 October 1916
Suffren (Fr) — torpedoed by U-Boat in Mediterranean 26 November 1916
Regina Margherita (It) — mined off Valona 11 December 1916
Gaulois (Fr) — torpedoed by U-Boat in Mediterranean 27 December 1916
Peresviet (Russ) — mined off Port Said 5 January 1917
Cornwallis (GB) — torpedoed by U-Boat in Mediterranean 9 January 1917
Tsukuba (Jap) — blew up at Yokosuka 14 January 1917
Danton (Fr) — torpedoed by U-Boat in Mediterranean 19 March 1917
Vanguard (GB) — blew up at Scapa Flow 9 July 1917
Slava (Russ) — wrecked by gunfire and scuttled in Moon Sound, Eastern Baltic 17 October 1917
Wien (A-H) — torpedoed by Italian MTB at Trieste 10 December 1917
Szent Istvan (A-H) — torpedoed by Italian MTB off Premuda 10 June 1918
Svobodnaya Rossia (Russ) — scuttled off Novorossiisk 18 June 1918
Viribus Unitis (A-H) — sunk by Italian limpet mine at Pola 10 October 1918
Britannia (GB) — torpedoed off Cape Trafalgar by U-Boat 9 November 1918

SMS Bayern *seen at the surrender of the High Sea Fleet. At last the enemy, last seen through the smoke of Jutland, was there in close-up. After 1916 the morale of the German fleet had been steadily eroded as key personnel were drafted to U-boats and destroyers. At Scapa, isolation, dirt and acute shortage of food contributed to a further drastic fall in morale. Main picture – the end, June 21, 1919 and SMS* Bayern *heads for the bottom of the Flow*

The Treaty for the Limitation of Naval Armament
'CUT DOWN BY WASHINGTON'

The brand-new battle-cruiser HMS Hood belches smoke as she ploughs through a heavy sea off the Isle of Arran while running her acceptance trials in 1920

When the First World War ended, the major navies seemed about to plunge into another battleship arms race like the one which had occurred between Great Britain and Germany from 1904 onwards. But this time there was a difference. The surrender and the scuttling of the High Seas Fleet at Scapa Flow in 1919 eliminated the second most powerful navy in the world. This left the Royal Navy still in an apparently unchallengeable position, followed by Japan and the United States, with France and Italy trailing some way behind.

These figures are misleading, for the British were in a much worse position than the Americans and Japanese, with all their existing battle-cruisers badly under-armoured and a third of their total strength armed with 12-in guns. By comparison the Americans had authorised in 1916 the construction of ten battleships and six battle-cruisers armed with 16-in guns, and in 1918 the Japanese had followed suit with eight battleships and battle-cruisers similarly armed. The Americans had made no secret of the fact that they wanted to overtake the British as the leading naval power in the world. Their main rival was Japan, for the United States wished to expand its trade in the Pacific, but some Big-Navy interests in Washington felt inclined to take on the British as well if they refused to accept with good grace. The entry of the United States

Battleship Strength of the Powers: 1919

	Battleships	Battlecruisers	Building
Royal Navy	33	9	1
US Navy	17	—	18
Japanese Navy	5	4	8
France	7	—	5
Italy	5	—	1

into the war in 1917 hamstrung the battleship programme, for steel and manpower were switched to building the destroyers and merchant shipping needed by the Allies. Only one of the 16 ships authorised by Congress was laid down in 1917; the others had to wait until 1919, and the last two were not actually started until mid-1921. The Japanese did slightly better, with two battleships begun in 1917 and 1918, but—like the Americans—they could not start the others until two or three years after the war. To match the American programme the Japanese drew up their so-called '8-8

Programme', eight battleships and eight battle-cruisers, all to be started by the beginning of 1927 at the latest.

It was not only the increase in gun-calibre to 16-in which made these ships remarkable. Displacement jumped from the 32,000-ton mark in the Japanese Nagato class and the American Colorado class to 40,000-43,000 tons in the Amagi and South Dakota classes. The Americans favoured a relatively modest speed of 23 knots for their biggest battleships, but the Japanese Nagato and Tosa classes were intended to be 26½-knotters. Against this the British had only the Queen Elizabeths, with 15-in guns and a speed of 24½ knots, and one survivor of the four Hood class, 41,000 tons and eight 15-in guns. The British, alone out of all the Allied navies, had first-hand knowledge of what happened to battleships when they were torpedoed, hit by shells or mined. Not only had their ships been much more exposed to action damage, but there had also been a chance throughout 1919 to study the design of German capital ships. German ships had suffered a certain amount of battle damage but not as much, and of course the extinction of the High Seas Fleet was followed by the dispersal of that talented group of constructors who had designed the battleships and battle-cruisers which fought at Jutland.

Armed with this knowledge and with the results of detailed tests against target ships, the British had good reason to be uneasy about their position. The Director of Naval Construction did not regard the new battle-cruiser *Hood* as a particularly suitable design, and had even suggested that the ship should be scrapped on the stocks to make way for something better. After a series of exhaustive tests against the German battleship *Baden* (the only large ship not to be successfully scuttled at Scapa Flow) and firing trials against the disarmed *Superb*, the British drew up a series of designs to outclass both the Japanese and American ships. Known as the '*G.3*' design, the first class consisted of four 48,000-ton battle-cruisers armed with nine 16-in guns and capable of 32 knots. They were to be followed by 43,500-ton battleships armed with nine 18-in guns, formidable weapons capable of firing a 3200-lb shell nearly 30,000 yards.

Bulge Protection

The '*G.3*'s were among the most powerful capital ships ever laid down, and were certainly the most advanced ships of their day. The armour arrangement was an extension of the 'all-or-nothing'. scheme pioneered in the *Nevada* of 1911, but the side armour was sloped inboard to increase its resistance to plunging shells, and the 'bulge' protection against torpedoes was incorporated into the hull to prevent a reduction of speed. The ships were 856 ft long overall, and to avoid spreading the belt armour over too great an area the triple 16-in turrets were concentrated forward, two before the extensive bridge structure and the third between the bridge and the funnels. The massive tower bridge was another bold step dictated by war experience. The windy platforms in older ships had provided little shelter for signalmen and bridge personnel, and it was decided to accept the risk of a large target in order to provide dry, comfortable accommodation for the key personnel who controlled the ship in action. This policy was amply vindicated in the Second World War, but no other navy followed the British lead.

The US Navy now found that it had a tiger by the tail. The 1916 programme was way behind schedule; the Japanese had responded with ships as powerful; and now, to make matters worse, the British had woken up and produced designs which would eclipse their own. The British ship-yards had shown their staggering pro-ficiency by building the *Renown* and *Repulse* (a completely novel design) in 18 months, and nobody in Washington doubted that the British would have their ships in service before the American giants.

The new arms race was also preoccupying the State Department in Washington. Rivalry with Japan was becoming more acute, with both the USA and Japan facing the

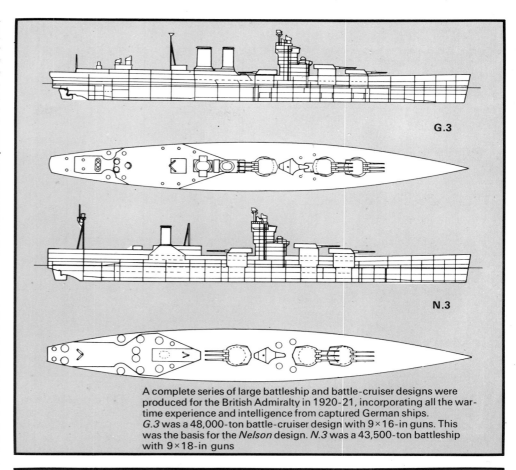

A complete series of large battleship and battle-cruiser designs were produced for the British Admiralty in 1920-21, incorporating all the war-time experience and intelligence from captured German ships. *G.3* was a 48,000-ton battle-cruiser design with 9×16-in guns. This was the basis for the *Nelson* design. *N.3* was a 43,500-ton battleship with 9×18-in guns

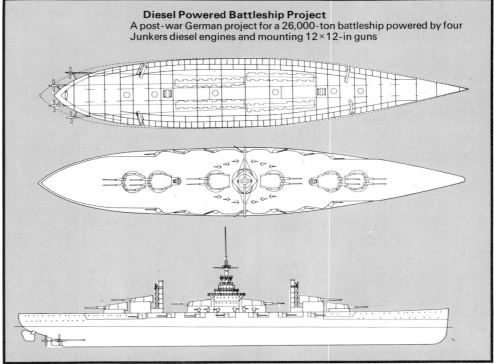

Diesel Powered Battleship Project
A post-war German project for a 26,000-ton battleship powered by four Junkers diesel engines and mounting 12×12-in guns

After 1919 the battle-cruiser Repulse *could be distinguished from her sister* Renown *by the strake of 9-in armour amidships. In 1936 she had a further partial modernisation giving her an aircraft hangar and catapult*

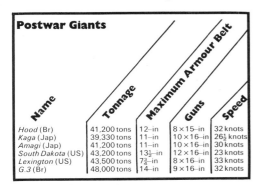

Postwar Giants

Name	Tonnage	Maximum Armour Belt	Guns	Speed
Hood (Br)	41,200 tons	12-in	8 × 15-in	32 knots
Kaga (Jap)	39,330 tons	11-in	10 × 16-in	26½ knots
Amagi (Jap)	41,200 tons	11-in	10 × 16-in	30 knots
South Dakota (US)	43,200 tons	13½-in	12 × 16-in	23 knots
Lexington (US)	43,500 tons	7¾-in	8 × 16-in	33 knots
G.3 (Br)	48,000 tons	14-in	9 × 16-in	32 knots

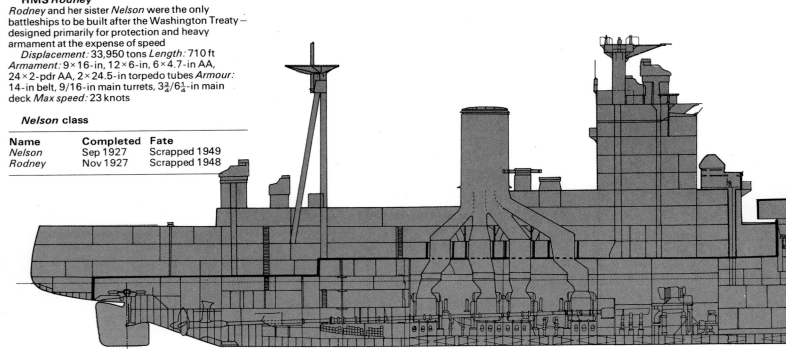

HMS Rodney
Rodney and her sister *Nelson* were the only battleships to be built after the Washington Treaty — designed primarily for protection and heavy armament at the expense of speed
Displacement: 33,950 tons *Length:* 710 ft
Armament: 9×16-in, 12×6-in, 6×4.7-in AA, 24×2-pdr AA, 2×24.5-in torpedo tubes *Armour:* 14-in belt, 9/16-in main turrets, $3\frac{3}{4}/6\frac{1}{4}$-in main deck *Max speed:* 23 knots

Nelson class

Name	Completed	Fate
Nelson	Sep 1927	Scrapped 1949
Rodney	Nov 1927	Scrapped 1948

problems of the post-war recession. Their respective economies had been greatly expanded to cope with war-production for the other Allies, and now these markets had virtually disappeared. Japan had clashed with the United States in 1915 over an attempt to coerce China, and when the US Navy began preparations to fortify its base at Cavita in the Philippines towards the end of the First World War the Japanese made it clear through diplomatic channels that they would regard any such move as a *casus belli*. The Japanese felt, with some justification, that they had not spent millions of yen and many thousands of soldiers' lives to expel the Russians from Manchuria only to have another American Port Arthur.

The Big-Navy party in Washington had a

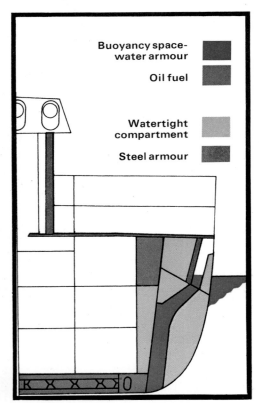

Buoyancy space-
water armour

Oil fuel

Watertight
compartment

Steel armour

simple answer to all these problems: scrap the 1916 programme entirely and replace it with bigger and better ships that would cow the British and the Japanese. But at this point Congress intervened to bring the whole discussion back to reality. There was no hope of getting the money to finish the existing programme, for the US taxpayer was not interested in financing a huge navy two or three years after the end of a costly 'war to end wars', to say nothing of widening the Panama Canal to take the 'Mark II' version battleships. Also, the British were linked to the Japanese by treaty, and the State Department was not wholly convinced by some of the admirals' arguments about fighting both the British and the Japanese simultaneously. The only sane solution was to bring the whole mad scheme to an end by negotiation, just as the British had done with the French in 1904 and the Japanese in 1902, to free themselves to concentrate on matching Germany.

In response to an invitation from President Harding, delegates from the USA, Great Britain, Japan, France and Italy met in Washington on 21 November, 1921 for a conference on naval arms limitation. It was an historic occasion, the first time that the principal naval powers had met to discuss ways of fixing the numbers of warships by treaty, and of fixing the characteristics of the ships themselves. The President began the proceedings by proposing a 'battleship holiday', a ten-year ban on the construction of capital ships; he went on to propose the scrapping of 845,000 tons of American battleship tonnage, 583,000 tons of British construction and 449,000 tons of Japanese construction. In this sense the Americans won the political side of the conference. They had more ships under construction than anyone else, and by offering to scrap them all they laid the onus of wrecking the possibility of peace, parsimony and international disarmament on the shoulders of the British and the other foreign delegations.

In the technical sense, however, it was the British who 'won' the conference. The Japanese and American delegates fought

tooth-and-nail to retain ships which had been designed without benefit of combat experience; the British fought for the right to build two ships in which they could incorporate all the lessons of the late war. Furthermore the British delegation at Washington had far superior technical briefing to the others; all technical points raised in the committees were referred back to the DNC and other technical departments for discussion. To cite one example, when the US Navy proposed limiting battleships to a tonnage of 32,500 tons the British immediately insisted on 35,000 tons on the DNC's advice. Design work on a smaller edition of the *G.3* to meet the probable size-limit which would be fixed was going on throughout the conference, so that the delegates could be constantly briefed on points that must not be conceded. The best example of this was the choice of Standard Tonnage. The displacement tonnage of warships had for the previous 60 years been listed as 'normal' or sometimes 'Navy List' for the tonnage of the ship as built, without complement, but with ammunition and the normal allowance of fuel and boiler feed-water. 'Full load' tonnage was the figure for the maximum fuel, reserve feedwater and ammunition and the ship's company.

The British delegation made a stand on the matter of defining tonnage, and insisted that a new tonnage definition should be drawn up, including men, ammunition and stores but not fuel and reserve feedwater. At the time this was put forward as necessary because British ships had to be capable of steaming greater distances in defence of the Empire; it was felt that if fuel and reserve feedwater were included in the tonnage, British ships would have to have thinner armour. The real reason was that the British had designed 'water protection' or liquid-loaded layers for the new battleships, a method of admitting fuel or seawater into a 'sandwich' compartment inside the anti-torpedo protection, with the aim of damping the effect of a torpedo hit. If fuel and feed-water could be left out of the tonnage total it would be much easier to conceal the existence of this novel type of protection,

The appearance of the Royal Navy's new battleships Nelson *and* Rodney *startled naval traditionalists. The* Nelson *was nevertheless a very battleworthy design*

National Maritime Museum

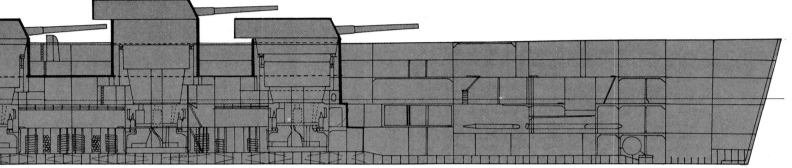

and in fact the British managed to hide it from the outside world for 40 years.

The delegates finally settled on a standard displacement of 35,000 tons and a maximum gun calibre of 16-in, but the bitterest wrangling was reserved for the discussion on total strength. Eventually it was agreed that the British should be allowed 22 capital ships (580,450 tons), to be reduced to 18 by 1927; the Americans 18 (500,650 tons); but the Japanese, the French and Italians 10 each. This was accepted by the Japanese with ill grace as a 'Rolls-Rolls-Ford' arrangement, but like all the other delegations present they knew that their government was not prepared to pay for a new fleet. On 6 February, 1922 the Washington Treaty, more properly known as the Treaty for the Limitation of Armament, was signed. The British could build two new 35,000-ton ships armed with 16-in guns, the US Navy could complete one of its 16-in gunned ships and the Japanese could complete both theirs. The French and Italians were in such financial difficulties that they had given up all ideas of completing their wartime construction.

Although the British negotiators had good reason to be satisfied with themselves, the DNC and his team still faced tremendous technical problems. The *G.3* design had been a 32-knot ship protected by 14-in armour on the side of 5½-in decks. Many features had to be sacrificed or modified to reduce this 48,000-ton design to 35,000 tons. The options were limited: the 16-in guns had to be retained and so either armour or speed must be reduced. With no hesitation the latter course was followed, and the installed power was slashed from 160,000 to 45,000 shaft horsepower. This meant a speed of only 23 knots, but even so it was two knots faster than the *Colorado* and only two knots less than the Japanese *Nagato*. To further reduce the hull length the third triple 16-in gun turret was moved forward to a position just behind the two foremost turrets, and the 6-in secondary guns were similarly bunched together aft. These changes saved 15,000 tons and 150 ft in length, but produced a most unusual profile,

With the Colorado *class the US Navy adopted 16-in guns for the first time, following the Japanese lead. Both navies were, however, following the layout of the British* Queen Elizabeth *design of 1915*

US Navy

particularly as the designers retained the massive 'tower' bridge which had been a feature of the original design.

HMS *Nelson* was completed on the Tyne in June 1927, and her sister *Rodney* followed her into service from her Birkenhead builders two months later. The decision to build two new battleships had not been received with unanimous approval, for a strong lobby in navalist circles wanted smaller battleships, and an even more vociferous air-power lobby wanted the battleship to be replaced by bomber aircraft. The outlandish appearance of the ships did not help, and as the critics knew nothing of the hidden factors in their design, particularly the 2000 tons of water protection not included in their declared tonnage under

the treaty, the battleships were compared unfavourably with foreign designs. They were known as the 'Cherry Tree' class, cut down by Washington, but the unkindest cut of all was the sailors' nickname for them—'Nelsol' and 'Rodnol'—in memory of a group of fleet oilers whose names ended in 'ol'; this was a reference to the position of the funnel so far aft.

6-in round uptakes	
14-in belt	
15-in round 16-in gun trunks	
6-in round 6-in gun trunks	
16-in armour round directors	
16-in round control position	

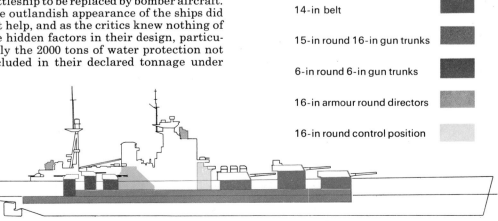

The Royal Sovereigns *were slower and smaller than the* Queen Elizabeths *but with some modernisation they gave extensive service in the Second World War*

National Maritime Museum

Ironically, in stopping the development of the battleship the Washington Treaty was responsible for advancing another type of warship, one which would eventually outstrip the battleship in destructive power, complexity and cost. Aircraft carriers had been developed during the First World War, but until 1922 the ships built or converted had all been relatively small. The large hulls made redundant by the treaty in 1922 all offered tempting opportunities to try out schemes for large aircraft carriers, but without the cost of building them from scratch. The US Navy took the incomplete battle-cruisers *Lexington* and *Saratoga* in hand and the Japanese announced that they would convert the similar-sized *Akagi* and *Amagi*. The British had already converted one of Fisher's freak 'large light cruisers', HMS *Furious*, from a paper tiger with two 18-in guns into a fleet carrier, and chose to disarm and convert her half-sisters *Glorious* and *Courageous* along similar lines. The Japanese had almost started work on their two battle-cruisers when the great earthquake of 1 September, 1923 wrecked the building slip at Yokosuka Dockyard. The hull of the *Amagi* was so badly distorted by the shock that it was decided to dismantle her, but the two *Kaga*-class battleship hulls were still in existence, and they were only 60 ft shorter. The hull of the *Kaga* was therefore reprieved and her conversion on similar lines to *Akagi* was started soon afterwards.

The 'battleship holiday' did not mean the end of work on battleships. For one thing the appearance of the 16-in gun made all the big navies conscious of the weak protection of their older battleships, and for another the lessons of the late war indicated many improvements that could be made. The British started immediately after the Armistice by re-armouring the thin-skinned *Repulse* with 9-in armour, an essential improvement which her sister did not get until 1926. In 1924 the first of the *Queen Elizabeth* class was taken in hand for improvements, including the addition of 'bulges' to the hull, strengthening anti-aircraft armament and trunking the funnels together to reduce the tendency to smoke out the bridgework. The single-funnelled *Royal Sovereigns* had no need of such drastic treatment, but some were given a funnel cap to reduce the smoke interference.

Maximum Fighting Value

With so many coal-fired ships the US and Japanese navies felt bound to devote money to reboilering their older ships and converting them to oil-burning. But the Japanese went even further. Still nursing a grievance over what they saw as a conspiracy beteen the Americans and their stooges the British to relegate Japan to second-class status, they planned a careful programme of reconstruction to extract the maximum fighting value out of their ships. Even if no new battleships could be built for ten years, each

Japanese battleship would exploit the reconstruction clauses of the treaty to the full. It was during this period that the complex 'pagoda' foremasts began to appear in Japanese ships. In reality these were only a cluster of platforms added to the original tripod masting in most cases, although the *Nagato*s went one better by having a pentapod mast.

In 1927 the Royal Navy received its two new battleships, the *Nelson* and *Rodney*, but had to say goodbye to the three *King George V* class and the *Thunderer* to reduce the numbers to 20, the same as the United States. The following year the Italians paid off the old *Dante Alighieri*, reducing their total of battleships to four, the four pre-dreadnoughts of the *Regina Elena* class having been disposed of between 1923 and 1927. The French retained their four old ships of the *Danton* class, for all their antique design, although after 1927 they were used only for training.

The French and Italian navies suffered even more than those of the major naval powers. Their ships were generally older and less powerful than the British, American and Japanese counterparts; the Italian vessels lacked heavy guns and the French ships were poorly protected. To compensate for this, special clauses in the treaty allowed France to start building a new capital ship in 1927 and another in 1929, while the Italians were permitted to build 70,000 tons of new construction. Neither the French nor the Italians took advantage of these clauses, although design work started in both countries. The French examined the idea of a

HMS *Malaya*
One of the *Queen Elizabeth* class extensively modernised between the wars. She was re-engined, the twin funnels were trunked into one, AA armament was increased and a central aircraft hangar with athwartship catapult was installed
Displacement: 31,000 tons *Length:* 600 ft
Armament: 8 × 15-in, 12 × 6-in, 8 × 4-in AA, 16 × 2-pdr AA

The Queen Elizabeths *were improved by the addition of anti-torpedo bulges, more effective anti-aircraft armament and the trunking of two funnels into one to reduce smoke effects.*

croiseur de combat, or battle-cruiser, capable of handling heavy cruisers and scouting for the Fleet—which sounds dangerously like the original *Invincible*. The Italians even went so far as to divide their 70,000 tons into three parts, and considered building three 23,000-tonners; the idea was dropped when it was pointed out that these vessels would be inferior even to the existing ships.

Two navies have not been mentioned so far, the German and the Russian. For the moment the Russian Navy, or Red Fleet as it had been christened, was wallowing in the chaos that followed the Revolution and the Civil War. Those ships that survived the vicissitudes of 1917–22 were in appalling condition, and Lenin wisely decided after the Civil War that Russia's industrial position was too weak to support a large fleet. All the pre-dreadnoughts were scrapped, and one of the four surviving dreadnoughts, the *Poltava*, was 'cannibalised' for spares. Only the *Petropavlovsk* (renamed *Marat*) and *Oktyabskaya Revolutsia* (ex-*Gangut*) were back in working order by 1925–26. Although the might of the High Seas Fleet had been obliterated in the depths of Scapa Flow, the Treaty of Versailles allowed Germany to retain eight old pre-dreadnoughts as coast-defence ships. Replacement of these was allowed, but only on a ship-for-ship basis, subject to a limit of 10,000 tons and guns of 11-in calibre. In 1926 the oldest ship, the *Zahringen*, was converted to a radio-controlled target. The *Preussen* and *Elsass* followed in 1931–32, and replacements were ordered in 1930. The Versailles Treaty was not concerned with naval limitations as such, but the framers of the Washington Treaty had laboured hard to separate the categories of battleship, coast-defence ship and cruiser. They reckoned without the tenacity and skill of German designers, however, who quite deliberately strove to build a ship which could fit into the 10,000-ton limit and yet act as a commerce raider on the high seas. And furthermore, by giving the ship the 11-in guns permitted under the Versailles Treaty, they made her much more than a match for all the big, expensive heavy cruisers permitted by the Washington Treaty.

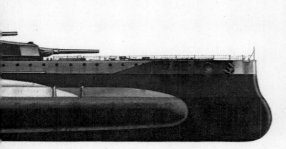

Fleet Reductions After Washington

Existing Ships to be Retained	Existing Ships to be Scrapped	New Ships to be Completed	New Ships to be Scrapped
Great Britain			
Hood	Indomitable	Nelson	Invincible*
Renown	Inflexible	Rodney	Inflexible*
Repulse	Bellerophon		Indomitable*
Royal Sovereign	Superb/Temeraire		Indefatigable*
Royal Oak	Collingwood		
Revenge	St Vincent		
Ramilles	New Zealand		
Resolution	Australia (RAN)		
Queen Elizabeth	Neptune		
Warspite	Orion		
Barham	Colossus		
Malaya	Hercules		
Valiant	Monarch		
Tiger	Conqueror		
Iron Duke	Lion		
Marlborough	Princess Royal		
Emperor of India	Courageous		
Benbow	Glorious		
King George V***			
Ajax***			
Centurion***			
Thunderer****			

*These names were unofficially allocated to the G.3 class
**To be converted to aircraft carriers
***To be scrapped in 1927 on completion of *Nelson* and *Rodney*
****Used for training, to be scrapped on completion of *Nelson* and *Rodney*

Existing Ships to be Retained	Existing Ships to be Scrapped	New Ships to be Completed	New Ships to be Scrapped
United States			
Florida	South Carolina	Colorado	Washington
Utah	Michigan	Maryland	South Dakota
Wyoming	Delaware	West Virginia	Indiana
Arkansas	North Dakota		Montana
New York			North Carolina
Texas			Iowa
Nevada			Massachusetts
Oklahoma			Lexington*
Pennsylvania			Constellation
Arizona			Saratoga*
New Mexico			Ranger
Mississippi			Constitution
Idaho			United States
Tennessee			
California			

*To be converted to aircraft carriers

Existing Ships to be Retained	Existing Ships to be Scrapped	New Ships to be Completed	New Ships to be Scrapped
Japan			
Kongo	Ibuki	Mutsu	Kaga
Kirishima	Kurama		Tosa
Hiei	Aki		Akagi*
Haruna	Satsuma		Amagi*
Fuso	Settsu		Atago
Yamashiro			Takao
Hyuga			
Ise			
Nagato			

Italy	
Napoli	
Regina Elena	
Roma	
Vittorio Emmanuele	
Dante Alighieri	
Conte di Cavour	
Giulio Cesare	
Leonardo da Vinci*	
Andrea Doria	
Duilio	

*Blown up at Taranto in 1916 and salvaged in 1919, but plans to reconstruct her were subsequently cancelled and she was scrapped in 1923

Existing Ships to be Retained	Existing Ships to be Scrapped		New Ships to be Scrapped
France			
Diderot	République*		Béarn**
Condorcet	Patrie***		Normandie
Vergniaud	Democratie		Languedoc
Jean Bart	Justice		Flandre
Courbet	Vérité		Gascogne
Paris			
France			
Bretagne			
Provence			
Lorraine			

*Disarmed and used as training ship
**To be converted to aircraft carrier
***Hulked as training ship at Toulon

THE SECOND NAVAL RACE

It was small wonder that the appearance of the *Deutschland* in April 1933 created a sensation, or that she was hailed with hysterical delight by the German public, now beginning to fret under the humiliating restrictions of the 1919 treaty. The outside world dubbed her a 'pocket battleship', but to the German Navy she was simply called a *Panzerschiff*, or armoured ship—the best translation of which was armoured cruiser. Despite the exaggerated reports of her capabilities she was not a battleship, but a high-endurance cruiser with ultra-heavy armament and only moderate speed and no better protection than most contemporary cruisers. Two novelties gave the clue to her success: the extensive use of welding to save weight, and the use of diesel motors to give high endurance. Unfortunately, she was not a 10,000-ton ship as defined by the Washington Treaty, and if her admirers had known that her standard displacement was actually 11,700 tons (17 per cent outside the limit) they might not have waxed so enthusiastic. Although contemporary reports had credited her with the staggering range of 19,000 miles at cruising speed, the actual service endurance was about 10,000 miles and the Germans admitted later that the diesel machinery had been something of a disappointment. Two similar half-sisters, the *Admiral Scheer* and *Admiral Graf Spee*, followed in 1934 and 1936.

The *Panzerschiffe* must be regarded as more of a political gesture than a significant contribution to the history of capital-ship design. The experience of the Second World War was to expose the myths about them, and in 1940 the *Kriegsmarine* admitted as much by re-rating the surviving pair as heavy cruisers. They were effective commerce raiders but heavily over-armed for the

The Reichsmarine's *coast-defence battleship* Schlesien *was modernised twice within the terms of the Versailles Treaty. The old ships' age was the excuse for building the pocket battleships*

Deutschland—*first of the pocket battleships—seen on completion in 1933. She was hailed in a frenzy of patriotic fervour as a symbol of the rebirth of German naval power*

Admiral Graf Spee
This pocket battleship saw action, in common with her sisters, during the Spanish Civil War and then carried out commerce raids in the South Atlantic until being intercepted by the British cruisers *Ajax*, *Achilles* and *Exeter*
Displacement: 16,200 tons maximum
Length: 186 m *Armament:* 6×280-mm,
8×150-mm, 6×105-mm, 8.37-mm, 8×20-mm
(from Oct 1939) *Armour:* 60/80-mm side,
140-mm main turrets *Max speed:* 28.5 knots

Deutschland class

Name	Completed	Fate
Lützow (ex-*Deutschland*)	Apr 1933	Blown up by crew May 1945
Admiral Scheer	Nov 1934	Capsized after bombing Apr 1945
Admiral Graf Spee	Jan 1936	Scuttled Dec 1939

job, and suffered from having the prestige value of a capital unit. They were five knots slower than the cruisers they were intended to elude, and their cumbersome arrangement of two triple 11-in gun mountings put them at a disadvantage in fighting faster and more manoeuvrable cruisers.

The appearance of the *Deutschland* caused a great disturbance in the carefully regulated balance of battleship strength. The French were immediately worried at the prospect of a German commerce raider cutting communications between France and North Africa, the routes by which troop reinforcements would be ferried in time of war, and if the French took fright the

Italians would inevitably respond to keep the balance. To complicate matters the Big Powers were again signing treaties, this time the London Naval Agreement of 1930, whereby Great Britain, America and Japan agreed to extend the 'battleship holiday' to the end of 1936 and to keep the limitations in force. France refused to ratify the treaty on the grounds that she needed new ships to counter the *Deutschland*, and Italy

predictably did likewise. For her the addition of even one new French capital ship would widen the gap between France's six ships and her own ageing quartet. It must never be forgotten just how important battleships still were as symbols of national prestige, and both France and Italy felt that they had been slighted at Washington, so that there was a degree of malicious pleasure in their refusal to ratify the London agreement. Another factor was the Italians' need to maintain employment in their shipyards as part of Mussolini's policy of using military expenditure to subsidise the economy.

The French decided to build two battle-cruisers of approximately 25,000 tons and armed with 13-in guns. The reason for this was that the British had been advocating a reduction in displacement and size of guns, as part of the constant search for mutual reduction of naval armaments in Europe. The Americans had been very cool about these proposals, and of course the Japanese had no intention of making a unilateral gesture of peace, but the French Navy cast its plans on the assumption that these proposals might become fact.

The ships which resulted were remarkable. Although they were lightly armoured, with a belt varying from 9¾-in to 5¼-in at its lower edge, a great deal of weight was saved by grouping the eight 13-in (330-mm) guns in two quadruple turrets forward, as in the *Nelson* class. But unlike the slow and rather ugly *Nelson*, the *Dunkerque* was an elegant ship with a long, flared forecastle and a balanced silhouette. She was also very fast, reaching 30½ knots on an 8-hr trial. Her sister *Strasbourg* was completed four years later (1936) and reached 31 knots. The 13-in/52 cal gun fired three 1258-lb shells per minute to a distance of 45,800 yards, and had a muzzle velocity of 2803 ft/sec.

The appearance of the *Dunkerque* made the Italians think again, and in 1930 they started work on a new series of 35,000-ton designs to be armed with 15-in or 16-in guns. The British convened another round of fruitless negotiations in Rome in 1931 in an attempt to head off a Franco-Italian arms race, but all that could be agreed was that both nations would be invited to a major conference to be held in London at the end of 1935. From then until the outbreak of the Second World War the naval treaties became less and less effective in controlling the rate of battleship building. Had the Germans not built their ingenious 'pocket battleships' the new arms race might have been delayed, but it should not be forgotten that the Washington Treaty—despite its limitations—did work remarkably well for a decade.

It was appropriate that the Italians should take the lead in designing the first of a new series of fast battleships. Their battleships had always been capable of a good turn of speed, even in the 1880s, and when they started design work on 35,000-ton designs in 1930 they plumped for a speed of 30 knots. The designers soon discarded the idea of

The impressive lines of the Graf Spee *seen from above as she surges through the water*

having 16-in guns, which would have to be designed from scratch. The Armstrong gun foundry at Pozzuoli was capable of producing the 15-in already designed in England in the First World War for the defunct *Francesco Caracciolo* class, and Ansaldo's factory at Genoa was able to produce a new and more powerful design which fired an 885-kg shell a distance of 42,800 metres at 36° elevation.

The Inspector of Naval Engineering, General Umberto Pugliese, was in charge of the project and designed a totally new scheme of underwater protection. This involved a cylindrical section running longitudinally down the length of the anti-torpedo 'bulge'. In theory a cylindrical

Reduction of Fleets: 1931-6

Retained	Scrapped
Great Britain	
Nelson	Iron Duke*
Rodney	Benbow
Hood	Emperor of India
Renown	Marlborough
Repulse	Tiger
Royal Sovereign	
Royal Oak	
Ramillies	
Resolution	
Revenge	
Queen Elizabeth	
Warspite	
Valiant	
Barham	
Malaya	
United States	
Colorado	Florida
Maryland	Utah*
West Virginia	Wyoming*
Tennessee	
California	
New Mexico	
Mississippi	
Idaho	
Pennsylvania	
Arizona	
Nevada	
Oklahoma	
New York	
Texas	
Arkansas	
Japan	
Mutsu	Hiei*
Nagato	
Hyuga	
Ise	
Fuso	
Yamashiro	
Kongo	
Haruna	
Kirishima	
France	
Dunkerque**	Jean Bart*
Strasbourg**	Condorcet*
Bretagne	Diderot
Provence	Voltaire
Lorraine	Vergniaud*
Courbet	
Paris	
Italy	
Littorio**	
Vittorio Veneto**	
Andrea Doria	
Caio Duilio	
Conte di Cavour	
Guilio Cesare	

*Retained demilitarised

**New Construction

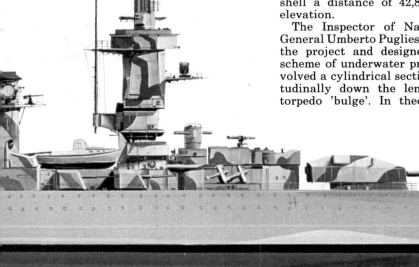

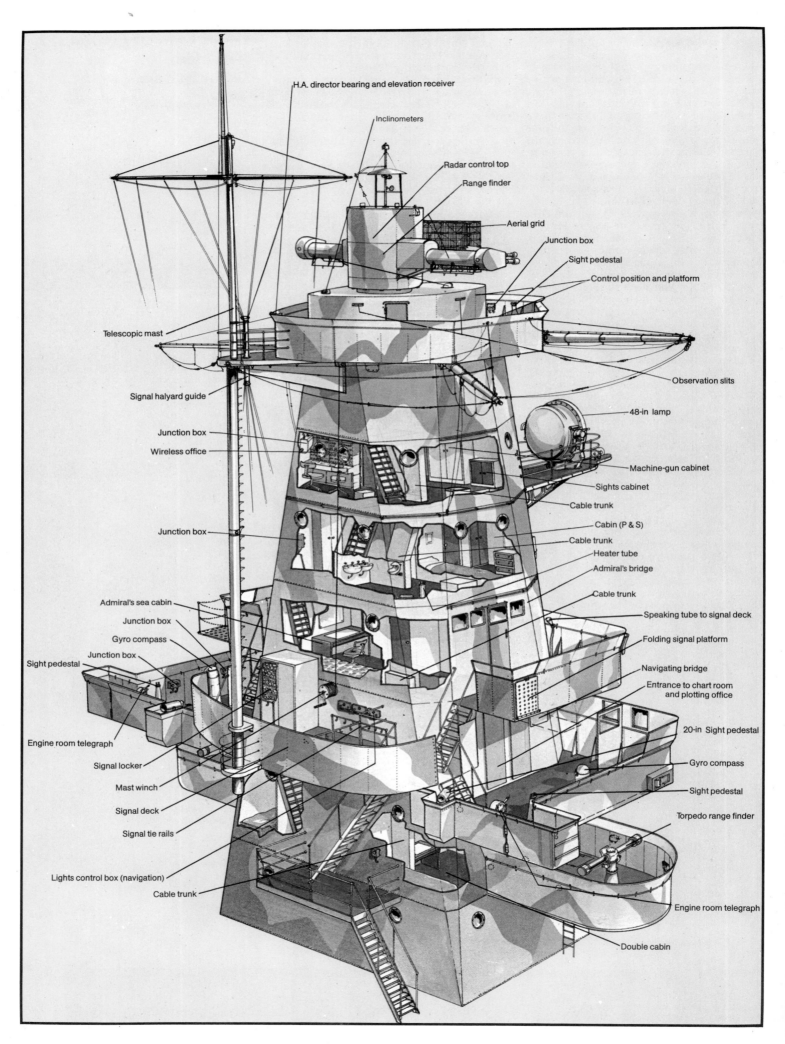

H.A. director bearing and elevation receiver

Inclinometers

Radar control top

Range finder

Aerial grid

Junction box

Sight pedestal

Control position and platform

Observation slits

48-in lamp

Machine-gun cabinet

Sights cabinet

Cable trunk

Cabin (P & S)

Cable trunk

Heater tube

Admiral's bridge

Cable trunk

Speaking tube to signal deck

Folding signal platform

Navigating bridge

Entrance to chart room and plotting office

20-in Sight pedestal

Gyro compass

Sight pedestal

Torpedo range finder

Engine room telegraph

Double cabin

Telescopic mast

Signal halyard guide

Junction box

Wireless office

Junction box

Admiral's sea cabin

Junction box

Gyro compass

Junction box

Sight pedestal

Engine room telegraph

Signal locker

Mast winch

Signal deck

Signal tie rails

Lights control box (navigation)

Cable trunk

The elegant French battle-cruiser *Dunkerque* was built in reply to the German pocket battleships to counter a potential threat to France's sea-route to North Africa

Strasbourg

Designed in response to Germany's construction of the *Deutschland* class of 'pocket battleships,' *Dunkerque* and her sister were fast and fairly heavily armed but had only light armour
Displacement: 35,500 tons full load
Length: 214.5 m *Armament:* 8×330-mm, 16×130-mm, 8×37-mm AA, 32×13.2-mm AA
Armour: 141/241-mm belt, 330-mm main turrets, 130/140-mm main deck *Max speed:* 29½ knots

Dunkerque class

Name	Launched	Fate
Dunkerque	Dec 1932	Scuttled at Toulon 1942
Strasbourg	Dec 1936	Scuttled at Toulon 1942, raised, bombed 1944, raised and scrapped

structure offered maximum resistance to the crushing effect of a torpedo hit and it was hoped that most of the effect would be expended in driving fragments of plating inwards. Another feature was the Ferrati 'triple hull', basically an additional floor to the double bottom to minimise the shock effect of mines. The belt armour was nearly 14 in (350 mm) thick, while the deck thickness reached a maximum of 8 in (207 mm).

Steaming Power
The most impressive aspect of the new ships was their machinery. Four Belluzzo geared turbines delivered 130,000 shaft horsepower for a projected speed of 30 knots —less than the French battle-cruisers, but considerably more than any battleships with comparable protection, apart from the British battle-cruiser *Hood*. In practice the four ships of the *Littorio* class reached an average speed of more than 31 knots on trials despite displacing over 41,000 tons in normal conditions. The trials, however, gave a misleading impression of the ships' steaming powers and in practice their sea speed (ie effective maximum at sea) was only 28 knots, making them equal to such ships as the British *King George V* class. Being designed for the Mediterranean, they had less endurance than British or American ships, but even so they carried 3700 tons of oil fuel, the same amount as the *King George V*. The eight Yarrow boilers were

not very economical, however, and endurance at full speed was a miserable 1770 nautical miles.

The first two ships were laid down on 28 October, 1934: the future *Littorio* at Cantieri Ansaldo, Sestri Ponente (Genoa), and the *Vittorio Veneto* at Cantieri Navali Riuniti dell'Adriatico, Trieste. The nameship of the class (littorio=lictor, the bearer of the fasces in ancient Rome) was launched

Dunkerque
Control tower and superstructure of the *Dunkerque* in close-up. *Dunkerque* differed from her sister *Strasbourg* in design of the control tower, superstructure and the position of the forward range-finder

Admiral Graf Spee
Left: The armoured control tower of the *Graf Spee* surmounted by a range-finder and primitive radar aerial. The Germans were a long way behind in seaborne radar development on the outbreak of war, but they were the first to use gunnery radar in action

The shallow waters of the baltic and the numerous islands forced the Scandinavian navies to retain small coast-defence battleships long after they had disappeared from other leading navies. The Swedish Drottning Victoria (seen below in 1921) resembled a small pre-dreadnought

Comparative Armour Protection Systems

British   **Italian**

The sandwich system of armouring battleships was typical of practise in Royal Navy and US Navy vessels, using void spaces and oil bunkers to maximise resistance to projectiles and blast damage. The Italian Pugliese system of cylindrical armour did not perform well in action.

Andrea Doria

The two ships in this class were designed in 1911 as half-sisters of the *Conte di Cavour* vessels, but they did not see action until the Second World War. By then they had been extensively modernised, but they remained under-armoured

Displacement: 25,200 tons *Length:* 186.9 m
Armament (after conversion): 10×320-mm, 12×135-mm, 10×90-mm, 19×37-mm, 16× 20-mm *Armour:* 130/250-mm belt, 240-mm main turrets, up to 44-mm main deck
Max speed: 27 knots

Duilio class

Name	Completed	Fate
Duilio	May 1915	Scrapped 1958
Andrea Doria	Mar 1916	Scrapped 1958

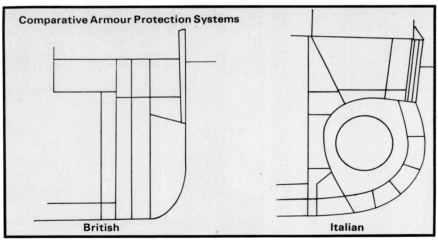

ANDREA DORIA

By the mid-1930s the Baltic navies were also being forced to modernise. The Swedish *Sverige* was given trunked funnels and increased anti-aircraft armament

two more battleships of the *Littorio* class. The *Impero* was started in May 1938 and the *Roma* followed in September. The possession of a squadron of four modern, fast and hard-hitting ships, backed up by the four older ships reconstructed to modern standards, was calculated by Mussolini to give him supremacy over the British in the Mediterranean and make it truly *Mare Nostrum*.

The reconstruction of the old Italian ships was one of the most remarkable feats of naval architecture, rivalling even the Japanese reconstructions in its ingenuity. The midships 12-in turret was removed and replaced by a modern two-shaft steam plant developing more than double the original power. The hull was lengthened and rebuilt to incorporate the Pugliese system of underwater protection, and the superstructure was entirely rebuilt to resemble that of the *Littorio* class. But sadly all this was achieved without increasing the protection. If the Italian constructors had been content with 24 knots to match the British *Queen Elizabeth* class, instead of aiming for 27 knots, they might have had weight to spare for better deck and side armour. The guns were relined to 12.6-in/44 cal (320-mm) to give higher velocity and range; at 27° elevation the 525-kg shell could reach a maximum of 28,600 metres.

With four modern capital ships projected it was not surprising that other countries were beginning to show signs of alarm. But it was Germany, still officially shackled by the Versailles Treaty, which made the next move. The 1933 programme included a fourth *Panzerschiff*, but after Adolf Hitler came to power in that year the German Government insisted on its 'right' to build a reply to the French *Dunkerque*—in other words a reply to the reply to the *Deutschland*. The democracies dithered and so tacitly conceded that they could do nothing to stop the Germans from building a 26,000-ton battle-cruiser armed with 11-in guns.

on 22 August, 1937, but she was preceded by nearly a month by her sister. It is interesting to speculate on what the delegates at the London Naval Conference in 1935 would have made of the proposals to build smaller battleships if they had known that Italy was building ships not only with 15-in guns but which exceeded the existing limit by the considerable margin of 6,000 tons. The Italians were to protest afterwards that they had to allow the tonnage to 'grow' during construction because they found that they could not meet the specified limits, but to the naval architect such excuses make little sense. A major project from a designer as skilled as Umberto Pugliese does not collect 18 per cent more than its designed weight in *standard* condition (all warships tend to increase their full-load tonnage, both during building and in service), and there must have been official connivance at the decision to violate the treaty limits.

As the international situation worsened, for reasons not unconnected with the territorial ambitions of Benito Mussolini, France replied to the two *Littorio*s with her own 35,000-tonners. By now Italy was heavily involved in supporting General Franco in the Spanish Civil War, and as she was already angered by international criticism of her war against Abyssinia in 1936 she decided to double her stakes by laying down

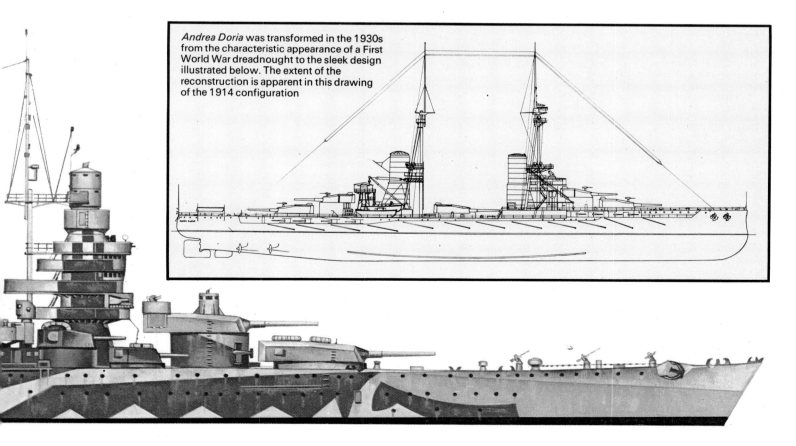

Andrea Doria was transformed in the 1930s from the characteristic appearance of a First World War dreadnought to the sleek design illustrated below. The extent of the reconstruction is apparent in this drawing of the 1914 configuration

The bluff bow of the Gneisenau *proved inadequate for sea-keeping. In 1939 she was rebuilt with a lengthened and raked 'Atlantic' bow*

Professional observers shrewdly suspected that the new ship, the *Scharnhorst*, would be much bigger. Indeed, when she was completed in 1938 she displaced 32,000 tons, an 'error' of 23 per cent which, if genuine, should have resulted in the dismissal of the designer. The choice of the 11-in gun was odd, in view of the *Dunkerque's* 13-in guns and the Italian 12.6-in and 15-in weapons, but in fact German heavy industry was not able to cope with Hitler's sudden expansion of military production. The 11-in triple turrets had been ordered for the next three *Panzerschiffe*, and it was decided to save time by using the six turrets for two nine-gunned battle-cruisers. The design allowed for eventual replacement by three twin 15-in mountings but nothing was done about it until much later.

The Versailles Treaty was now a dead letter. The *Kriegsmarine* (formerly the *Reichsmarine*) did not reveal the laying down of the *Gneisenau*, a sister ship for the *Scharnhorst*, under the 1934 programme. In the early part of the following year Hitler denounced the treaty, however, and presented a shocked world with a *fait accompli*: a new and powerful navy already well advanced. The 1935 programme added a battleship, eventually to be named

Scharnhorst

The two vessels in this class, orginally designated armour-clad ships, gradually grew as design work progressed and heavier armament than originally intended was installed. They were intended partially as replacements for two older battleships

Displacement: 32,000 tons *Length:* 226 m
Armament: 9×280-mm, 12×150-mm, 14× 105-mm, 16×37-mm, up to 24×20-mm, 6×533-mm torpedo tubes (from 1941)
Armour: up to 350-mm side, 360-mm main turrets, 50-mm deck *Max speed:* 31.5 knots

Scharnhorst class

Name	Completed	Fate
Scharnhorst	Jan 1939	Sunk in Battle of North Cape, Dec 1943
Gneisenau	May 1938	Scuttled at Göten-hafen Mar 1945

Bismarck, armed with eight 15-in guns; her sister *Tirpitz* was ordered in 1936.

The British Rearmament Programme

As early as 1934 the British Government realised that a war with either Germany or Japan—and possibly both—was likely by 1941, with Italy thrown in to lengthen the odds. What disturbed the Admiralty was the fact that the Royal Navy was considerably under-strength for such a struggle. Although nominally still the largest in the world, the RN had a large proportion of elderly capital ships, the majority of which would be unfit to fight their opposite numbers. It must be remembered that the aircraft carrier had not yet developed its full potential, and no major navy dared think of countering battleships with anything but its own battle fleet.

The leading naval powers were anxious to continue the limitations enshrined in the treaties, but not at the cost of their fighting efficiency. The London Naval Treaty was due to expire in December 1936, and a new conference was due to be convened to discuss how to continue the limitations on the world's fleets. With a view to rectifying what they saw as a serious weakness in the Royal Navy's strength, the Admiralty advised the Cabinet in May 1934 that the new naval treaty must allow Great Britain to build new battleships. The Admiralty was particularly anxious that they must be laid down as soon as the existing treaty expired, even if the new agreement reduced the permitted displacement and armament.

Design studies for new capital ships had begun in the spring of 1933 to allow the British delegates to have clear objectives at the 1935 conference, just as they had at Washington. Armour protection was given top priority, as it was recognised that even if the conference agreed to reduce gun calibre the new ships would have to face opponents with 15-in and 16-in guns for some years. Air attacks with bombs of up to 2000 lb weight were to be taken into account. Speed was to be no more than 23

knots, the same as foreign battleships and the *Nelson* class. The decisive battle range was held to be 12,000–16,000 yards; it was felt that although high speed (30 knots) would permit action at greater distances, experience showed that destruction of an enemy battleship would only take place at the shorter ranges.

The question of speed vexed the designers of what had now been labelled the '1937 Capital Ships'. The 1935 conference led to the Three-Power Treaty among Great Britain, the USA and France. But the French, with a nervous eye on Italy, would not renounce their right to build 35,000-ton ships with 15-in guns. The battle-cruisers *Dunkerque* and *Strasbourg* were also fast, as were the German replies to them, the *Scharnhorst* and *Gneisenau*. Gun calibre was also the subject of violent changes of policy. At the conference in 1935 the British

Top: Scharnhorst *fires a salvo from one of her three triple 280-mm turrets*

Construction of the Scharnhorst *effectively torpedoed the Versailles Treaty*

were still pressing for a reduction to 12-in guns for battleships, although the Americans wanted to retain the 16-in, while the French and Italians had secretly already committed themselves to 15-in guns for their new ships. But the British remained optimistic about a reduction to 14-in calibre, and won the Americans round. As naval guns and their massive mountings take a long time to design and even longer to build, the guns had to be ordered before the end of 1935 if the first two battleships were to be ready in 1940.

The result was that in October 1935, two months before the convening of the London Naval Conference, the Board of Admiralty recommended that the new capital ships should be 35,000-ton, 28-knot ships armed with twelve 14-in guns. The United States insisted on a clause to allow 16-in guns to be reinstated if the Japanese refused to accept the treaty terms by April 1937. In the event this happened, and so Great Britain ended up as the only country to build 14-in-gunned battleships. This was at the core of most of the criticism levelled at these ships, although experience during the Second World War was to indicate that the theoretically greater range and hitting power of 15-in and 16-in shells made little difference in action. But in 1935 the British designers

felt that to compensate for the lighter shell they should increase the number of guns from eight or nine to 12 in three quadruple mountings, a solution adopted by the Americans as well in their 14-in design.

As work on the new ships progressed several radically novel features were incorporated. A new 5.25-in surface/anti-aircraft gun mounting was adopted for the battleships in place of the planned 4.5-in gun; this was the first example of a dual-purpose armament. The thick horizontal armour against plunging shells and bombs was raised from the middle deck to the main deck to improve stability if the ship was damaged and to reduce the volume of structure vulnerable to semi-armour-piercing (SAP) bombs. The original requirement for six aircraft had been altered, but now provision was to be made for two aircraft hangars in the superstructure, the first time this had been done in any battleships. The underwater protection system which had proved such an important feature of the *Nelson* class was retained in a much improved form.

In February 1936 a provisional programme was drawn up for the two ships. It is quoted below to give some idea of the time-scale for building battleships, and the actual completion dates are given for comparison:

	Provisional date	Actual date
1 Order for the gun mountings	Apr 1936	Apr 1936
2 Order for two ships	Sep 1936	Jul 1936
3 Laying down of ships	Feb 1937	Jan 1937
4 Launch	Jan 1939	Feb and May 1939
5 1st turret installed	Mar 1939	Feb 1940
6 2nd turret installed	May 1939	Apr 1940
7 3rd turret installed	Dec 1939	May 1940
8 Completion of ships	Jul 1940	Dec 1940, Mar 1941

It can be seen clearly from this table that the main source of delay was the armament. The guns themselves presented no problems, unlike the turrets. Three quadruple

turrets had been stipulated to achieve the maximum weight of broadside, although for a time the designers toyed with the idea of nine 14-in guns in three triple mountings. Finally it was decided to alter the number of guns to ten by substituting a twin mounting for one of the quads to save weight. As time was so short this sudden change can only be described as capricious. With hindsight it is clear that nine 14-in would have been nearly as good as twelve, for the simple reason that a triple turret was roomier and easier to work than a quadruple one. But either arrangement was preferable to incurring further delay while a new twin 14-in turret was designed. In any case the design of the new turrets proved more complex than the Director of Naval Construction had envisaged, and the quadruple turrets were eleven months late because of a shortage of draughtsmen.

The first two ships were the *King George V*, ordered from Vickers-Armstrongs, Barrow, and the *Prince of Wales* from Cammell Laird, Birkenhead. The Board of Admiralty wanted to go to a 16-in-gunned design to match the ships which it believed the Japanese were building, but to save further delay the next three battleships authorised under the 1937 programme were repeats of the *King George V*. Despite all the delays it was still hoped to have the first ship at sea in September 1940 and the others in 1941, and *King George V* began her trials in October 1940. During the crisis at the time of Dunkirk, work on the last two—*Anson* and *Howe*—was stopped, but only for a few months; they joined the Fleet in 1942.

US Battleships

Like the British, the Americans had their '1937 Battleships', and it is interesting to see that they came to much the same conclusions: that 27–28 knots was all that was needed to provide tactical flexibility without sacrificing armour. They also chose three quadruple 14-in mountings and a dual-purpose secondary armament for dealing with surface and air attack. All other contemporary designs still retained the cumbersome arrangement of low-angle guns for

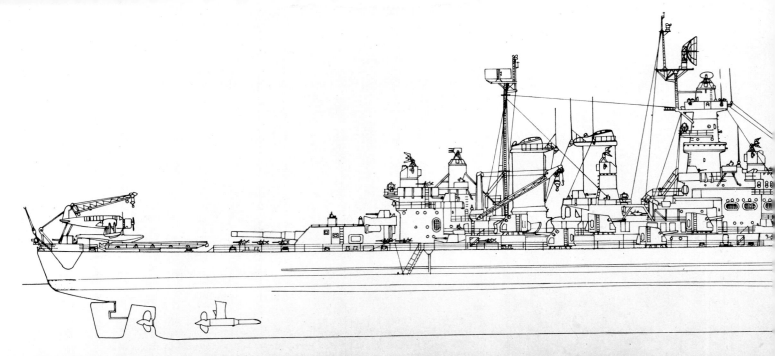

fending off destroyers and a separate lighter-calibre armament against aircraft. But, as we have seen, the Americans reserved the right to drop 14-in guns and revert to 16-in if the Japanese refused to sign the 1936 naval treaty. Nobody knows what the reaction of the British and Americans would have been if they had known just how far the Japanese had decided to depart from the spirit of the treaties, but by the time it was learned that the Japanese might be building 18-in-gunned ships it was too late to change the design of the British ships. The Americans were prepared to wait a little longer, and so the two ships of the *North Carolina* class were altered during construction from twelve 14-in guns to nine 16-in.

The *North Carolina* class had 12-in inclined armour belts with external 'bulges', a relatively light scale of protection. This was the result of being designed to fight 14-in-gunned ships, but it makes an interesting comparison with the British *King George V*, which had equally heavy deck armour but much thicker side armour. This fault was rectified in the next class, the four *South Dakotas* projected for the 1939 programme. These ships were possibly the best of the battleships designed within the restrictions of the international treaties,

and certainly the most ingenious balance of offensive and defensive qualities. The first criterion was to increase protection while keeping the displacement the same, and so it was necessary to make drastic savings in weight. The waterline length was reduced to save structural weight, but as the stubbier hull needed more horsepower than the *North Carolinas* to reach the same speed it was necessary to redesign the steam plant, and in any case the short hull meant smaller engine rooms. But once the intricate problems of squeezing 130,000-shp turbines and boilers into less space than the *North Carolina* needed for 121,000 shp, there were many compensating factors. The shorter hull reduced the areas vulnerable to damage by 7 per cent, and the compact superstructure made for good anti-aircraft defence. The armour was only slightly thicker, but it was inclined at 19° in a different way to that in the previous class, with the belt mounted internally as in the British and Japanese designs of 1920–21. The disadvantages were the risk of increased listing as a result of damage to the thin outer plating, and the loss or contamination of large quantities of oil fuel, but the overriding need was to provide protection against 16-in shells and so the risks were accepted. Like the

British ships, the *South Dakotas* concentrated deck armour in a single 5-in deck, a far more effective defence against bombs than the *North Carolinas* total of three decks.

Production time for the new US battleships was similar to the British ships, and the *North Carolina* was built in roughly the same time as the *King George V*. Both ships were commissioned in the spring of 1941. The *South Dakotas* were laid down between July 1939 and January 1940; three were ready by the spring of 1942 but the last, the *Alabama*, was not commissioned until August 1942. The two classes looked very different, the *North Carolinas* being elegant ships with two slim funnels whereas the *South Dakotas* were squat and purposeful, with a single funnel faired into the superstructure. Both classes retained the old feature of a separate bridge and conning tower, unlike the British *Nelson* and *King George V*, which incorporated both into the tower bridge. This was a weak point, for it split the command organisation in action and the slender pyramidal tower tended to suffer much more from vibration than the solid 'Queen Anne's Mansions' introduced in the *Nelson* class. These features of battleship design were of vital importance.

US Navy

USS *North Carolina*

The two vessels in this class were laid down in response to the construction of the Royal Navy's *King George V* class and similar Japanese ships. Weight-saving construction methods were used, but speed was sacrificed for the sake of firepower
Displacement: 46,770 tons full load
Length: 729 ft *Armament:* 9×16-in, 16×1.1-in AA *Armour:* $6\frac{5}{8}$/12-in belt, 7/16-in main turrets, $3\frac{5}{8}$/$4\frac{5}{8}$-in main deck *Max speed:* 28 knots

North Carolina class

Name	Completed	Fate
North Carolina	Apr 1941	Moored in Cape Fear river as memorial
Washington	May 1941	Scrapped 1961

While the disarmament treaties remained effective, warship designers were set almost impossible tasks in accommodating more powerful guns, higher speed and increased anti-aircraft armaments. The South Dakota class were the last battleships built under these conditions and were a very ingenious solution to the problem

Challenge in the Pacific
RISING SUN

US Navy

The old Japanese battleships were largely inferior to their Western contemporaries and so required a much greater degree of modernisation. The Hyuga *(seen above at Tsingtao in 1938) was re-engined and totally reconstructed to improve her fighting capacity*

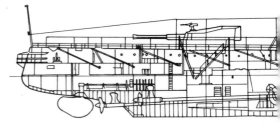

Kongo (above) in her three-funnelled configuration before the first rebuilding 1929-31. The second conversion in 1936 brought her up to modern standards. She is seen below as in 1944 equipped with a Nakajima 'Rufe' floatplane

From 1934 onwards the Imperial Japanese Navy grew more and more ambitious. Under strong political pressure from the Army to support grandiose schemes for conquest in the Far East, the Navy Staff drew up plans for rebuilding the older capital ships and building new ships which could defeat the British and Americans in battle. But at every turn the designers were hampered by the treaties' limits on tonnage and numbers. Eventually the grave decision was taken to renounce the treaties, and Japan gave the statutory two years' warning of her intention not to renew the 1930 treaty when it expired in 1936. It was this announcement which led the Americans to drop their plans for 14-in-gunned ships, but Japan did agree to keep to the spirit of the 1936 treaty, although reserving the right to build ships of up to 45,000 tons. This was agreed to in June 1938 in a protocol signed by Great Britain, the United States and France.

The first step in rebuilding the Fleet was to reconstruct the four *Kongo*-class battle-cruisers, which had been completed in 1913–15 and partially modernised. Between 1933 and 1940 first the *Haruna* and then her sisters, including the officially 'demilitarised' *Hiei*, were rebuilt as 'fast battleships'. The ships were lengthened by 25 ft, extra deck armour was added and elevation of the 14-in guns was increased to 30° to increase their range. The machinery was completely replaced, so that horsepower went up from 64,000 to 136,000, raising speed from just under 26 to 30½ knots. When the British saw the rebuilt *Kongos* (which they had designed originally) they reflected ruefully that they could have done the same with the battle-cruiser *Tiger*, which had been prematurely scrapped in 1933 to comply with the Washington Treaty. The *Kongos* were no better

protected against other battleships than the Italian *Cavour* and *Doria* classes, but they were ideal escorts for the new fast carriers being built.

The *Fuso* class, the similar *Hyuga* class and the two *Nagatos* were also reconstructed to bring them into line with modern requirements. In all six ships this involved massive 'bulge' protection, heavy anti-aircraft armament, new deck armour and huge 'pagoda' foremasts. But these measures only brought the Japanese battle fleet up to the standard of the latest British and American ships in quality, not in numbers. Japan's aggressions in China made her many enemies, particularly the United States, which joined the League of Nations in condemning Japan for invading Manchuria. And when Russia, in a new mood of conciliation, restored diplomatic relations with China and the United States, Japanese extremists saw this as evidence that Japan was hemmed in by hostile nations just as Germany had been 30 years before.

Japanese shipbuilding could not hope to outbuild either Great Britain or the United States and so the Naval General Staff planned for ships of the maximum fighting power in conjunction with a massive fleet of submarines to wear down the strength of the opposing fleets. In fact the Japanese strategy was only an up-dated version of Togo's Tsushima campaign—to lure the enemy fleet into Japanese waters and there finish it off in one decisive battle. The attrition was to be accomplished mainly by torpedo attacks from destroyers and submarines attacking enemy supply lines in the Pacific, but there was still the question of how to ensure that the final fleet action would go in Japan's favour. To achieve this the Naval General Staff decided that they wanted the most powerful battleships that could be built, whatever the treaties said.

The Road to Pearl Harbor

Once the decision had been taken to defy the treaties the necessary justification was created—provided that Japan signified her intention to withdraw from the international agreements, there was nothing to stop her from planning and building ships which would not be completed until after the expiry date! And with that dubious logic the Imperial Japanese Navy took the first positive step down the road to Pearl Harbor. The next step was to ask the Bureau of Naval Construction to determine what size of ship was needed. It was recognised that the US Navy had a priceless asset in being able to move its battleships from the Atlantic to the Pacific through the Panama Canal, and so the Japanese Staff demanded a battleship of such size and power that the only possible American rival would be too big to pass through the canal. This was an echo of the *Dreadnought* era, when the Germans had been forced to widen the Kiel Canal to allow them to compete in the naval race in the North Sea.

To meet this condition the new battleships would have to displace at least 63,000 tons, have a speed of 23 knots and be armed with ten 16-in guns. But the Naval General Staff wanted 18-in guns to achieve the other requirements of superior range and hitting power. Now it became clear what a monster had been hatched, for it was not possible merely to scale up, say, the *Nagato* design to produce an 18-in-gunned battleship. As the British had found in 1917, the increase in calibre caused many headaches; shell weight jumped from about 2200 to 3200 lbs, and a triple turret would weigh more than 2500 tons. Blast effects went up from about 50 lbs/sq inch from one of the *Nagato's* twin 16-in turrets to nearly 100 lbs/sq inch from three 18-in guns at a point 50 ft from the muzzles. It should be remembered that a muzzle blast of $\frac{1}{4}$ lb/sq in could damage boats nearby and as little as 15 lbs/sq in was capable of rendering a man unconscious. The new battleship would have to have all secondary and light guns enclosed in blast-proof shields, and weather-deck fittings would have to be reduced to a minimum.

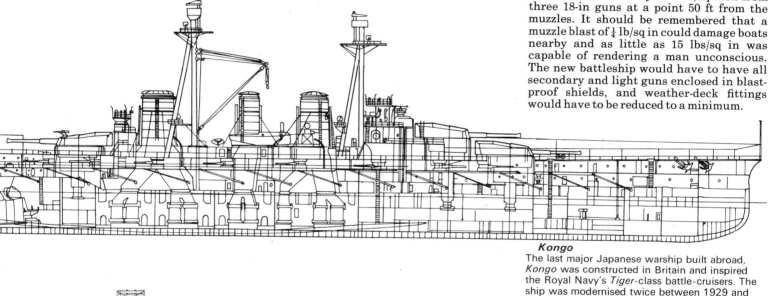

Kongo

The last major Japanese warship built abroad, *Kongo* was constructed in Britain and inspired the Royal Navy's *Tiger*-class battle-cruisers. The ship was modernised twice between 1929 and 1937

Displacement: 27,500 tons *Length:* 214 m *Armament:* 8×356-mm, 16 (later 14)×152-mm 16×76-mm, 12×127-mm (from 1944), 118 (max)×25-mm *Armour:* 76/203-mm belt, 229-mm turrets *Max speed:* 27.5 knots

Kongo class

Name	Completed	Fate
Kongo	Aug 1913	Sunk by US submarine *Sealion* 1944
Hiei	Aug 1914	Sunk by US aircraft 1942
Haruna	Apr 1915	Sunk by US aircraft 1945
Kirishima	Apr 1915	Sunk by US battleships 1942

The go-ahead for the new design was given in October 1934, with a request from the Staff to the Bureau of Naval Construction for a 30-knot ship armed with nine 18-in guns and protected by the thickest armour possible. By March 1935 a design had been produced for a 69,500-ton monster 294 metres (965 ft) long and having a beam of 135 ft; with 200,000-hp steam turbines she would have had a speed of 31 knots. With great reluctance the Staff accepted that this design was too big, and a lower speed was requested to allow better protection and more endurance. To improve endurance and to save weight steam was abandoned in favour of high-speed diesels, presumably because of favourable reports about the Germans' success with the 'pocket-battle-ships'. The Japanese were very proud of a new 10,000-bhp two-cycle double-acting diesel which had been used in a series of submarine tenders, and it was hoped that this unit would propel the new battleships,

in conjunction with steam on the inner shafts for top speed.

In two years the Bureau produced 23 designs, but in July 1936 a sudden setback threw the project into the melting pot again. The high-speed diesel was found to have a major design fault, and had to be abandoned. In the battleship design the diesel room was covered by 7¾-in armour, and it would have been impossible to replace the engines if they gave any trouble, so there was nothing to be done but redesign the machinery. Finally four-shaft steam turbines as in the original 1935 design were chosen, but reduced to 150,000 shp making 27 knots.

Protected Vitals
Nothing has been said so far about armouring, but, as might be expected, the Japanese had not gone to the trouble of driving a coach and horses through the naval treaties to build a poorly protected ship, and the new class would outstrip all

Nagato and her sister Mutsu *underwent a total reconstruction between the wars, which involved widening of the hull and rebuilding of the superstructure to accommodate a heavy anti-aircraft battery*

others in the scale and thickness of armour. The vitals were protected by 16.1-in Vickers face-hardened armour capable of stopping an 18-in shell at 22,000 yards, and the 7¾-in deck armour could keep out an 18-in shell at 33,000 yards. This deck armour could also stop a 2200-lb bomb dropped from 15,000 ft and even the extremities of the ship were plated with light armour capable of keeping out small bombs. The funnel was armoured, not by conventional coaming armour, but by a huge 15-in plate inside the uptakes, with 7-in-diameter perforations to allow the smoke to pass through; the coaming of the funnel was protected by 2-in plating. Even the bottom plating was armoured with two 3-in plates under the magazines to protect

Mutsu
Japan was able to forge ahead with battleship design while the European powers were locked in combat, and some of the lessons of Jutland were incorporated in their design. *Mutsu* and her sister were fast, heavily armed and were considered extremely successful

Displacement: 34,100 tons full load *Length:* 215 m *Armament:* 8×406-mm, 18×140-mm (from 1936), 8×127-mm (from 1933, 20×25 -mm (from 1936), 4×533-mm torpedo tubes *Armour:* 100/300-mm belt, 356-mm turrets, up to 75-mm decks *Max speed:* 26.7 knots

Nagato class

Name	Completed	Fate
Nagato	Nov 1920	Sunk during A-bomb test 1946
Mutsu	Oct 1921	Blew up 1943

them from mine or torpedo explosions. Even though the ship was 860 ft long the armour absorbed 34.4 per cent of the displacement.

The 18-in guns were actually 46-cm (18.1-in) 45 cal weapons which weighed 157 tons each and had a muzzle velocity of 2559 ft/sec. At 45° elevation they could fire a 3220-lb shell a maximum of 45,000 yards. The triple turrets were the most massive ever built, with 24.8-in faces, 9-in sides, 6.7-in backs and 9.8-in roof plates. The rate of fire was one round per gun every 90 sec, and the whole moving structure weighed 2730 tons.

Although the Japanese constructors were not limited by considerations of size and cost there were nevertheless restraints imposed by practicability. For example, the draught had to be restricted to allow the ships to enter Japanese harbours, a factor which contributed to the great beam. To try to save weight the lower side armour formed part of the longitudinal strength of the ship, and welding was used wherever possible.

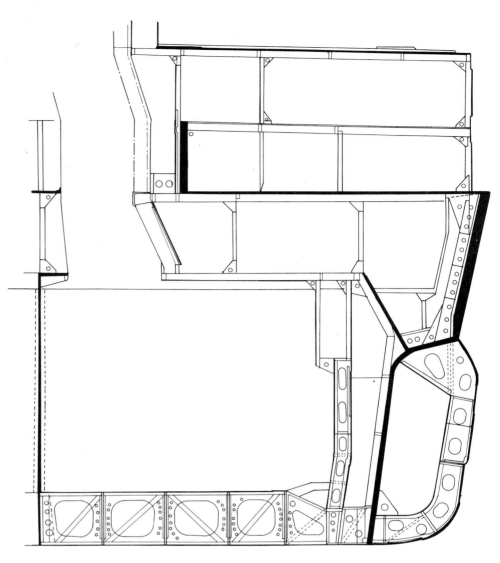

Amagi: Armour Diagram
Midship section of the cancelled battle-cruiser *Amagi*, showing the inward slope of the armour designed to increase the angle of impact of shells and hence increase resistance to penetration

Unfortunately the Japanese shipbuilding industry had severe problems with welding, partly through lack of proper rods. The structure of the new battleships was much heavier than that of contemporary British and American ships, with all the important parts of the hull riveted for safety. When tests showed that armour plates had less resistance at their edges the Japanese spent $10 million on new steel mills to make large armour plates. The 16.1-in plates for the side armour were 19.36 ft × 11.81 ft and weighed 68½ tons. The great thickness of these plates forced the Japanese to use a new process for hardening the surface, one which proved to be more effective and

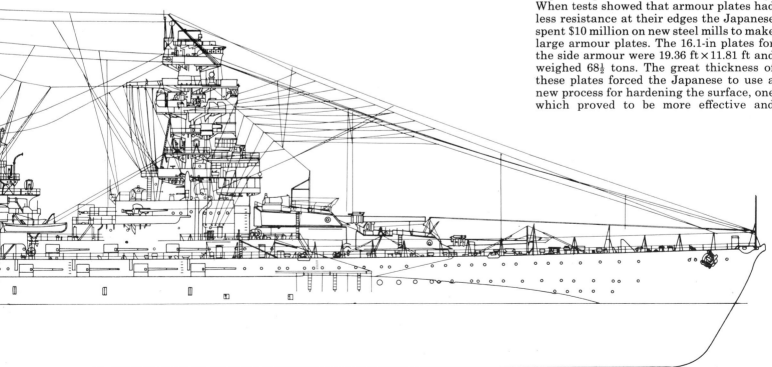

The first public outing of the Soviet Navy was in 1936 when the Marat *appeared at the Coronation Naval Review. A quaint reconstruction failed to conceal the original 1915 outline of the* Petropavlovsk

quicker than the traditional method of cementing.

The first of the super-battleships was given the name *Yamato* when her keel was laid in November 1937, while her sister *Musashi* was laid down in March 1938. Work started in 1940 on two more ships of slightly modified design, but a fifth unit and two more of even larger type with six 50.8-cm (20-in) guns were never started. Kure Dockyard, the builder chosen for the *Yamato*, had to deepen its building dock by 3 ft and strengthen the gantry crane to allow for the weight of the bigger armour plates. A special transport, the *Kashino*, had to be built to carry the 18-in guns and part of the mountings from the Kamegakubi Ordnance Works to the four yards selected. A special new dock was built at Yokosuka for the *Shinano*, but Mitsubishi at Nagasaki built the *Musashi* on a conventional slipway. Never before had any Japanese shipyard launched a hull weighing more than 30,000 tons, although the British had recently launched the *Queen Mary* at a weight of 37,387 tons. Because of the need to delay any announcement about these ships as long as possible there was total secrecy. At Kure the *Yamato* was hidden from prying eyes by a roof built at the landward end of the berth, while the *Musashi's* hull was covered by a gigantic camouflage net weighing 408 tons and made out of 1370 miles of sisal rope.

The appearance of the *Yamato* and *Musashi* was unusual, with a long undulating flush deckline and a massive funnel raked well aft to take smoke clear of the tall tower mast. Two catapults at the stern could launch six floatplanes, but to avoid blast damage these aircraft had to be kept in a large hangar a deck below the boat stowage. A large lift hoisted both aircraft and boats to the deck, where a crane put the aircraft on positioning trolleys.

Russia

Despite the efforts made to revive the Red Fleet, the Soviet Union found that its industrial potential was not sufficient to produce the guns and heavy armour needed for new battleships. But to Stalin this was merely a temporary problem. Between 1935 and 1938 Italy and the United States were approached for designs of ships and asked to supply guns

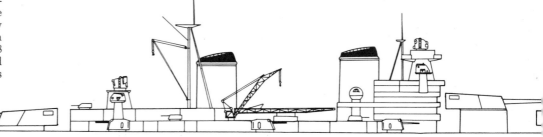

The old battleship Sebastopol *was renamed* Parishkaya Kommuna *in 1928 but in 1942, as part of Stalin's drive to rekindle the spirit of Russian patriotism, she reverted to her old Tsarist name*

Sovietski Soyuz

Construction of two battleships in this class was begun, the name-ship being laid down in 1938. Work proceeded slowly, but by the time of the German invasion in 1941 the first vessel was almost ready for launching. In November of that year construction was abandoned, however, and the hull was scrapped after the war
Displacement: up to 60,000 tons *Length:* 262 m *Armament:* 9 × 406-mm, 12 × 130-mm or 12 × 150-mm, 12 × 76-mm or 8 × 100-mm *Max speed:* nearly 30 knots

and armour. In 1939 the Germans were also asked to supply plans of the new *Bismarck* class as well as guns, but on Hitler's orders the negotiations were spun out to avoid giving away any secrets. In 1938 two very large battleships were laid down, one at Leningrad and the other at Nikolaiev in the Black Sea. Neither was launched, and naturally nothing of any value has ever been released by the Russian authorities, but in August 1941 German forces captured the dockyard at Nikolaiev and so we have a fairly good idea of how big the ship would have been. What was gradually realised was that if the Second World War had not broken out the Russian Navy would have had two battleships nearly as big as the *Yamato* class. On a displacement of 59,000 tons they would have been a little shorter but with similar beam. The armour was lighter and nine 16-in guns would have been carried at a speed of 30 knots. During the war Stalin assured his allies that the two ships would have been stationed in the Pacific, but it is clear that the Russians were on the brink of a massive expansion to challenge both British and German seapower in the West.

Germany

In 1937–38 the German Navy drew up plans for a naval war against Great Britain and France, at about the same time as the British were putting their own naval programme in hand. Lists were drawn up of the ships needed for a successful sea war against British trade as follows:

German Z-Plan

6 battleships to be ready by 1944
8 heavy cruisers, 4 by 1943 plus 4 by 1948
4 aircraft carriers, 2 by 1941 plus 2 by 1947
223 submarines, 128 by 1943 plus 95 by 1947

The plan was modified several times, and subsequently some of the heavy cruisers were replaced by a trio of battle-cruisers. The battleships were 56,000-ton diesel-driven ships to be armed with eight 16-in guns, and the battle-cruisers would have been 15-in-gunned versions of the *Scharnhorst* class.

The 'Z' Plan showed little sense of reality, for the German Naval Staff seems to have ignored what effect it might have on British naval programmes. The magic date of 1944 was chosen because Adolf Hitler claimed to guarantee that war between Britain and Germany could not break out before then, and it had nothing to do with the capacity of German shipyards. In fact the British had already started to lay down more ships than the Germans in every category except submarines (a type for which they had less need), and the news of the 'Z' Plan only helped to strengthen the British determination to use their superior shipbuilding resources to outbuild the *Kriegsmarine*. An improved *King George V* design with 16-in guns, known as the *Lion* class, was started in 1939 and the modernisation of the older ships was accelerated. The results can be seen below:

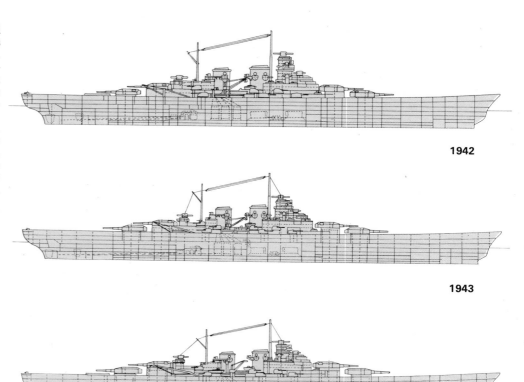

1942

1943

1944

***Schlachtschiff Entwurf* (Battleship Project)**
Hitler's constructors laboured arduously throughout the war to avoid the Eastern Front by producing ever more colossal designs. The steel alone would have equalled a years Tiger tank production

The Second Naval Race

	Begun	Completed
British		
King George V	1937	1940
Prince of Wales	1937	1941
Duke of York	1937	1941
Anson	1937	1942
Howe	1937	1942
German		
Bismarck	1936	1940
Tirpitz	1936	1941
'H'	1939	—*
'J'	1939	—*

*Stopped in October 1939 and scrapped on slipway in 1940

During the same period the British also modernised the *Queen Elizabeth*, *Valiant* and *Renown* to a degree which made them virtually new ships. The four *Lions* were fine ships, but the slow progress of German shipbuilding made them superfluous, and their cancellation in 1940 released much-needed steel and manpower for better purposes. The only way in which the 'Z' Plan could have worked would have been for the British to build no more ships whatsoever between 1937 and 1941, an eventuality so remote as to be absurd, and Hitler's naval expansion plans must be pigeon-holed alongside Stalin's megalomaniac plans for the *Sovietski Soyuz* class.

Right: *A navy band crashes out* Deutschland über Alles *as Hitler attends the launching of the* Tirpitz *in 1937. In 1941 the German surface fleet was still a threat to the Royal Navy, but by 1943 the remaining big ships would be completely overshadowed by the submarine offensive*

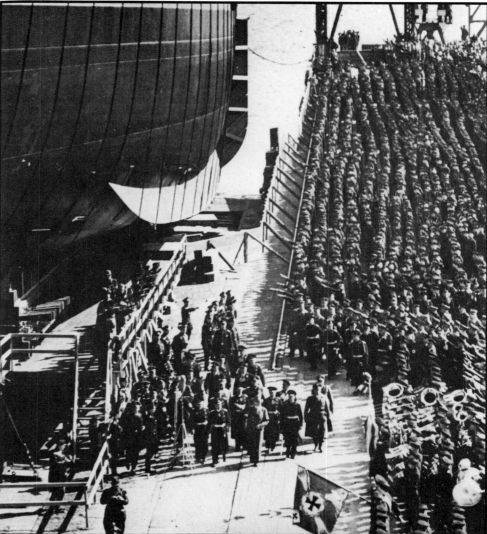

THE SECOND TEST

When war broke out in September 1939 none of the new generation ships was in commission, unless one counts the French *Dunkerques* and the German *Scharnhorsts*. The British had a total of 13 ships in commission, with the *Queen Elizabeth* and *Valiant* still completing reconstruction, whereas the Germans had only two battle-cruisers and four new ships under construction. The French and Italians were more evenly matched, with two new ships each due to commission from mid-1940 and another pair apiece which could be ready by 1942–43. The Japanese had nearly completed their programme of reconstructing their battleships, but the *Yamato* and *Musashi* would not be ready until 1941–42. The Americans expected to have six 16-in-gunned ships in commission in the same time and were about to lay down the first two of a class of six 45,000-tonners.

The first battleship casualty of the war was the old British *Royal Oak*, which was torpedoed by a U-Boat in the supposedly safe anchorage at Scapa Flow. Under K/Lt Gunther Prien *U.47* was sent to force her way through the defences of Kirk Sound, which had not been overhauled since 1918. Prien's daring paid off, and he found himself inside the Flow on the night of 13–14 October, 1939. The first salvo of three torpedoes (one tube was faulty) had no effect, either because the single torpedo which hit struck an anchor cable, or more likely because it only detonated partially. Nearly threequarters of an hour later Prien had reloaded his forward torpedo tubes and returned to the attack. This time his three torpedoes ran true and the magnetic pistols detonated the warheads underneath the *Royal Oak's* keel. The old ship, which had been at Jutland 23 years before, blew up and sank with the loss of 833 officers and men.

The *Royal Oak* was not a modern ship, and would have been scrapped in another

Battleship Strength of the Powers: 1939

Great Britain

Nelson
Rodney
Hood
Renown
Repulse
Royal Sovereign
Royal Oak
Revenge
Ramillies
Resolution
Queen Elizabeth
Valiant
Warspite
Barham
Malaya

United States

Colorado
Maryland
West Virginia
Tennessee
California
New Mexico
Mississippi
Idaho
Pennsylvania
Arizona
Nevada
Oklahoma
New York
Texas
Arkansas

Germany

Scharnhorst
Gneisenau

Japan

Nagato
Mutsu
Hyuga
Ise
Fuso
Yamashiro
Haruna
Kirishima
Kongo
Hiei

Note: Only units operational in September 1939 are indicated

France

Dunkerque
Strasbourg
Bretagne
Provence
Lorraine
Courbet
Paris
Ocean

Italy

Andrea Doria
Duilio
Conte di Cavour
Guilio Cesare

Russia

Marat
Oktyabrskaya Revolutsia
Parizhskaya Kommuna

Chile

Almirante Latorre

Argentina

Moreno
Rivadavia

Brazil

Sao Paulo
Minas Geraes

Turkey

Yavuz

The twisted hulk of the Graf Spee blazes in Montevideo harbour after demolition charges had ripped through her hull

three years if war had not broken out, but the brilliant attack by *U.47* shook the Home Fleet. As in 1914 the battle fleet had to desert its main base for bases in the west of Scotland until Scapa Flow could be made safe once more, and for a few crucial months the Home Fleet had to leave the exit to the North Sea unguarded. Furthermore the extemporised bases like Loch Ewe were even less secure than Scapa Flow; the Home Fleet flagship *Nelson* was badly damaged by a magnetic mine laid by a U-Boat in the entrance to Loch Ewe and the *Barham* was torpedoed by *U.30*. The defences were not fully strengthened until early in 1940, but no further casualties resulted.

Another casualty of the early months of the war was the myth of the 'pocket-battleship'. In December 1939 the *Admiral Graf Spee* was caught off the River Plate by three British cruisers, the *Exeter*, *Ajax* and *Achilles*. The *Panzerschiff* had left Germany before the outbreak of war with her sister *Deutschland* to evade the British patrols, and they had been cruising in the Atlantic spreading confusion by sinking random merchantmen and adopting disguises. No fewer than eight hunting groups, including the battle-cruisers HMS *Renown* and the French *Dunkerque* and *Strasbourg*, hunted them from Halifax, Nova Scotia, down to Pernambuco. The *Deutschland* sank only two ships before being recalled but the *Admiral Graf Spee*, under her skilled and humane captain Hans Langsdorff, sank nine ships totalling 50,000 tons. One of the ruses adopted by Langsdorff was to paint a dummy tripod on his control tower and rig a dummy triple 11-in turret. He was reported on more than one occasion as a French battleship, which tells a lot about the average merchant navy officer's skill at warship recognition.

When the *Graf Spee* met the three British cruisers off Montevideo early on the morning of 13 December, 1939 she soon showed her shortcomings. She had radar, but the rapid changes of bearing of her three adversaries made it impossible for the two triple 11-in turrets to register long enough to score hits. Eventually by concentrating on the 8-in-gunned *Exeter* the German ship was able to damage her severely, but she was unable to finish her off because the *Ajax* and *Achilles* behaved like picadors drawing off the bull from a wounded matador. The *Graf Spee* was not fast enough to out-manoeuvre the cruisers and eventually, with relatively light damage, she was forced to make for neutral Uruguayan waters, from which she eventually emerged to scuttle herself. The vaunted 'pocket-battleship' had turned out to be too slow to out-distance cruisers and not well enough protected to ignore their shells.

'Salmon and Gluckstein'

The Norwegian Campaign of April 1940 saw no great fleet action, but capital ships on both sides played their part from the beginning. The British moved first, wanting to lay mines in Norwegian territorial waters to stop the flagrant violation of neutrality by German iron ore ships, and their mine-laying forces ran into German naval forces covering an invasion of Norway intended to pre-empt a British occupation. The *Renown* and four destroyers narrowly missed the heavy cruiser *Admiral Hipper* on 6 April but one of her escorts, HMS *Glowworm*, was sunk in a gallant but hopeless action after becoming detached two days later. On 9 April the Germans started to land troops at Narvik, Trondheim and other Norwegian ports, and on the same day the *Renown* and nine destroyers ran into the *Scharnhorst* and *Gneisenau* about 50 miles off Vestfjord. The British ship was keeping a sharp look-out and spotted the German battle-cruisers at 3.37 am in bad weather, amid intermittent snow squalls. The *Renown* closed the range to about nine miles, and her opening salvo about 30 minutes later came as an unpleasant surprise. 'Salmon and Gluckstein' (as they were known in Britain after a chain of teashops) turned to fight, but it was the *Renown*'s 15-in guns which scored the first hit ten minutes later, putting the *Gneisenau*'s forward fire-control out of action. Hitler's orders were explicit; no German capital ships were to expose themselves to the risk of loss, and so there was little choice for Admiral Lütjens but to break off. But the *Renown* pursued the Germans and hit the *Gneisenau* twice more, crippling one of her forward turrets. She herself was hit by two 11-in shells, one of which clipped the top of her funnel, but she suffered no damage. The rising sea prevented her from catching her quarry, despite working up to 29 knots.

On 10 April a British destroyer flotilla fought the First Battle of Narvik in an attempt to dislodge the German destroyer force which had landed troops to seize the vital iron-ore port. But in spite of sinking two destroyers the British lost two of their own and had left the Germans in possession of Narvik, and so the Admiralty ordered the Commander-in-Chief of the Home Fleet to finish off the remaining destroyers. This time Admiral Whitworth was given permission to take the *Warspite* up Ofotfjord to reinforce the nine destroyers, a gamble which could have resulted in the battleship's grounding or being torpedoed. This was the same *Warspite* which had been at 'Windy Corner' at Jutland, after two reconstructions, and far from being damaged she was about to start her glorious Second World War career. The destroyers hurried up the fjord with the *Warspite* bringing up the rear. Her Swordfish floatplane was catapulted off to reconnoitre, and soon sighted and sank a U-Boat in the small Herjangsfjord. The booming of 15-in guns warned the German destroyers of the approach of the British force, but there was little they could do to avoid their fate. By the end of the day all eight German destroyers had been sunk, at a cost of two British destroyers damaged. Narvik was left in German hands for lack of troops to occupy the port, but a large part of the German Navy's entire destroyer force had been wiped out.

Off Norway the Home Fleet learned for the first time just how effective dive-bombing could be. The *Rodney* was hit by a heavy bomb and, although she was not seriously damaged, losses of smaller ships showed that anti-aircraft gunnery alone could not ward off bombers. The multiple pom-pom was found to be useful in breaking up massed attacks but fire-control was still at too crude a state of development to enable aircraft to be shot down except by a random hit. Another weapon was introduced in 1940, a multiple rocket-projector

The pre-dreadnought Schleswig-Holstein, *which had bombarded the Polish coastline in 1939, is seen here at Götenhafen (Gdynia) in 1940. The old ships in Hitler's navy survived until the end of the war*

known as the UP (Unrotated Projectile) mounting. This fired a salvo of rockets, which released parachutes and trailing wires in the hope of entangling an aircraft propeller. Its main disadvantages was that if it was fired too soon the aircraft could dodge the row of parachutes, and it was almost impossible with the predictors of 1940 to plant a salvo in the right place.

The *Scharnhorst* and *Gneisenau* had their moment of glory at the end of the Norwegian Campaign, during the evacuation by the British and French. On the afternoon of 9 June they met the aircraft carrier HMS *Glorious* and two destroyers. The carrier had just evacuated the last shore-based RAF Hurricanes and Gladiators from Norway, and although she had a few Swordfish torpedo-bombers still left on board she does not appear to have been able to fly any off. Thus she was defenceless when the German ships opened fire at 28,000 yards, and it was left to the destroyers *Acasta* and *Ardent* to make a desperate attack. The fight was hopelessly one-sided, but the *Acasta* managed to hit the *Scharnhorst* with a single torpedo abreast of the after turret.

The *Gneisenau* did not escape either, for on 20 June she was also badly damaged by a torpedo from a British submarine. Both battle-cruisers were out of action for a considerable time, and their absence from the scene had a considerable bearing on the German Navy's reluctance to support Hitler's plans for invading the British Isles after Dunkirk. The Norwegian Campaign was full of disappointments and mistakes on the British side but it also cost the Germans losses in ships that they could ill afford.

Right: The world had forgotten the two ex-US pre-dreadnoughts passed to the Greek Navy in 1914 until Stukas found and sank the Kilkis (ex-*Mississippi*) *in Salamis harbour, 1941*

HMS Warspite
A battleship which saw extensive service in two wars, *Warspite* was the most heavily engaged warship at the Battle of Jutland. She served throughout the Second World War, from Norway, through the Mediterranean to the Indian Ocean and back to Europe to support the D-Day and Walcheren landings
Displacement: 31,000 tons full load
Length: 600 ft *Armament:* 8×15-in, 8×6-in, 8×4-in AA, 16×2-pdr AA

The French Eclipse

The fall of France in June 1940 did not mean the immediate collapse of the French Navy. The old battleships *Courbet* and *Paris* escaped to England and the incomplete *Jean Bart* and *Richelieu* reached North Africa after incredible exertions. The *Dunkerque, Strasbourg, Bretagne* and *Provence* were at Mers-el-Kebir near Oran when the Armistice was signed, while the *Lorraine* was at Alexandria. The Italians had finally moved against France in her most desperate hour, and to the British it seemed unarguable that whatever sincere intentions the French Navy might give about their ships not falling into German hands, they were not in a good position to offer such guarantees. Neither Hitler nor Mussolini had a good track record as far as guarantees went, and furthermore both the *Regia Navale* and the *Kriegsmarine* needed ships badly. Means and motive existed, and only opportunity was needed for the deed to be done. On 3 July Admiral Somerville was ordered to use his new Force 'H' to back up a British 'offer' to the French, one which they could not refuse. The ultimatum offered five choices to the French:

1 Put to sea and join forces against Germany.
2 Sail with reduced crews to a British port for internment.
3 Sail with reduced crews to a French West Indian port to be laid up in a demilitarised condition.
4 Scuttle the ships within six hours.
5 Demilitarise the ships where they lay, within six hours.

Admiral Gensoul was in a difficult position. The first two conditions contradicted the conditions of the Armistice, and the third condition could also be construed that way. The fourth condition was insulting to a proud navy, and the fifth was physically impossible to fulfil in the time allowed. Probably Gensoul and Somerville were not the right people to handle such a delicate matter; Somerville seems to have been needlessly brusque, while Gensoul inexplicably reported to the French C-in-C Admiral Darlan that he had been simply ordered to sink his ships in six hours or surrender them. Not unexpectedly Darlan, who had devoted his career to building up the French Navy, instructed Gensoul to resist, and so the stage was set for the unhappiest action of the war, with the British and French fighting one another only weeks after both navies had heroically evacuated their soldiers from Dunkirk.

All that day (3 July) Force 'H', which included the battle-cruiser *Hood*, the battleships *Resolution* and *Valiant* and the carrier *Ark Royal*, patrolled to seaward of Mers-el-

Kebir. At 1730 a final signal was sent to Admiral Gensoul by Somerville, warning him that if no answer was received his ships would be fired upon. At 1754 the British ships began to fire into the crowded anchorage, and soon the 15-in salvoes were causing havoc. The French ships tried to return fire, and obtained two straddles on the *Hood*, but the British had the range and had no difficulty in silencing their fire. The *Bretagne* blew up and the *Provence* and *Dunkerque* were seriously damaged. At 1809 the attackers shifted fire to the coastal batteries, and three minutes later the 'melancholy action' was over. The only important unit to escape the carnage was the

Strasbourg, which managed to work clear of the crowded anchorage under cover of the huge pall of smoke from burning ships. The *Hood* gave chase but her 28 knots was insufficient to catch the Frenchman, and when two French aircraft attacked her with torpedoes she turned back. To give some idea of the pace of the action, the *Hood* fired 56 15-in shells and 120 4-in in only 18 minutes, or 14 salvoes.

The *Richelieu* had reached Dakar in Senegal, but that did not put her beyond the reach of the British. On 8 July she was attacked with great daring by a motor boat, which attempted unsuccessfully to drop depth charges under her stern to wreck the

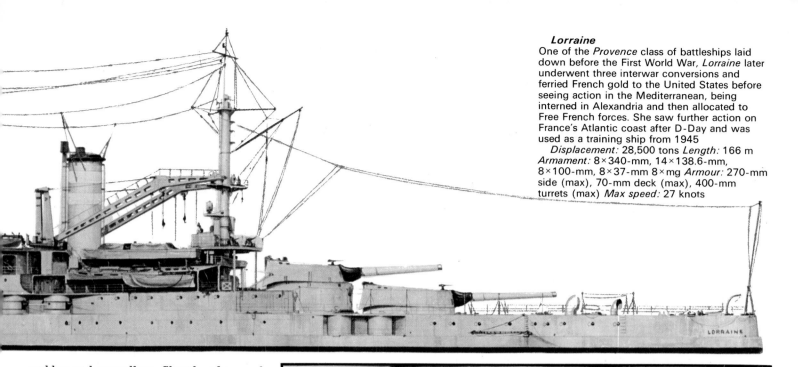

Lorraine
One of the *Provence* class of battleships laid down before the First World War, *Lorraine* later underwent three interwar conversions and ferried French gold to the United States before seeing action in the Mediterranean, being interned in Alexandria and then allocated to Free French forces. She saw further action on France's Atlantic coast after D-Day and was used as a training ship from 1945
Displacement: 28,500 tons *Length:* 166 m *Armament:* 8×340-mm, 14×138.6-mm, 8×100-mm, 8×37-mm 8×mg *Armour:* 270-mm side (max), 70-mm deck (max), 400-mm turrets (max) *Max speed:* 27 knots

rudder and propellers. Shortly afterwards a torpedo-bomber from HMS *Hermes* scored a hit with a torpedo right aft, but the *Richelieu* remained capable of putting to sea. When the British and the Free French attempted to take Dakar in September (Operation 'Menace') her 15-in guns were a major factor in driving off the attackers. The British battleships *Barham* and *Resolution* failed to silence her or the shore batteries, and when a French submarine put a torpedo into the *Resolution* British enthusiasm for Operation 'Menace' waned noticeably. Fortunately the *Resolution*'s 'bulge' took the main force of the explosion and she was not out of action for long.

Jean Bart
Larger and better protected than the ships of the *Dunkerque* class, which they resembled, *Jean Bart* and her sister *Richelieu* sailed to African ports while still incomplete when France was invaded
Displacement: 47,500 tons full load *Length:* 248 m *Armament:* 8×380-mm, 9×152-mm, 12×100-mm, 16×37-mm AA, 8×13.2-mm AA *Armour:* 327-mm belt, 430-mm main turrets, 170-mm main deck *Max speed:* 30 knots

Richelieu class

Name	Launched	Fate
Richelieu	Jan 1939	Scrapped 1968
Jean Bart	Mar 1940	Scrapped 1969

The French battleship Provence *trains her 13·4-in turrets to starboard before opening fire on the British Force H at Mers-el-Kebir. In the background the* Strasbourg *slips her moorings—one of the few ships to escape the holocaust*

ECP Armées

ACTION IN THE MEDITERRANEAN

The entry of Italy into the war meant that the British now had to send battleships back to the Mediterranean urgently if they were to maintain their hold on the vital Suez Canal. There were no fast battleships to spare, for the first two of the *King George V* class were earmarked for the Home Fleet to 'mark' the *Scharnhorst* and *Gneisenau* and the *Bismarck* when she appeared. The *Warspite* was sent to the Mediterranean as the flagship of Admiral Sir Andrew Cunningham, shortly to make his name as the most brilliant fighting admiral since Nelson. In May 1940 Cunningham was also given the old *Royal Sovereign* and *Malaya*, and shortly afterwards the aircraft carrier *Eagle* and the *Ramillies* came through the Suez Canal from the Far East. For all too short a period the Mediterranean Fleet was also strengthened by the modernised French battleship *Lorraine*, but she and her squadron-mates were interned at Alexandria in July when France surrendered. At first the British thought that they would have to abandon Malta, their priceless base in the central Mediterranean, but with Cunningham in command there was no need for such a concession.

On 9 July Cunningham met the Italian Fleet off the coast of Calabria; each squadron was covering the passage of a convoy at the time. After the *Eagle*'s torpedo-bombers failed to score hits the battleships came within range, and the *Warspite*'s 15-in guns scored a hit on the *Giulio Cesare* at the great range of 24,600 yards. An orange-coloured flash shot up from the Italian flagship, followed by a pillar of smoke. Admiral Campioni's flagship was not slowed down by the damage but the single shell had made a shambles out of the topsides gun positions, and the whole force turned away under cover of a smokescreen. The *Malaya* was unable to get within range and *Royal Sovereign* had been left behind, which meant that the *Warspite* had been unsupported. To complete the Italian discomfiture in what they called the Battle of Point Stilo (Punta di Stilo), the retreating squadron was bombed by Italian aircraft.

The next brush with the Italian Fleet, the Battle of Cape Spartivento on 25 November, 1940, was less satisfactory. This time the new battleship *Vittorio Veneto* was Admiral Campiano's flagship, with the repaired *Giulio Cesare*, and they faced the *Ramillies* from the Mediterranean Squadron and the *Renown* from Somerville's Force 'H'. Again, the slower *Ramillies* could not get within

range and it was only the *Renown* which was able to fire a few salvoes at extreme range. Campioni over-estimated the strength of the British squadron and broke off the action before any damage could be inflicted on either side.

Taranto

Cunningham was sent another modernised battleship, the *Warspite*'s sister *Valiant*, at the end of August 1940, but the arrival of a modern aircraft carrier, HMS *Illustrious*, was even more important. The next blow against the Italians was to be a deadly one which could have affected the outcome of the entire war and marked a turning point in naval history.

The attack on Taranto was carried out on the night of 11–12 November by the new armoured carrier *Illustrious*, using 21 Swordfish biplane bombers. For the price of a few bombs and eleven 18-in torpedoes these slow aircraft sank the battleship *Conte di Cavour* outright and damaged the new *Littorio* and the *Caio Duilio*. The shallowness of the harbour at Taranto meant that the two damaged ships would eventually return to service, but at a crucial moment three out of the six battleships of the Italian Navy were out of action, and the British could pass reinforcements through the central Mediterranean with impunity. For the first time in history a battle fleet had been crippled in harbour without a shot being fired by the opposing side's fleet. Strangely enough, a similar attack had been planned by the British for 1919, using Sopwith Cuckoos to drop torpedoes against the German Fleet. The lesson of Taranto

was not lost on the Japanese, who studied the plan very carefully when preparing their own air strike against Pearl Harbor a year later.

The *Conte di Cavour* never sailed again. She was refloated and towed to Trieste, but was still incomplete at the time of Italy's surrender. The Germans captured the ship in September 1943 but Allied bombs sank her in February 1945. The other two ships were refloated and put back into service in 1941, but the blow to the Italians' confidence was a heavy one. Like the Germans, they could build fine ships, but the High Command was reluctant to accept any risk. The Italians could easily have sacrificed two of their ships without being outnumbered by the British, and if in so doing they had cut British communications between Gibraltar, Malta and Alexandria the strategic consequences could have been overwhelming—the Germans would have reached the Middle East oil that they needed so desperately and the Mediterranean would indeed have become an Italian lake. But the advantages of boldness were obscured by anxiety about losses, and Italian fleet commanders were never given any encouragement to show a bold front to their opponents.

The next time the Italian Fleet met the British was in March 1941, when the Mediterranean Fleet was covering the ill-fated expedition to Greece. Under prodding from the German Naval Liaison Staff in Rome the Italians were persuaded that only HMS *Valiant* was ready for action, and that the time was propitious for another sortie by the 15-in-gunned *Vittorio Veneto*, accompanied by a force of heavy cruisers. But

Giulio Cesare

By 1942 the two surviving battleships of the *Conte di Cavour* class were very different in appearance from their First World War outline. Speed, armament and protection were increased, modernisation having been spurred partly by construction of the French *Dunkerque*, and *Giulio Cesare* survived the Second World War only to mysteriously sink in the Black Sea in 1955 while serving with the Russian Navy
  Displacement: 29,100 tons *Length:* 186.4 m *Armament:* 10×320-mm, 12×120-mm, 8×100-mm, 16×37-mm, 12×20-mm *Armour:* 250-mm max side, 100-mm max decks, 280-mm max turrets *Max speed:* 28 knots

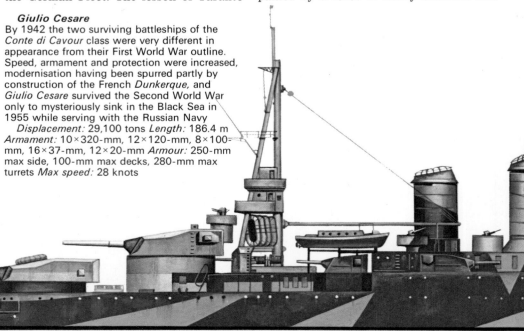

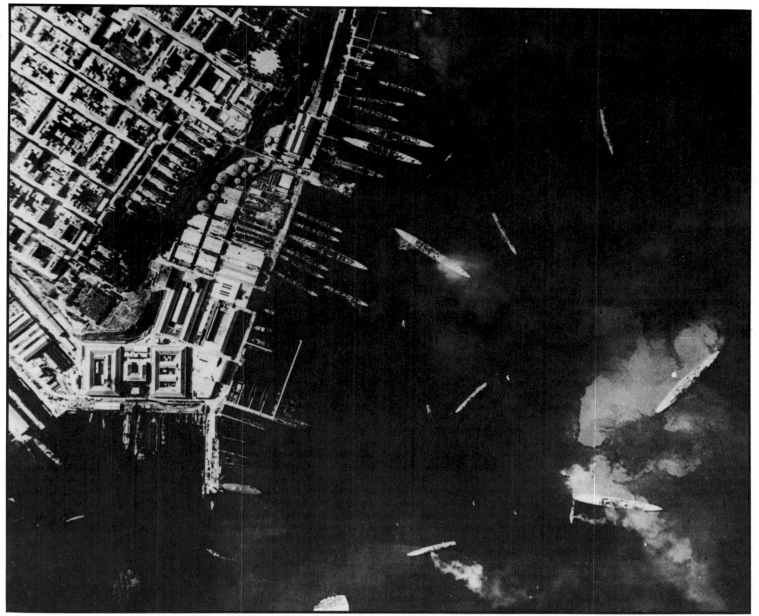

Reconaissance pilot's view of the agony of the Italian Fleet at Taranto. Battleships are surrounded by tell-tale oil slicks, and some already have their bows beneath the water. The major surface threat to Allied control of the Mediterranean had been removed at a stroke, and the aircraft had supplanted the big gun as the arbiter of power at sea

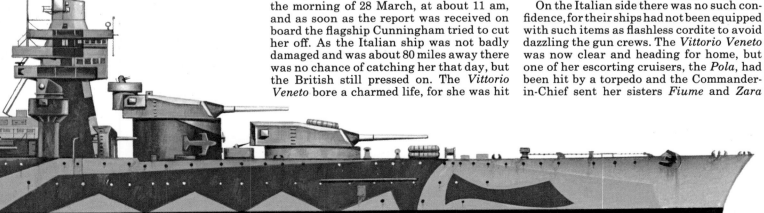

there were three British battleships at sea: the *Warspite, Barham* and *Valiant*, all veterans of Jutland but modernised to varying degrees. With the invaluable carrier *Formidable* in company Cunningham was ready to take a few chances to bring the Italians to battle, and this time his wish was granted.

The *Vittorio Veneto* was hit by a torpedo from one of the *Formidable*'s bombers on the morning of 28 March, at about 11 am, and as soon as the report was received on board the flagship Cunningham tried to cut her off. As the Italian ship was not badly damaged and was about 80 miles away there was no chance of catching her that day, but the British still pressed on. The *Vittorio Veneto* bore a charmed life, for she was hit

again near the stern but managed to maintain a fair speed, varying between 12 and 15 knots. At dusk the pursuers were still there, about 65 miles astern, and Cunningham made up his mind to accept the risk of night action. It was a far cry from Jutland, when action had been declined because of the risks; this time, even though only a few ships had radar, Cunningham knew that his ships were fully exercised in night fighting.

On the Italian side there was no such confidence, for their ships had not been equipped with such items as flashless cordite to avoid dazzling the gun crews. The *Vittorio Veneto* was now clear and heading for home, but one of her escorting cruisers, the *Pola*, had been hit by a torpedo and the Commander-in-Chief sent her sisters *Fiume* and *Zara*

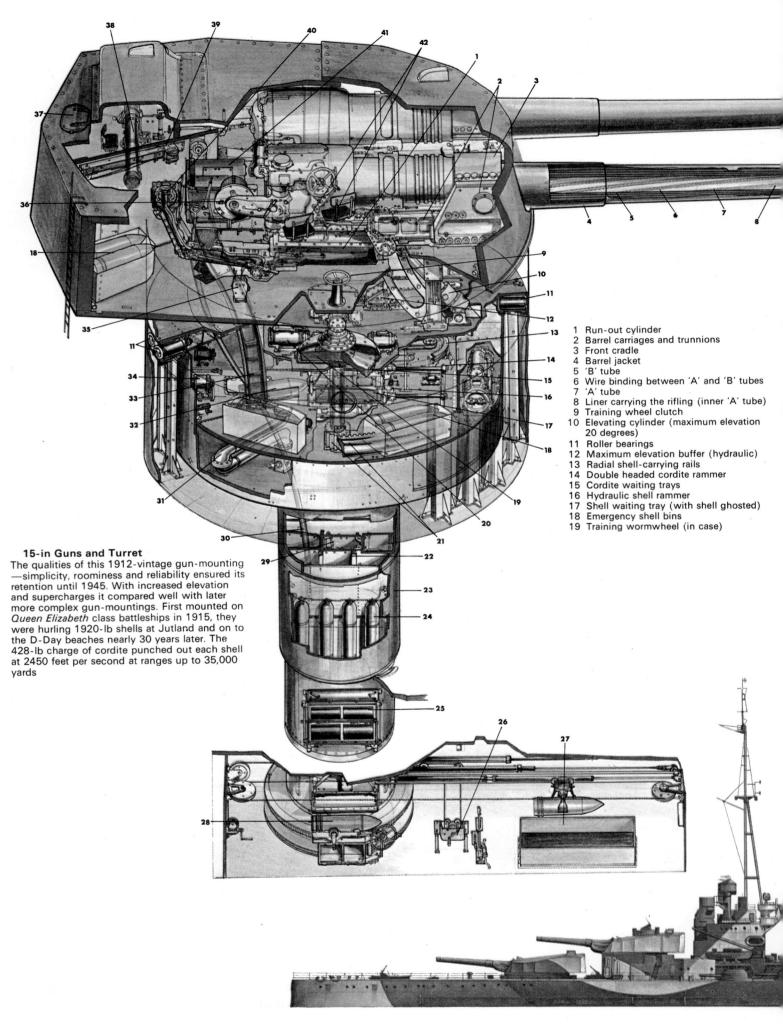

1 Run-out cylinder
2 Barrel carriages and trunnions
3 Front cradle
4 Barrel jacket
5 'B' tube
6 Wire binding between 'A' and 'B' tubes
7 'A' tube
8 Liner carrying the rifling (inner 'A' tube)
9 Training wheel clutch
10 Elevating cylinder (maximum elevation 20 degrees)
11 Roller bearings
12 Maximum elevation buffer (hydraulic)
13 Radial shell-carrying rails
14 Double headed cordite rammer
15 Cordite waiting trays
16 Hydraulic shell rammer
17 Shell waiting tray (with shell ghosted)
18 Emergency shell bins
19 Training wormwheel (in case)

15-in Guns and Turret

The qualities of this 1912-vintage gun-mounting —simplicity, roominess and reliability ensured its retention until 1945. With increased elevation and supercharges it compared well with later more complex gun-mountings. First mounted on *Queen Elizabeth* class battleships in 1915, they were hurling 1920-lb shells at Jutland and on to the D-Day beaches nearly 30 years later. The 428-lb charge of cordite punched out each shell at 2450 feet per second at ranges up to 35,000 yards

98

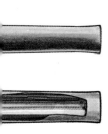

20 Turret training engine
21 Turret training rack and pinion gears
22 Ammunition hoist cage rails
23 Turret trunk
24 Breech air blast cylinders (four each side)
25 Cordite hopper (when empty ammunition hoist cage returns, flash proof doors open, and cordite drops onto carriers inside turret trunk)
26 Hand lifting winch
27 Shell bin
28 Shell bogie (in this position it collects shell from overhead rail. Should turret be turned to either side, the bogie is hand wound to position opposite flash proof doors)
29 Auxiliary shell supply hoist tube
30 Auxiliary cordite supply rail (used if normal supply fails)
31 Walking pipes with radial joints (allow systems to function properly while the turret is turning)
32 Emergency supply shell waiting tray (from this point shell is lifted with block and tackle up to the guns)
33 Gun loading cage rails (shape of these allows the cage to line up with breech no matter where the turret is trained)
34 Local fire control dynamo
35 Interlocking gear for gun loading cage and telegraph gear
36 Hydraulically operated breech mechanism (in open position)
37 Turret entrance through armour
38 Range finder
39 Radial crane for lifting shells from bin to emergency folding breech tray in front of open breech
40 Rammer engine and gun loading arm
41 Gun loading cage with cordite in two top sections and shell in bottom chamber (cage lines up with gun at any elevation)
42 Breech operator's and loader's seats

back to look for her. These two ships were suddenly confronted by the terrifying sight of three battleships which had been tracking them steadily on radar. Cunningham himself describes the scene:

'In the dead silence, a silence that could almost be felt, one heard only the voices of the gun control personnel putting the guns on to the new target. One heard the orders repeated in the director tower behind and above the bridge. Looking forward, one saw the turrets swing and steady when the 15-in guns pointed at the enemy cruisers. Never in the whole of my life have I experienced a more thrilling moment than when I heard a calm voice from the director tower: "Director-layer sees the target"; sure sign that the guns were ready and that his finger was itching on the trigger. The enemy was at a range of no more than 3800 yards—point blank.

'It must have been the Fleet Gunnery Officer . . . who gave the signal order to open fire. One heard the "ting-ting-ting" of the firing gongs. Then came the great orange flash and the violent shudder as the six big guns bearing were fired simultaneously. At the very same moment the destroyer Greyhound *. . . switched her searchlight on to one of the enemy cruisers, showing her up momentarily as a silvery-blue shape in the darkness. Our searchlights shone out with the first salvo, and provided illumination for what was a ghastly sight. Full in the beam I saw our six great projectiles flying through the air. Five out of the six hit a few feet below the level of the cruiser's upper deck and burst with flashes of brilliant flame. The Italians were quite unprepared. Their guns were trained fore and aft. They were hopelessly shattered before they could put up any resistance.'*

Partial Success

The *Valiant* and *Barham* dealt similarly with the other cruisers, and in a matter of a few minutes both were glowing torches. The Italian destroyers made a gallant attempt to torpedo the British squadron but they were driven off. The destroyers found the damaged *Pola* and torpedoed her, and as dawn was approaching Cunningham wisely decided to head for home. This Battle of Cape Matapan, otherwise known to the Italians as the Battle of Gaudo Island, was in Cunningham's eyes only a partial success as he had wanted to trap the *Vittorio Veneto*, but its strategic value was to be demonstrated very soon. In May the Mediterranean Fleet had to evacuate troops from Crete under constant German air attack. The *Warspite* was hit and badly damaged by a large bomb, and several smaller ships were sunk. If the Italian Fleet needed to put to sea now was the time, but it did not. The memory of Matapan was too recent.

The Italians did eventually get their

revenge for Matapan, but still they failed to reap the proper benefit. On the night of 18–19 December, 1941 the submarine *Scire* launched three 'human torpedoes', really small self-propelled craft driven by two operators wearing underwater breathing apparatus and sitting astride the body of the craft. At about 4 am sentries found two frogmen clinging to the anchor cable of HMS *Valiant*, and a few minutes later charges detonated under her and the flagship *Queen Elizabeth*. The *Valiant* was seriously damaged, but could steam, whereas the *Queen Elizabeth* was much worse, with a hole about 40 feet square under her forward boiler rooms. Both ships were quite unfit for action, and, had the Italians but known it, they had virtually sunk the last two British battleships in the Mediterranean. But the harbour at Alexandria is shallow and both ships settled on the mud, revealing very little to the snooping aircraft which flew over next day. After strenuous efforts both battleships were eventually refloated; the *Valiant* went to Durban in April 1942 for a three-month repair but the *Queen Elizabeth* needed nine months in an American yard, and did not rejoin the Fleet until June 1943.

The other battleship in the Mediterranean had been the *Barham*, but on 24 November she had been exercising with the rest of the Mediterranean Fleet off the coast of Egypt when *U.331* penetrated the screen without being detected. Three torpedoes hit the old ship, she rolled over to port and after about four minutes lay on her beam ends and blew up. She and the *Malaya* had never received the full modernisation given to the other *Queen Elizabeth*s and her loss was probably caused by her inferior underwater protection. The Board of Inquiry concluded that 4-in ammunition stored in what had once been the port underwater torpedo-tube compartment might have caught fire and set off the 15-in magazines. In the modernised ships such spaces had been given protection and converted to other uses, but in the unmodernised ships the compartments were outside the main citadel and were often used for storing the vast quantities of anti-aircraft ammunition which were needed. It is significant that four out of the five British capital ships sunk in the war were old ships which had not had their underwater and magazine protection overhauled. It is also interesting to note that the *Barham* was the only Allied battleship to be sunk at sea by a U-Boat.

HMS *Queen Elizabeth*
Queen Elizabeth, seen here in 1941, was substantially modernised a second time before the war. The superstructure was completely replaced, anti-aircraft armament was increased and a hangar and catapult were provided. Weight saved on new machinery was used to increase protection
Displacement: 36,000 tons *Length:* 639 ft
Atmament: 8×15-in, 20×4.5-in, 32×40-mm up to 52×20-mm, 16×mg *Armour:* 13-in max side, 3-in max deck, 11-in max turrets
Max speed: 24.5 knots

TWILIGHT OF THE KRIEGSMARINE

Bismarck: Breakout and Destruction

It is opportune now to return to the Atlantic, for the German Navy was ready by April 1941 to send its newest and most powerful battleship to sea. On 21 May the *Bismarck* sailed from her Norwegian fjord with the 8-in gunned cruiser *Prinz Eugen*, and as the Home Fleet had been alerted it was not long before two cruisers patrolling in the Denmark Strait made contact. In the early hours of 24 May the battle-cruiser HMS *Hood* and the new battleship *Prince of Wales* moved from Iceland to intercept the German squadron. Vice-Admiral Holland in the *Hood* hoped to come into action on the most advantageous bearing, but during the night he had made an alteration of course, and as a result found that his ships would have to engage on a fine bearing which masked their after guns and so reduced the weight of fire. The *Prince of Wales* had been completed only two weeks before and was suffering teething troubles in her 14-in gun mountings, so a reduction of 40 per cent in her firepower added to her already severe problems.

The British ships turned in line ahead to close the range as fast as possible, for Admiral Holland knew that his flagship was vulnerable to 15-in shellfire down to about 18,000 yards. Vulnerability in this sense refers to the 'immunity zone' conferred by the side and deck armour, and it is interesting to compare this with *Prince of Wales'* immunity zone, which extended down to 13,000 yards. Below 18,000 yards the trajectory of shells flattened and the thinness of

Hood's deck armour would matter less and less, while her 12-in side armour was only .6-in less than that of the *Bismarck*. Another problem for Holland was that *Hood's* speed was now only about 28½ knots, the same as that of the *Prince of Wales*; although the *Bismarck's* sea speed was only 29 knots she was credited with 31, and he must have felt that he could be out-manoeuvred by the German ships.

Massive Explosion

Many commentators claim that *Hood* made a mistake in identifying the leading ship as the *Bismarck* instead of the *Prinz Eugen* but German survivors reported that *Hood* was firing at *Bismarck* very well and found the range in three salvoes. The next salvo might well have been a hit, but *Prinz Eugen* had already scored a hit on *Hood's* boat deck which started a fire. The range was now down to just over 18,000 yards, and the *Hood* ordered a turn to port to bring full broadsides to bear, but just as she started her turn she was hit by one or possibly two shells from the *Bismarck*. Suddenly the *Hood* vanished in a sheet of flame and a massive explosion engulfed her. When the smoke cleared her shattered hull could be seen disappearing below the water.

To the onlookers in the *Prince of Wales*, as much as to the Germans, the explosion was horrifying, but there was no time to think of reasons. The *Prince of Wales*, with one forward 14-in gun defective and the after turret

jammed by a shell which had fallen out of the hoist, now faced the *Bismarck* and *Prinz Eugen* alone. She was hit seven times in quick succession by three 8-in and four 15-in shells. Six caused little damage but one hit was deadly; it passed through the bridge without exploding but shattered the binnacle on its way out. Fragments of metal scythed across the compass platform, killing or wounding everyone except Captain Leach. But the *Prince of Wales* was not put out of action, and although her gunnery radar set was not working she was able to get the range from her Type 281 air-warning set and obtained several straddles on the *Bismarck*. Two 14-in shells penetrated the German ship's hull and started a leak in a fuel bunker, but it was clearly foolhardy to allow a new ship to face two apparently undamaged German ships, and the rear-admiral commanding the cruisers, now the

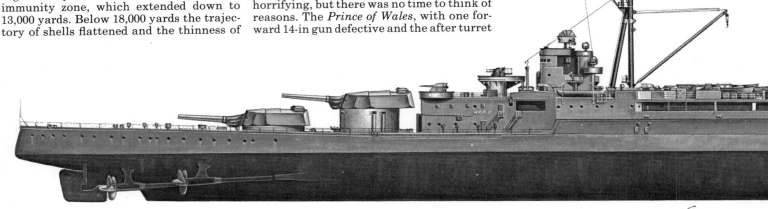

HMS *Hood*

The battle-cruiser *Hood* was the only one of her class to be completed, the other three being suspended in 1917 when Germany stopped work on the *Mackensen* class. The loss of three battle-cruisers at Jutland resulted in additional armour being incorporated in the *Hood's* design, adding 5000 tons to the displacement and reducing top speed by 2 knots. The explosion which destroyed the ship in her action against the *Bismarck* and *Prinz Eugen* is thought to have resulted from anti-aircraft shells or rockets being ignited by a fire following a shell hit, rather than by the main armour being penetrated

Displacement: 41,200 tons *Length:* 860 ft
Armament: 8×15-in, 14×4-in, 24×2-pdr (3×8),. 20×mg, 5×UP batteries, 4×21-in TT *Armour:* 12-in belt, 3-in deck (max), 15-in turrets (max)
Max speed: 28½ knots

senior officer present, ordered Leach to break off action.

It will never be known just what caused the *Hood* to blow up, and two boards of inquiry were unable to do more than make educated guesses. There were hardly any witnesses; the three survivors could not provide any clue, and the majority of people on board the *Prince of Wales* were either watching the German ships or fully engaged elsewhere. Several interesting points did come to light, however. First, the *Hood* was carrying a large amount of rocket ammunition for her anti-aircraft 'UP' (Unrotated Projectile) rocket mountings, stowed in light steel lockers under the boat deck, which was the site of the fire caused by the 8-in shell from *Prinz Eugen*. Second, four out of the seven shells which hit the *Prince of Wales* did not explode, and the remaining three only detonated partially. Third, the after magazines in the *Hood* had been surrounded by additional 4-in anti-aircraft stowage outside the armoured barbettes. If

Right: The breakout and destruction of the *Bismarck*. Once she had fought her way out into the Atlantic and given the Royal Navy a bloody nose by sinking the *Hood*, the convoys were easy prey. Through a mixture of luck, the long arm of airpower, and finally the gunpower of superior surface forces, the *Bismarck* was sunk only a few hundred miles from the safety of Brest

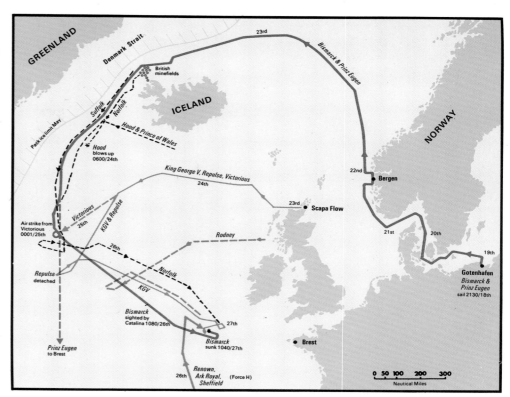

May 20, 1941 and the Bismarck *prepares in the Baltic for her final sortie against the Atlantic convoys. The aircraft recognition bands were painted out at Bergen*

Bismarck

The *Bismarck* was the *Kriegsmarine*'s first modern battleship, built under the terms of the Anglo-German Naval Agreement. Basically an enlarged version of the 1915 *Baden*, she displayed many old-fashioned features— particularly separate high-angle and low-angle batteries and a lack of vertical sandwich protection against underwater damage. In fact her most important asset was her massive beam
Displacement: 41,000 tons *Length:* 245 m *Armament:* 8×380-mm, 12×150-mm, 16× 105-mm, 16×37-mm, 12×20-mm *Armour:* 320-mm side (max), 120-mm deck (max), 360-mm turrets (max) *Max speed:* 29 knots

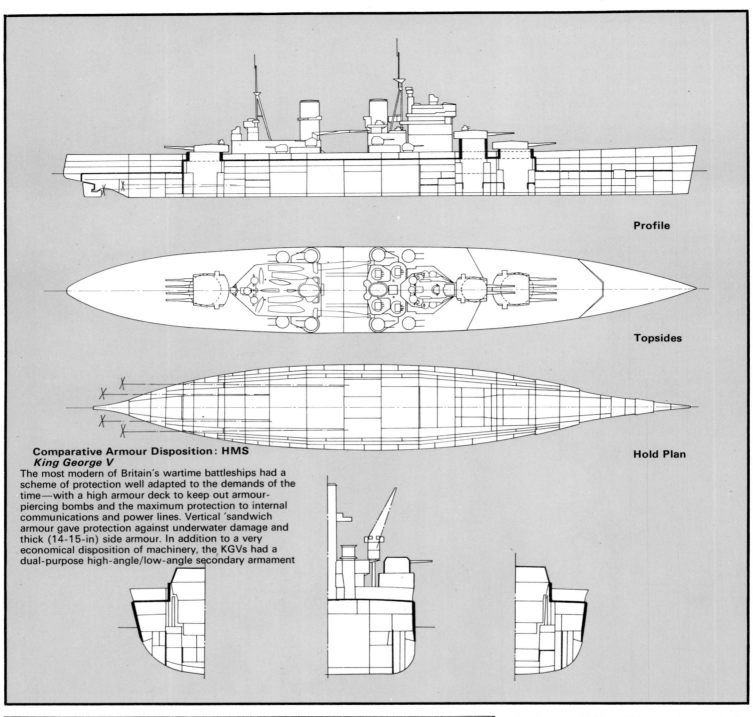

Profile

Topsides

Hold Plan

Comparative Armour Disposition: HMS *King George V*

The most modern of Britain's wartime battleships had a scheme of protection well adapted to the demands of the time—with a high armour deck to keep out armour-piercing bombs and the maximum protection to internal communications and power lines. Vertical 'sandwich' armour gave protection against underwater damage and thick (14-15-in) side armour. In addition to a very economical disposition of machinery, the KGVs had a dual-purpose high-angle/low-angle secondary armament

the fire amidships did not detonate the above-water torpedo tubes, and there is no direct evidence of this, and if the *Bismarck*'s shells were defective, as we know they were, then the most tenable conclusion is that the *Hood* was sunk by a fire which somehow spread to the 4-in ammunition below and thence to the after 15-in magazines. Stemming from this, the probability is that *Hood* was sunk by a fire caused by an 8-in shell, and not by a 15-in shell penetrating her side or deck armour.

The *Bismarck* and *Prinz Eugen* now succeeded in shaking off the shadowing cruisers, and during the confusion the cruiser broke away and proceeded independently to Brest. Admiral Lütjens decided that his flagship had lost too much fuel from the two shell hits, and decided to make for St Nazaire, where there was a dock large enough to take her. Late on the night of 24

Left: HMS Anson, *launched in 1942, fourth of the* King George V *class*

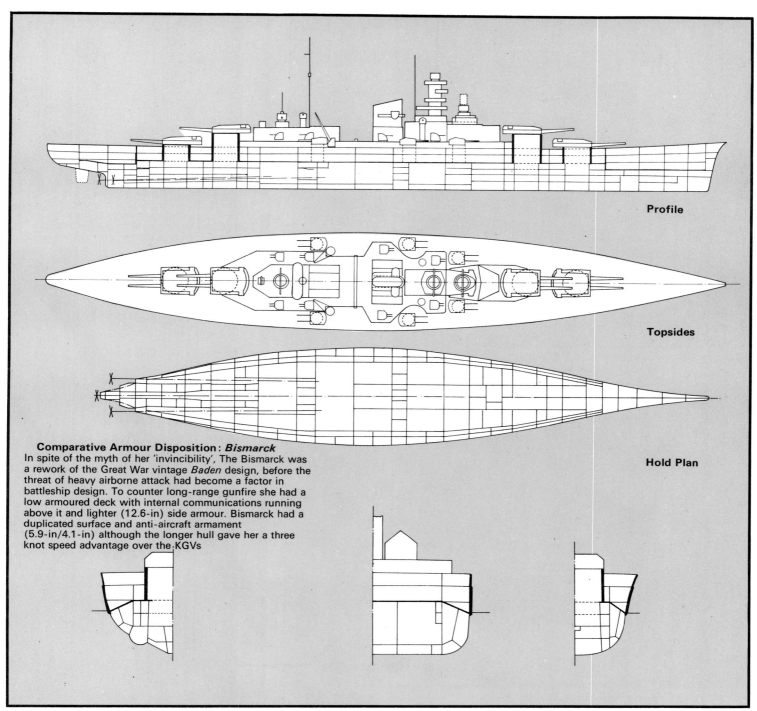

Profile

Topsides

Hold Plan

Comparative Armour Disposition : *Bismarck*
In spite of the myth of her 'invincibility', The Bismarck was a rework of the Great War vintage *Baden* design, before the threat of heavy airborne attack had become a factor in battleship design. To counter long-range gunfire she had a low armoured deck with internal communications running above it and lighter (12.6-in) side armour. Bismarck had a duplicated surface and anti-aircraft armament (5.9-in/4.1-in) although the longer hull gave her a three knot speed advantage over the KGVs

May she was attacked by Swordfish torpedo-bombers from the aircraft carrier *Victorious,* and although one torpedo hit the 18-in weapon did not carry a warhead big enough to make much impression on the thickest part of a battleship's armour belt.

Throughout the next day the British hunted the *Bismarck* with ships and aircraft in the most massive co-ordinated search of the war. Not until 26 May did a Catalina flying boat spot the *Bismarck*, but she was so far away from any ships strong enough to bring her to battle that it seemed as if she might reach safety after all. In a French port she could be repaired and then sail again, and this time she would be closer to the Atlantic shipping routes. It was essential to slow her down, and the carrier *Ark Royal* coming up from Gibraltar with the battle-cruiser *Renown* was ordered to fly off a strike. The first was unsuccessful, as the

Right: Bismarck, *greatest of her time, or a rework of an outdated design?*

Drüppel

Pulling through a 38-cm gun aboard the Tirpitz *after firing practise*

10.5-cm High-Angle Anti-Aircraft Gun
Main AA armament on *Bismarck* and *Tirpitz*.
A triaxial stabilising system ensured that the
gun and crew were on a level platform whatever
the sea conditions and angle of the ship.
Illustration bottom right shows the gun at
maximum angle of roll

The 10·5-cm high-angle anti-aircraft guns of the Tirpitz

*The 10·5-cm and 3·7-cm anti-aircraft armament
aboard German capital ships was supplemented
by 2-cm automatics in single and quadruple
mountings*

Swordfish attacked the cruiser *Sheffield* by mistake in the murky weather, but the second strike was successful. One 18-in torpedo spent itself on the armour belt as before, but the second wrecked the *Bismarck*'s steering gear and jammed her rudders.

The giant battleship was doomed; although she survived torpedo attacks from destroyers during the night she was steering erratically and trailing oil fuel. Next morning the Home Fleet flagship *King George V* and the *Rodney* hove into view, and the *Bismarck* prepared to fight her last battle. The two British battleships selected their own courses, the *Rodney* choosing to engage end-on while the flagship attacked on the broadside. All three ships opened fire at about 8.47 am, but the *Bismarck*'s firing was soon erratic; the nearest she came to scoring a hit was a straddle on the *Rodney,* and within half an hour her guns were silent and she had sustained heavy damage. By now she was so low in the water

and the range was so short that the shells were passing straight over the armoured deck. To try to get a plunging hit the *King George V* opened the range to 14,000 yards, leaving the *Rodney* to reduce the superstructure to a shambles from a range of 4000 yards. At 10.15 the C-in-C Home Fleet, Admiral Tovey, ordered his ships to cease fire and the cruiser *Dorsetshire* fired two torpedoes into the *Bismarck*'s starboard side and another one into the port side. At 10.36 she rolled over and sank, leaving a few score of dazed survivors in the water.

Myth of Invincibility

Surprisingly the last fight of the *Bismarck* has become a subject for myth and misunderstanding, with claims made to the effect that she was 'unsinkable', that she was scuttled without her armour being perforated, or even that the British could have towed her into port. Myths also surround the subject of her design; she is credited with the heaviest protection in the

world, with a 'secret formula' nickel-steel armour twice as resistant as any previous steels, etc, etc. True, she was a powerful ship but her design basically was old-fashioned. The haste with which Hitler had expanded the *Kriegsmarine* had prevented a full evaluation of designs and many of the brilliant ship designers had left the service after 1918. With nothing like the action experience of the British and the lengthy tests on target ships carried out by them, the Americans and the Japanese, there was little choice but to update the *Baden* design of 1915, just as the *Mackensen* of 1916 had served as the model for the *Scharnhorst*. Of course the machinery was more modern and far more powerful, but the essential details of armouring were more First World War than Second in conception.

Among the principal features which stamp the *Bismarck* design as elderly are the triple gun-battery, main 15-in, secondary 15-cm (5.9-in) and anti-aircraft 10.5-cm, and the relatively low level at which the main armoured deck was positioned. As we have already seen, the US Navy and the Royal Navy had independently reached the conclusion that bombs were a bigger danger than long-range gunfire, and had sited the armoured deck as high as possible. Nor was there any 'sandwich' protection against torpedoes; instead the *Bismarck* relied on

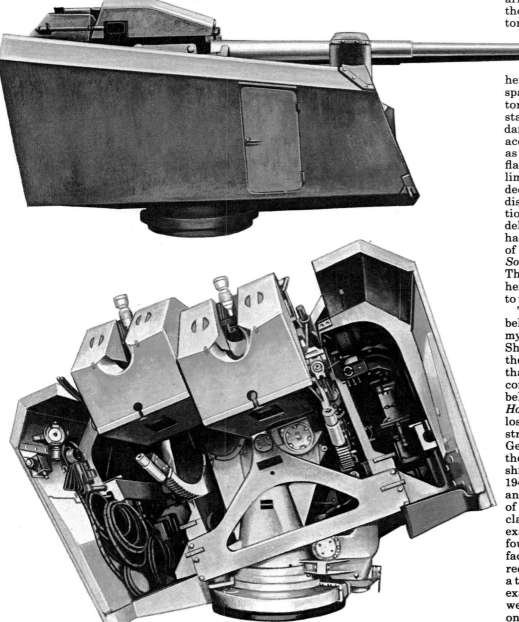

her massive 118-ft beam to provide a deep space between the ship's side and the anti-torpedo bulkhead. This gave great initial stability and resistance to underwater damage, but eventually resulted in an accelerated tendency to capsize, especially as the freeboard was quite low. Despite a flagrant evasion of the international treaty limits, involving a jump from 35,000 tons declared standard tonnage to an actual displacement of 41,700 tons, and the installation of high-pressure steam machinery delivering 138,000 horsepower, the *Bismarck* had a sea speed of only 29 knots, a fraction of a knot more than that of the smaller *South Dakota* and *King George V* classes. The belt armour was 12.6-in thick, making her equal to the *South Dakota* but inferior to the *King George V* and other classes.

These comparisons are quoted not to belittle the *Bismarck* but to debunk the myths which have grown up around her. She and the *Tirpitz* were powerful ships but they were by no means the ultimate design that many people think they were. This contrast between the facts and popular belief probably stems from the loss of HMS *Hood*. The British were downcast by the loss of a ship that had been imbued with strength she did not possess, and the Germans were correspondingly elated by the feat and justifiably proud of their battleship's last stand. Be that as it may, since 1941 there has been a flood of ill-informed and half-baked speculation about the loss of the *Bismarck*. One ludicrous report claimed that a diver had gone down to examine the hull of the *Bismarck* and had found 'no holes in the hull'. Apart from the fact that the diver could claim a world record for diving off the Continental shelf, a team of expert divers took three months to examine the hull of the *Prince of Wales* and were still unable to find the radar aerials; on such a large hull a bottom search in deep water would be impossible.

The Channel Dash

The elimination of the *Bismarck* led the German naval command to reconsider the wisdom of leaving the *Scharnhorst* and *Gneisenau* at Brest. The two battle-cruisers had cruised in the Atlantic from January to March 1941—Operation *Berlin*—during which they sank or captured 22 ships. After steaming a total of 17,800 miles they docked at Brest on 23 March, but soon the RAF began to bomb their berths. Despite an ever-increasing weight of bombs dropped, neither ship was seriously damaged, apart from a torpedo hit on the *Gneisenau* on 6 April, 1941 and bomb damage to *Scharnhorst* on 24 July. But it was only a matter of time before a lucky hit caused serious damage, and if the ships were not to be allowed to make another foray into the Atlantic better use could be made of them elsewhere. On 1 January, 1942 Naval Group Command West brought up the subject of what to do with the two battle-cruisers and the cruiser *Prinz Eugen,* and 12 days later Hitler announced his plan for a breakout through the English Channel.

The naval staff was aghast, for on the face of it three large ships had no chance of slipping through the narrow Straits of Dover without being sunk by air attack, surface torpedo attack or coastal guns. But Hitler once again showed that his imagination and skill at divining his opponent's weaknesses could out match conventional wisdom; he banked on the British convincing themselves that a daylight run could never happen. And so it turned out. The RAF failed to spot the German ships until they were off Le Havre at 10.42 am on the morning of 12 February, and even then no co-ordinated attack could be mounted. Piecemeal attacks by motor torpedo boats and aircraft were beaten off with ease, for the *Luftwaffe* had for once co-operated with the *Kriegsmarine* totally, and had provided a massive fighter 'umbrella' for Operation *Cerberus*. The coastal guns at Dover were not allowed to open fire until the German ships were almost out of range, for fear that they might hit their own MTBs' Although a small force of destroyers got within 4,000 yards their torpedoes were dodged, and an incredulous Admiral Ciliax slowly realised that the Führer's intuition had been right. Apart from mine damage to both ships late in the day, the most audacious, not to say insolent, excursion of the war had been achieved without loss.

The British were furious, and heads rolled as Churchill investigated what *The Times* chose to call the greatest humiliation inflicted on the Royal Navy since the Dutch burned the fleet at Chatham in 1667. But it was a hollow victory, for the three German ships were far less dangerous in Germany than they had been at Brest. Operation *Cerberus* was in fact a strategic withdrawal, that time-honoured euphemism for a retreat, and the high command was hard-put to work out what to do with the battle-cruisers now that they were safe in German waters. Both ships went to Kiel for repairs, and *Scharnhorst* rejoined the Fleet in August 1942. But *Gneisenau* was not so lucky. On the night of 26-27 February she was set on fire by a bomb during an air raid on Kiel, and an explosion of oil fumes wrecked the entire forepart of the ship, from the bow as far back as 'A' turret.

The ship was towed to Götenhafen

Above: *The* Scharnhorst *arms at Brest in preparation for Operation* Cerberus. *Her Arado Ar 196 is on the dockside*

Drüppel

(Gdynia) in April, and a long-cherished plan to re-arm the class with 15-in guns was revived. The barbettes had been designed to take the weight of the twin 38-cm turret, but the opportunity was also taken to improve seaworthiness by lengthening the bow. The wreckage of the forecastle was cut off in 1943, but by this time the Third Reich was desperately short of steel and labour. The work ground to a halt in 1944, and eventu-

ally she was no more than an inert hulk. On 27 March, 1945 she was scuttled in the entrance to the harbour of Götenhafen to deny the port to the Russians. The Poles took four years to salvage the wreck, and the work was not completed until September 1951.

The Destruction of the Scharnhorst and Tirpitz

After the sinking of the *Bismarck* the German naval command fell back on its older and safer doctrine of the 'fleet in being'. When the Allies stopped their convoys to North Russia in the summer of 1943 this was largely due to the presence of the *Scharnhorst* and *Tirpitz* in northern Norway. Despite Hitler's rage over the bungled action in the Barents Sea in December 1942, when the failure of the 'pocket battleship' *Lützow* (formerly the *Deutschland*) and the heavy cruiser *Admiral Hipper* to deal with a convoy escorted only by destroyers led to the resignation of Admiral Raeder as Commander-in-Chief.

Raeder had resigned largely because Hitler had threatened to pay off the large warships, using their steel to make tanks and their guns for coastal defence. His successor, Admiral Dönitz, was well known for his advocacy of U-Boat warfare, but even he recognised the value of the few remaining large ships in tying down large numbers of British ships and preventing supplies from reaching Russia. Not only did Dönitz win a reprieve for the surface fleet, but he even initiated a request to Hitler early in 1943 for permission to use the big ships offensively once more. Dönitz and his admirals Schniewind (Flag Officer Group North) and Kummetz (Flag Officer Northern Task Force) were determined that the commanders would have freedom to engage, without inhibiting orders of the sort that had resulted in so many abortive operations in the past.

The subject acquired new urgency in November 1943, when two convoys slipped through to Russia without loss. This was despite doubts expressed by Kummetz, who pointed out that *Tirpitz* would not complete her repairs until March, and the undeniable fact that in an action during the long Arctic winter the much superior British radar would put his ships at a disadvantage. Kummetz then went on long leave, and command of the Northern Group was handed over to Admiral 'Achmed' Bey, who commanded the destroyers. Bey seems to have been under the impression that action would be limited to a destroyer raid on a convoy but on 29 December he was told that it might be expedient to use the *Scharnhorst* as well. On 19 December Dönitz informed Hitler that the battle-cruiser would attack the next Allied convoy if the circumstances were favourable.

Dunking Dönitz

The circumstances were not very favourable, had Dönitz known, and now that the 'Ultra' story has been revealed, of how much of the highest level German intelligence was known to the Allies, we can wonder how much knowledge the C-in-C Home Fleet, Admiral Fraser, was acting upon when he took his flagship, the battleship *Duke of York*, the cruiser *Jamaica* and four destroyers as distant cover for an outward convoy (JW.55B) and an inward convoy (FA.55A) between Loch Ewe and the Kola Inlet. The *Scharnhorst* sailed from Altenfjord at 7 pm on Christmas Day, accompanied by five destroyers. Recon-

naissance had detected convoy JW.55B but not the one heading for home, and Admiral Bey did not know that Admiral Fraser had already transferred some of his destroyers to JW.55B's escort, bringing it up to 14 destroyers to oppose the *Scharnhorst*. The weather and visibility were worsening, and Bey was forced to ask permission to send his destroyers back as they could not keep up with his flagship. Despite the risk of operating a capital ship without escort he was told to press on alone if he felt justified. All the time the *Duke of York* and the *Jamaica* were pounding through the heavy seas at a steady 17 knots, closing on the *Scharnhorst*.

The bad weather grounded the *Luftwaffe*'s reconnaissance aircraft, and although U-boats provided good estimates of the convoy's escort they failed to spot the other convoy or the Home Fleet. Mindful of the way in which his forces were scattered, Admiral Fraser took care to inform them of his own position and established the whereabouts of all ships; even the risk of breaking wireless silence was preferable to any misunderstanding about the tactical dispositions. By contrast the *Scharnhorst* lost contact with her destroyers at about 7.30 am on 26 December, thanks to a mix-up in signals, and they were not able to rejoin the flagship.

It was 8.40 am when Admiral Burnett, commanding the cruisers covering the convoy, learned that the *Belfast* had picked up the *Scharnhorst* on her radar screen, only 30 miles away. The *Duke of York* was still nearly 200 miles distant, and the three

HMS *Duke of York*
Construction of the *King George V* class was spurred by the laying down of new battleships in France, Germany and Italy. The ships were more heavily armoured than those of the *Nelson* class
Displacement: 44,790 tons max *Length:* 745 ft
Armament: 10×14-in, 16×5.25-in, 48×2-pdr AA
Armour: 15-in belt, 9/16-in main turrets, 1/6-in deck *Max speed:* 29 knots

King George V class

Name	Completed	Fate
King George V	Dec 1940	Scrapped 1958
Prince of Wales	Mar 1941	Sunk by Japanese aircraft 1941
Duke of York	Nov 1941	Scrapped 1958
Anson	Jun 1942	Scrapped 1957
Howe	Aug 1942	Scrapped 1958

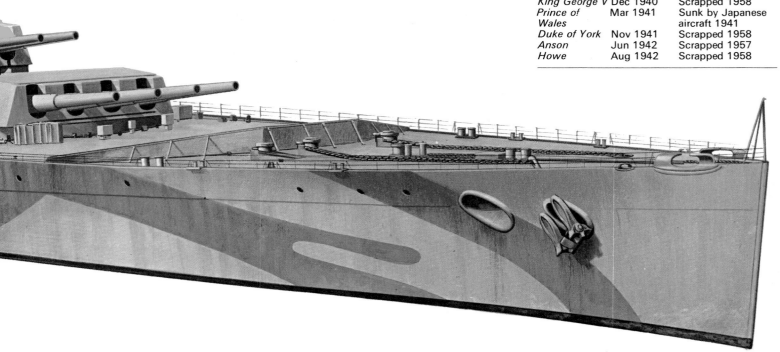

cruisers would have to hold off the *Scharnhorst* for a long time. At 9.24 the *Scharnhorst* was suddenly illuminated by starshell from the *Belfast* and two minutes later an 8-in shell from HMS *Norfolk* burst on her foretop, destroying the forward radar fire-control director. With one of her 'eyes' blinded the *Scharnhorst* was in a bad position, but she was able to turn to the south and outstrip the cruisers, which could not maintain top speed in such bad weather. The cruisers therefore rejoined the convoy, putting themselves between the *Scharnhorst* and her quarry. There were terrible fears aboard the Home Fleet flagship that contact might have been lost for good, but Admiral Burnett in the *Belfast* was confident that the *Scharnhorst* would be back, and he was proved right when his flagship regained radar contact at about mid-day.

Just after 12.21 the *Scharnhorst* opened fire on the cruisers, and as the range was down to 11,000 yards she hit both *Sheffield* and *Norfolk;* the latter had an 8-in turret and all but one of her radar sets put out of action. Once again the *Scharnhorst* turned away, but this time she unwittingly steamed directly towards the *Duke of York*, with the result that the British battleship picked her up on radar at 4.17 pm.

The range rapidly came down to 12,000 yards as the *Duke of York* manoeuvred to bring her full broadside to bear on her luckless target. At 4.50 pm the dreaded starshell burst in the darkness overhead, followed by 14-in and 6-in salvoes from the *Duke of York* and *Jamaica*. Admiral Bey was taken completely by surprise by this attack from an unexpected bearing, and it was some minutes before the German guns could reply. The range quickly opened as the *Scharnhorst* tried to break away, but the *Duke of York* hung on her heels. By 5.40 the cruisers had fallen back and the two big ships fought their duel alone at range varying from 17,000 to 20,000 yards. The *Scharnhorst's* gunnery settled down, but the only two hits she scored against the *Duke of York* went through the legs of her tripod masts and failed to explode. The British shooting was excellent, and at one stage the *Scharnhorst* was reduced to making small alterations to port to throw off the enemy fire-control, just as Hipper's battle-cruisers had done against the 5th Battle Squadron at Jutland many years before. But this time radar plotting was able to pick up these variations, and the *Duke of York's* gunnery was good enough to be able to fire the 14-in to hit the target by aiming at her next likely position.

Glow Through the Smoke
At least one of the 14-in shells had damaged one of the *Scharnhorst's* propeller shafts, but this did not slow her down sufficiently, and Admiral Fraser's fear was still that she would escape. After the gun action was broken off, just as Bey signalled 'We shall fight to the last shell', the four destroyers were ordered to attack with torpedoes. While two drew fire on the port side the other pair crept up to within 3000 yards on the starboard side before they were seen. The *Scorpion* hit her with at least one torpedo, and in the confusion that followed the *Savage* and *Saumarez* hit with another three. At 7 pm the *Duke of York* again opened fire, this time at only 10,400 yards, and the cruisers joined in. In half an hour the *Scharnhorst* was crawling at 5 knots, with shells bursting everywhere and fires

The topography of her fjord lair rather than any inherent invincibility of the ship protected the Tirpitz *from air attack. The* Tirpitz *never took part in any major surface action and was finally sunk by 'Tallboy' 12,000-lb bombs delivered by Lancaster bombers*

glowing through the clouds of smoke. The *Jamaica* closed in to finish her with torpedoes, and reported that she could see only a dull glow through the smoke.

No-one saw the *Scharnhorst* go down, but she must have sunk at about 7.45. Only 36 survivors were found in the icy water, out of nearly 2000 men. She had been sacrificed in an operation which had been badly planned, and with her went the last credible threat to the Arctic convoys for the time being. Once again it had been proved that only a capital ship could do the job, for at that distance from land and in such weather conditions air attacks could not have been made.

The last capital ship left to the *Kriegsmarine* was the *Tirpitz*, the sister of the *Bismarck*. Since late 1941 she had led a life of masterly inactivity. She was sent to Norway to threaten the Russian convoys, and in 1942 the threat of her going to sea was enough to cause the Admiralty to order convoy PQ.17 to scatter. In April 1943 the Royal Navy started to plan an attack on her Norwegian anchorage, using midget submarines to penetrate the net defences in Altenfjord. In this sense the X-Craft, as they were known, were the modern equivalent of the fireship, sent in to reach a ship which would not come out to fight. In this the midgets were successful, and on the night of 20-21 September, 1943 the *Tirpitz* was badly damaged by a ½-ton charge which exploded under her keel. All three sets of turbines were seriously damaged, putting the ship out of action for at least seven months.

The *Tirpitz* has acquired a formidable reputation for the way she stood up to attacks, but the reason she survived so many is because the anchorage she used afforded a superb natural defence against air attack. It was all but impossible to aim a bomb or torpedo at her when she nestled under the side of the fjord, and the story of the many attacks on her is really the story of attempts to overcome the geographical problems. On the occasion that a bomb did hit her, it went right through most of her decks but failed to explode. Once she was surprised at sea by Fleet Air Arm torpedo-bombers, and was very lucky to dodge the

torpedoes. Finally in August 1944, with the Allied Joint Planning Staff increasingly irritated at the way in which she was tying down ships urgently needed for the Pacific, it was decided to use Lancaster bombers and 12,000-lb 'Tallboy' bombs. On 15 September, 1944, 28 Lancasters flying from a Russian airfield scored a hit and two near misses.

The damage caused was too serious to be repaired so far north, and as the Germans were in any case thinking of abandoning Altenfjord they decided to move her to Tromsö, where she could act as a floating battery to defend against the invasion which Hitler was sure would be launched against Norway. Now she was 200 miles nearer to British air bases than before, and after a false start on 18 October, when low cloud obscured the anchorage, 32 Lancasters attacked on 12 November. This time all went well; the *Luftwaffe* failed to put any fighters up and in clear weather, without any distractions, the RAF bomb-aimers were able to hit the *Tirpitz* three times. She heeled over 30° to port, her after magazine exploded, and then she turned turtle. Some thousand men were trapped inside the hull, but a few trapped in an air pocket were heard, and a hole was cut in the bottom plating to allow them to escape.

In all 16 air attacks were made on the *Tirpitz,* 7 by the RAF and 9 by the Fleet Air Arm. For many years the wreck of the *Tirpitz* lay in Tromsö Fjord oozing oil, but she yielded a useful bonus to the Norwegian people who had been her unwilling hosts for three years, in the form of hundreds of electrical generators salvaged and put to good use ashore.

BATTLESHIPS IN SHADOW

American battleships blaze at Pearl Harbor, struck by the massive Japanese carrier-launched attack. Since Taranto the message had been clear. The mighty battleship as king-pin of surface fleets was now overshadowed by air power

Across the other side of the world the Japanese had set in train events which rocked the world, and incidentally finished the reputation of the battleship. Profiting by the lessons of the British attack on Taranto, the Japanese planned an air strike against the United States' Pacific Fleet in its base at Pearl Harbor on Oahu in the Hawaiian Islands. They were acutely aware that the Americans outnumbered them, and it was hoped, just as at Port Arthur in 1904, to start the war with a knockout blow. Commercial rivalry between the United States and Japan had been growing for years, but above all the Japanese needed the strategic raw materials of Malaya and the East Indies—oil, rubber and minerals— to maintain their economic growth. It needed only the military ardour of young middle-rank officers who believed themselves invincible to turn these economic imperatives into a bold and imaginative war plan.

On 26 November, 1941 a large fleet of six aircraft carriers, two battleships and three cruisers put to sea for a secret rendezvous; they were actually heading by a roundabout route for Pearl Harbor, and avoided shipping routes. The deception was a complete success and the attack position 275 miles north of Pearl Harbor was reached on the night of 6-7 December. At 7 am the first wave took off, and an hour later the first bombs shattered the Sunday tranquility of the great naval base.

In just under two hours two waves of aircraft wrought havoc with the unprepared Pacific Fleet. Despite having radar warning and despite a destroyer reporting a midget submarine outside the harbour, nothing was done to sound the alarm. By midday the battleships *Arizona* and *Okla-*

homa had been destroyed, and the *California, Maryland, Pennsylvania, Tennessee* and *West Virginia* all seriously damaged. Burning furiously, the *Nevada* had nearly sunk in the entrance to the harbour, but had managed to beach herself before blocking the channel. Casualties were heavy in men and aircraft, but above all the Americans' pride was hurt. They could draw some comfort from the knowledge that all four of their own aircraft carriers had been away at sea and so had escaped the holocaust, and that the ships' gunfire had punished the second wave of Japanese aircraft severely. But the fact remained that the US Pacific Fleet had been neutralised, and nothing stood between the Japanese Fleet and conquest of the Pacific.

The British had rashly sent the *Prince of Wales* and the old battle-cruiser *Repulse* to Singapore in the vague hope that their

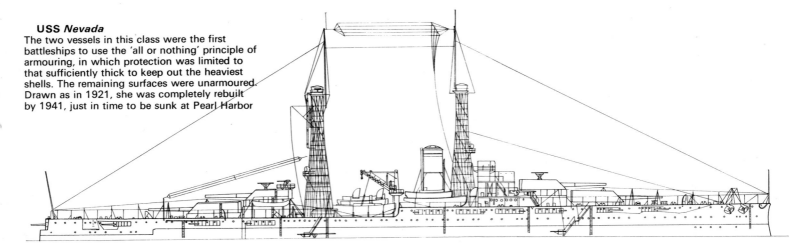

USS *Nevada*
The two vessels in this class were the first battleships to use the 'all or nothing' principle of armouring, in which protection was limited to that sufficiently thick to keep out the heaviest shells. The remaining surfaces were unarmoured. Drawn as in 1921, she was completely rebuilt by 1941, just in time to be sunk at Pearl Harbor

Displacement: 34,000 tons full load *Length:* 583 ft *Armament:* 10×14-in, 12×5-in, 8×5-in AA *Armour:* 8/14-in belt, 5/18-in main turrets, 4-in main deck *Max speed:* 20.5 knots

Nevada class

Name	Completed	Fate
Nevada	Mar 1916	Sunk as target 1948
Oklahoma	May 1916	Sank under tow 1947

presence would overawe the Japanese. With the destruction of the US Fleet these two capital ships now found themselves in a hopeless position, close to powerful land-based air squadrons in Thailand and lacking anything but the most rudimentary air cover from the obsolescent fighters of the RAF. On 8 December, six days after the two ships had arrived, Admiral Sir Tom Phillips took them to sea to carry out a 'search and destroy' mission against a reported Japanese landing at Singora and Kota Bharu. Next day the force was sighted by aircraft, and although it altered course during the night it was relocated next morning. Just after 1100 high-level bombing attacks started, and then torpedo attacks. The *Repulse* was slightly damaged by a bomb but the *Prince of Wales* was hit aft by a torpedo, which wrecked her steering.

The *Prince of Wales* was in a bad way. The torpedo hit warped the port outer shaft, and as the turbine was not stopped the bent shaft churned up the structure, opening out the bulkheads and allowing about 2500 tons of water to flood the machinery compartments. The ship listed about 11½°, and when

HMS *Repulse*
Repulse was another victim of that precocious child, the aircraft, and only three days after Pearl Harbor she succumbed to Japanese bombers while steaming off Malaya in the company of *Prince of Wales*. The birds let loose at Taranto were finally coming home to roost
Displacement: 32,000 tons *Length:* 740 ft *Armament:* 6×15-in, 9×4-in, 8×4-in AA, 24×40-mm, 8×21-in torpedo tubes *Armour:* 6-in max side, 3½-in max decks, 11-in max turrets, *Max speed:* 29 knots

the shock effect of near-misses knocked out the electrical generators the anti-aircraft gun turrets were unable to train. A second wave of aircraft scored no hits on either *Prince of Wales* or *Repulse* but the third wave hit *Prince of Wales* with four torpedoes on the starboard side. The great ship heeled over further to port but was still able to steam and made off slowly to the north. She was hit by another bomb at 12.44 but continued until 13.20, when she lurched suddenly and capsized. Two destroyers rescued 1285 officers and men but 327 officers and men including Admiral Phillips and Captain Leach were lost with their ship.

Striking Force
The *Repulse* had skilfully dodged both bombing and a torpedo attack and had even tried to help the flagship, but she was struck by a torpedo from a third wave, just after the *Prince of Wales* was hit, at 12.23 pm. Her steering was hit, and now she was at the mercy of the bombers. Three more hits finished her and Captain Tennant ordered his crew to abandon ship. The old battlecruiser hung at an angle of 60–70° to port for several minutes and then rolled over and sank at 12.33. Again destroyers were able to save 796 out of a total company of 1309 officers and men.

If Pearl Harbor was a blow to the supremacy of the battleship, this disaster marked the end. The Japanese 22nd Air Flotilla, a striking force of some 30 bombers and 50 torpedo-bombers, had taken less than an hour-and-a-half to sink two capital ships, at a cost of only eight aircraft. True, the *Repulse* had an obsolescent anti-aircraft battery, but the *Prince of Wales* had not only the most modern anti-aircraft gunnery system with radar control but also a modern scheme of protection. Until December 1941 people fondly hoped that the battleship could hold its own against aircraft at sea; thereafter it remained a valuable but vulnerable asset which had to be given the right

protection. The loss of the two ships could nevertheless have been avoided. Had some degree of air cover been provided the Japanese pilots would not have been able to execute such perfectly co-ordinated attacks, and a properly organised standing air patrol such as became standard in the Mediterranean and Pacific would have given virtual immunity to anything but a chance hit.

The Battle of the Coral Sea was fought in May 1942 without any capital ships, and at Midway only a month later a force of American carriers forced the Japanese Commander-in-Chief to turn back, despite the fact that he had under him no fewer than seven battleships, including the giant *Yamato*. It was inevitable, if hard to grasp, that three thin-skinned carriers could deter ships armed with the heaviest guns afloat, but from that moment the Japanese too regarded the battleship as no longer relevant. All the existing construction programmes were thrown out, and a new plan for more carriers was drawn up; its most grandiose element was the conversion of the third *Yamato*-class battleship, the *Shinano*, to a 62,000-ton carrier. An even more extreme move was to convert the *Hyuga* and *Ise* to hybrid 'battleship-carriers'. Work began on *Ise* at Kure in March 1943 and she

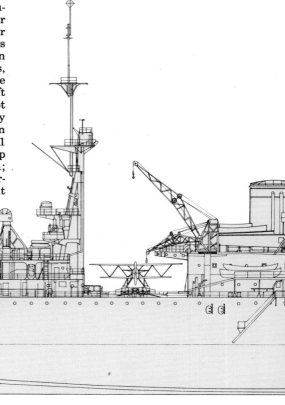

was ready seven months later; her sister started her conversion in July 1943 and was ready in only four months. The two aftermost 14-in gun turrets were removed and replaced by a large flight deck and hangar which extended from the mainmast to the stern. The aircraft were intended to be 22 floatplane bombers, launched from two catapults which effectively masked the fire of the midships turrets, but by the autumn of 1943 there were neither aircraft nor pilots available.

Battleships were still destined to fight their own kind for the time being, however. On the night of 11–12 November, 1942, during the US amphibious landings on Guadalcanal in the Solomon Islands, a Japanese force including the fast battleships *Kirishima* and *Hiei* tried to shell the newly captured airstrip at Henderson Field. In a fierce night action at relatively short range the *Hiei* was detected on radar and then savagely mauled by gunfire from a force of five cruisers and eight destroyers. She was badly damaged by 8-in shells from the *Portland* and *San Francisco* and possibly a torpedo from one of the destroyers, made a half-circle turn and then lurched northwards along the east side of Savo Island.

The *Kirishima* withdrew with only a single hit from an 8-in shell—relying totally on radar, the Americans could only aim at the largest radar echo—and joined up with another bombarding force next day. The *Hiei* was hunted down when daylight came, and aircraft from the carrier *Enterprise* found her. Throughout the day she twisted and turned in frantic efforts to dodge the bombs and torpedoes. Eventually, after 300 of her crew had died in the fires and explosions, she was abandoned the following evening. When destroyers had taken off the survivors she was torpedoed and sunk.

The new American battleships *South Dakota* and *Washington* arrived too late to join in this first part of the battle, but they were in position the following evening when a fresh bombardment force was reported making for Henderson Field. At 2316 the two ships opened fire on the Japanese cruiser *Sendai* at a range of 16,000 yards, but suddenly the tables were turned. The Japanese ships, trained to concert-pitch in night fighting, opened a furious fire with guns and torpedoes. Within minutes all four US destroyers were disabled without

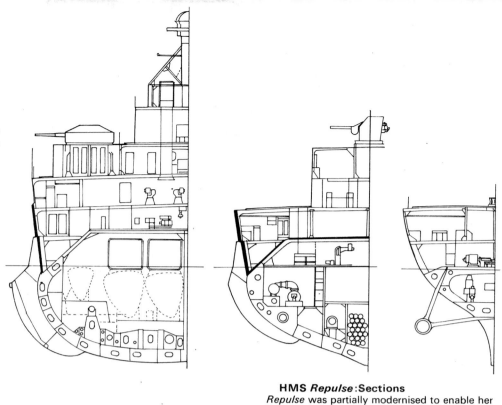

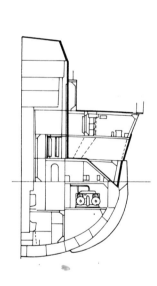

HMS *Repulse*:Sections
Repulse was partially modernised to enable her to fight a modern war on something approaching equal terms. Sectional views show added AA armament—high angle 4-in mountings and 2-pdr pom-poms

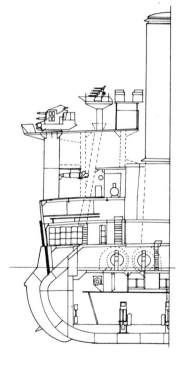

USS South Dakota *somewhere in the North Atlantic. The 'Sodak' and the* Alabama *were attached to the British Home Fleet escorting convoys to North Russia in 1942*

having fired a single torpedo. As for the *South Dakota*, her performance was less than brilliant; about 17 minutes after the start of the action the concussion from a 5-in twin gun mounting caused a short-circuit in the secondary fire-control system, and by a series of errors this 'blew' the entire electrical system for the ship. For three endless minutes the ship was in darkness without power for any of the guns, gyros or fire-control. She made a turn to avoid the burning destroyers, but then the surface-warning radar blacked out. To add to the confusion gun blast set fire to the two floatplanes on their catapults aft, but by a lucky stroke the next salvo's blast blew the aircraft overboard and put out the fires. But the battleship was now off course and blundered towards the Japanese, unable to get a 'fix' on the *Washington*. She was silhouetted by the glare from the burning destroyers and at a range of 5800 yards was illuminated by Japanese searchlights. The *Kirishima* and the cruisers *Atago* and *Takao* opened fire immediately, and although the American ship aimed at the searchlights and was successful in putting them out she was hit by a deluge of 8-in shells. Fortunately the *Washington* had kept her searchlights switched off and was free to concentrate her fire on the *Kirishima*, and so the *South Dakota* was only hit by one 14-in shell. She had 38 killed and 60 wounded, and was hit 27 times in 22 minutes; structural damage was mostly superficial but she had only one radar set still functioning, had many small fires burning, and had lost most of her fire-control and internal communications. She was clearly in no fit state for further fighting and withdrew just after midnight.

The *Washington* took advantage of the *South Dakota*'s plight to approach the Japanese unobserved, and from about 8400 yards opened a devastating fire on the *Kirishima*. Nine 16-in and about 40 5-in shells hit the *Kirishima*, her steering gear was wrecked and her upperworks were soon ablaze. Like the *Hiei*, she was eventually abandoned, and at about 0320 next morning friendly destroyers torpedoed the wreck after taking off the remnants of her crew. In only seven minutes the *Washington* had fired 75 16-in shells and 522 5-in, and had saved the day, but the Battle of Guadalcanal had shown up grave weaknesses in the American night-fighting organisation. As at Jutland 26 years earlier, one side had lavished a lot of attention to the subject of night action while the other had not, and if the US Navy had not had radar the battle could have gone against it and the Marines might have been forced to abandon Guadalcanal.

Two years later another battleship action took place in the Pacific, but this time the older American battleships were involved. Like the old Japanese ships, the battleships sunk at Pearl Harbor had been rebuilt. The *West Virginia*, *California* and *Tennessee* had been completely transformed, while the *Pennsylvania* and *Maryland* had also been repaired and given modern equipment. The first three boasted the new Mark 8 fire-control radar, which gave precise ranges as far as 44,000 yards and could pick up surface echoes out to 60,000 yards. Although these old ships were not intended to face the latest Japanese ships they were more than a match for their First World War contemporaries of the *Fuso* and *Ise* classes.

By October 1944 the tide of war had turned against the Japanese. Fast carrier task forces, composed of the new carriers and their battleship escorts, hit at the perimeter of island bases seized by the Japanese in the early days of 1942, while submarines preyed on the shipping which fed and supplied their garrisons. All this time the grand battle of annihilation, for which the Japanese had originally planned their giant battleships, remained elusive. The American invasion of the Marianas finally forced the Japanese to make a decisive move, for at last their leaders began to admit that they might soon face defeat. The Commander-in-Chief of the

USS *Iowa*

The fastest battleships ever built, the *Iowa* class were 10,000 tons heavier and 200 ft longer than the preceding *South Dakota* class. They were widely used in the Pacific for shore bombardment and anti-aircraft escorts

Displacement: 57,450 tons full load
Length: 887 ft *Armament:* 9×16-in, 20×5-in, 60×40-mm AA, 60×20-mm AA *Armour:* 12¼-in belt, 17½-in turrets, 4¾-in main deck *Max speed:* 33 knots

Iowa class

Name	Launched	Fate
Iowa	Aug 1942	Decommissioned 1958
New Jersey	Dec 1942	Decommissioned 1969
Missouri	Dec 1942	Decommissioned 1955
Wisconsin	Dec 1943	Decommissioned 1958

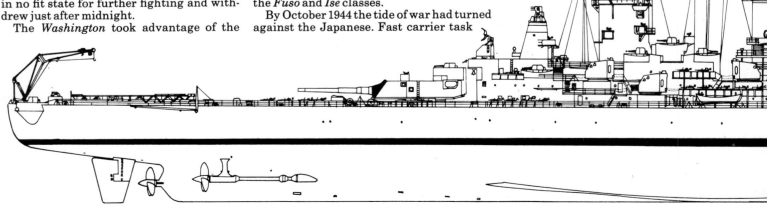

Combined Fleet, Admiral Toyoda, and his staff had little difficulty in predicting that the next American move would be against the Philippines. The *Sho-1* or Victory Plan was to make use of the entire surface fleet in a final gambler's throw to draw the American Fleet into a battle. It was recognised that there were now too few trained

Top: USS Iowa *off Pearl Harbor in the early 1950s*

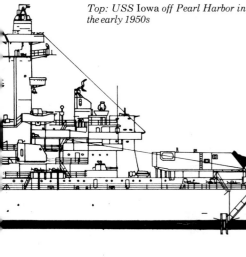

aircrew to provide adequate carrier strike forces, and so the surface forces were to be used as a bludgeon to smash their way through to the invasion beach-head, at which point the Americans would have to commit their main fleet to save the landing.

The Japanese Fleet was divided into four sections:

1 The Main Body under Vice-Admiral Ozawa, comprising the carriers *Zuikaku, Chitose, Chiyoda* and *Zuiho* and the battleship-carriers *Hyuga* and *Ise*, these last two without aircraft as we have already seen, and three cruisers and eight destroyers.
2 Force 'A' under Vice-Admiral Kurita, comprising the battleships *Yamato, Musashi, Nagato, Haruna* and *Kongo*, 12 cruisers and 15 destroyers.
3 Force 'C', divided into a Van Squadron

under Vice-Admiral Nishimura, the battleships *Fuso* and *Yamashiro*, a heavy cruiser and destroyers.
4 The Rear Squadron under Vice-Admiral Shima, with only three heavy cruisers and destroyers.

To the Americans these forces were known only by their locations: the Main Body was labelled the 'Northern Force', Force 'A' the 'Centre Force' and Force 'C' as the 'Southern Force'.

Admiral Ozawa's Force 'A' was the decoy force to lure Admiral William Halsey's Fast Carrier Task Force, comprising the cream of the US Pacific Fleet, away from the invasion fleet. The Main Body would unite with Force 'C' to sink, burn and destroy the invasion fleet, and then deal with any forces which tried to stop them. As soon as the Americans began to land in

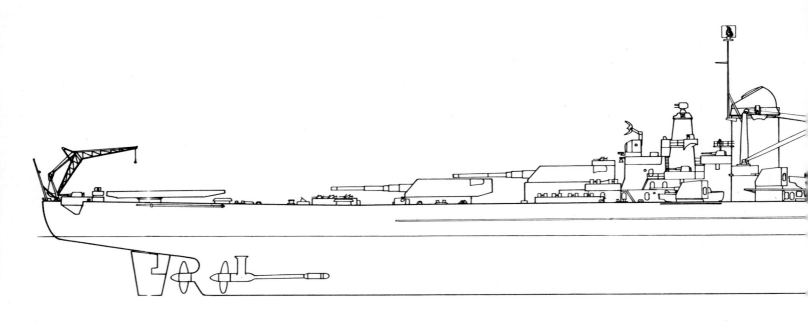

Leyte Gulf on 17 October the units of the *Sho* Plan knew the parts that they had to play: Force 'A' steamed southwards from Japan, the Main Body sailed from Borneo heading for the San Bernardino Strait and Leyte Gulf, and Force 'C' headed for Leyte Gulf via the Surigao Strait between Leyte and Mindanao.

Against this the Americans could muster the most powerful fleet ever seen. Halsey had organised Task Force 38 under Vice-Admiral Mitscher into four powerful Task Groups:

TG.38.1 carriers *Wasp, Hornet, Monterey* and *Cowpens*, four heavy cruisers and 15 destroyers.

TG.38.2 carriers *Intrepid, Hancock, Bunker Hill* and *Independence*, fast battleships *Iowa* and *New Jersey* (flagship), three light cruisers and 16 destroyers.

TG.38.3 *Essex, Lexington, Princeton* and *Langley*, battleships *Massachusetts* and *Indiana* and four light cruisers and 12 destroyers.

TG.38.4 carriers *Franklin, Enterprise, San Jacinto* and *Belleau Wood*, battleships *Washington* and *Alabama*, two cruisers and 16 destroyers.

In addition there was the Landing Support Group of six older battleships, the *Mississippi, Maryland, West Virginia, Tennessee, California* and *Pennsylvania*, but as they were intended purely for shore bom-

bardment the shellrooms were largely stocked with high explosive (HE) rather than armour-piercing (AP) or semi-armour-piercing (SAP) shells.

Usually American submarines provided outstanding reports of Japanese movements, but this time things went wrong and Admiral Ozawa's departure from the Inland Sea went unreported. The decoy force was thus not functioning as a decoy yet, whereas Kurita's Main Body was seen passing through the Palawan Passage three days later, and part of Admiral Shima's group was also seen. It was assumed that both forces were heading for Surigao Strait and three of the Task Groups were stationed to the east of the Philippines, 125 miles from one another.

Death of a Giant

On 24 October Admiral Halsey ordered air searches in every sector except the vital north and north-east, and so Ozawa's presence was still unsuspected. Halsey decided to concentrate his three task groups and ordered the fourth, TG.38.1, back from its position much further east. Although Ozawa's aircraft attacked the carrier *Princeton* a search could not be made for his ships until late in the day, by which time he was too far away. In the meantime strikes had been launched against Admiral Kurita's Main Body by carrier aircraft, and the 64,000-ton *Musashi* was under constant

attack from 1015 to 1500. The bombs mostly bounced off her massive decks and even a torpedo hit did not slow her down, but finally a third wave hit her with three torpedoes. These opened up the bow, slowing her down to 22 knots, and further attacks reduced this to 12 knots, making a total of seven bombs and nine torpedoes. More than a hundred aircraft suddenly arrived and in the confusion the *Musashi* took another 11 torpedoes; soon she was sinking by the bows and capable of only 6 knots, as progressive flooding began to beat the frantic countermeasures. At 1700 the captain ordered his crew to abandon ship, and at 1735 she suddenly lurched to port and rolled over, taking with her 1039 officers and

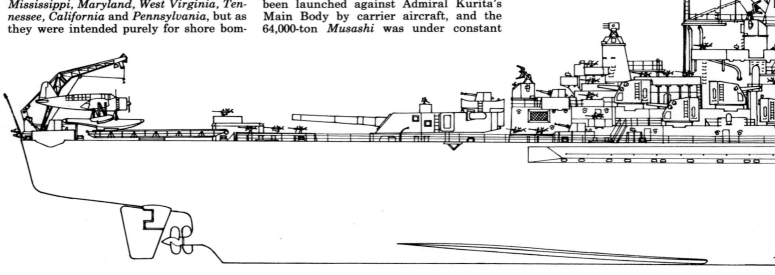

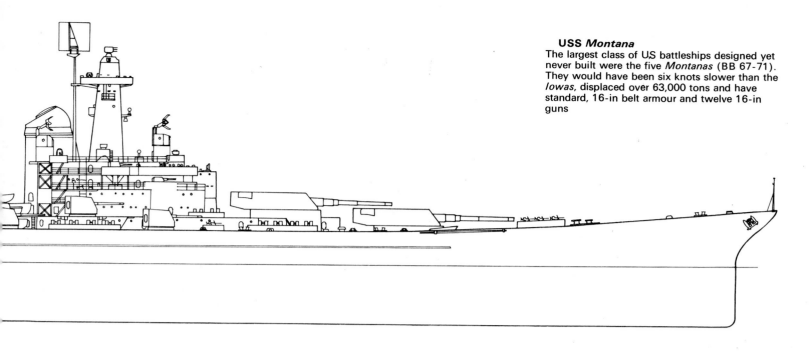

USS *Montana*
The largest class of US battleships designed yet never built were the five *Montanas* (BB 67-71). They would have been six knots slower than the *Iowas*, displaced over 63,000 tons and have standard, 16-in belt armour and twelve 16-in guns

men out of her complement of 2400. She had withstood more punishment than any previous battleship but even her massive protection could not cope with 20 torpedoes, 17 bombs and at least 15 near misses, most of them within a space of three to four hours.

Apart from damage to the cruiser *Myoko*, Kurita's force had otherwise escaped further loss during these attacks, but he still insisted on maintaining his withdrawal to avoid further attacks until he had confirmation that Halsey had been successfully decoyed by Ozawa. Halsey obliged by deciding that the 'Centre Force' was so badly mauled that it no longer constituted a threat to the invasion fleet. He compounded this misplaced optimism by declaring Ozawa's force to be the main Japanese fleet and ordered all his ships in pursuit. Toyoda's plan had worked perfectly.

What now occurred was poor staffwork, but it turned an error into a major blunder which nearly cost the Americans the battle. At 1512 on 24 October Halsey had signalled his intention of forming a new task force of battleships and carriers off the San Bernardino Strait to stop Kurita's Main Body. Although only an intention it was taken by Kinkaid's 7th Fleet to mean that the force had actually been formed, whereas the exit was not guarded by any ships at all. To the south, off Surigao Strait there were at least the six old battleships under Rear-Admiral Jesse B. Oldendorf and, as we have seen, they had been alerted to the Japanese Force 'C' heading for the area. When Kurita reversed course and headed for Leyte Gulf once more, however, there were no units heavier than escort carriers and destroyers to stop him from slaughtering the invasion transports.

At mid-day Oldendorf was warned to prepare for a night action, and he disposed his forces as best he could. Using destroyers and radar-equipped PT-Boats (motor torpedo boats) as an advance guard, he had his battleships steam across the 12-mile wide strait, with the two cruiser divisions extending the patrol line to the north of the destroyers and PT-Boats. The first sighting of Nishimura's Van Squadron was made at about 1030 that night, but the first attacks by PT-Boats had no effect. Nishimura ploughed on, with four destroyers leading the line, followed by his flagship *Yamashiro*, the *Fuso* and the *Mogami* at one-kilometre intervals. Even when US destroyers attacked at 0300, from a range of 8000-9000 yards, and hit three destroyers and the two battleships he did not waver, and continued to steam majestically towards the unseen line of American battleships.

Eventually at 0349 the *Fuso* blew up, breaking in two parts which drifted southwards, but the flagship seemed indestructible. She took another two torpedo hits at about 0411 but was not stopped. When she was within 22,000 yards the *California*,

USS *Alabama*
Battleships of the *South Dakota* class were shorter than their *North Carolina* predecessors, to give better protection both above and below the waterline. This resulted in the layout of the secondary armament being altered
Displacement: 44,375 tons full load *Length:* 680 ft *Armament:* 9×16-in, 20×5-in, 56×40-mm AA, 40×20-mm AA *Armour:* 12¼-in belt, 18-in turrets, 5-in main deck *Max speed:* 28 knots

South Dakota class

Name	Launched	Fate
South Dakota	Jun 1941	Scrapped 1962
Indiana	Nov 1941	Scrapped 1964
Massachusetts	Sep 1941	State memorial
Alabama	Feb 1942	State memorial

Tennessee and *West Virginia* poured in devastating broadsides of 14-in and 16-in shells, followed by the *Maryland* and *Mississippi* (fleet flagship). The *Yamashiro* could not withstand such a lethal concentration of fire and was soon blazing from end to end. She wheeled southwards with the *Mogami*, but at 0419 she suddenly capsized, taking the admiral and most of her crew with her. As the last battleship to be sunk in a straight fight with her own kind she had faced 3100 6-in and 8-in shells and 285 14-in and 16-in shells. The *Mississippi*'s last salvo, a full broadside of 12 guns, was, in the words of Samuel E. Morison, the 'funeral salute to a finished era of naval warfare'.

Just about the time that Nishimura was being wiped out by Oldendorf someone finally thought to check which ships were guarding the San Bernardino Strait, but even so a proper answer was not obtained from Halsey's staff until 0645 on the morning of 25 October. Ten minutes later the escort carriers off Samar learned the facts for themselves, when the *Yamato*'s 18-in shells began to fall around them—the Japanese were only 17 miles away. These small carriers were almost defenceless because their aircraft, like Oldendorf's battleships, had been armed for bombing shore targets and had only light bombs. But the destroyers sacrificed themselves in an heroic attempt to save the carriers and, although three of them were sunk, only the carrier *Gambier Bay* was lost. Sprague's forces were at the end of their tether, and his pilots were reduced to making dummy passes at the Japanese ships because they had no bombs left, but suddenly Kurita's ships vanished as quickly as they had appeared.

HMS *Nelson*
Being the Royal Navy's most modern capital ships in 1936, the *Nelson* and *Rodney* were never reconstructed. By 1945 their close-range armament had been vastly increased. She is seen here with a mixture of 2-pdr pom-poms, US-supplied quad 40-mm Bofors, 20-mm Oerlikon guns as well as numerous radar sets. (see *Rodney* for specifications)

USS *Tennessee*
These battleships were originally based on the *New Mexico* class but were extensively modified during their lives, especially after having been damaged at Pearl Harbor
Displacement: 35,190 tons full load
Length: 624 ft 6 in *Armament:* 12×4-in, 12×5-in 8×5-in AA *Armour:* 8/14-in belt, 5/18-in main turrets, 3½-in main deck *Max speed:* 21 knots

Tennessee class

Name	Completed	Fate
Tennessee	Jun 1920	Scrapped 1959
California	Oct 1921	Scrapped 1959

HMS Nelson *finished her wartime career of continuous service with the East Indies Fleet in 1945. She is seen here entering the harbour of Trincomalee in Ceylon with all her wartime modifications and final combat paint scheme*

APC

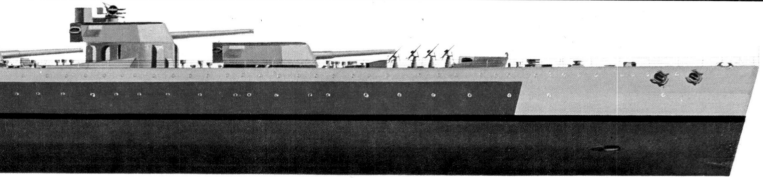

The old US battleships, some of them rebuilt after Pearl Harbor, proved their worth until the end. Here an Idaho *class battleship bombards the coast of Okinawa in 1945*

US Navy

In all probability the prolonged strain of air attacks and the lack of reliable intelligence cause Kurita to change his plans so suddenly. He knew now that Nishimura's forces had been annihilated and he had used a lot of fuel, but whatever his reasons he now threw away the last chance to affect the outcome of the war. After wasting time in manoeuvres of no consequence he withdrew at noon and headed for home, leaving Ozawa to Halsey. That gallant admiral now suffered the full wrath of the American carrier strikes, and quickly lost three carriers. But it was a paltry substitute for the general action with the main fleet, which would have earned Halsey laurels comparable to Nelson's or Togo's and his (Halsey's) wrath could not mask the fact that his intemperate handling of the battle had nearly lost it.

The Japanese were now finished as a naval power, but characteristically they used the Yamato in one final gesture of futile defiance. When the Americans landed on Okinawa Vice-Admiral Ito was given enough fuel for a one-way trip (not that there was enough left for the return voyage, even if it had been contemplated) and orders to hurl his 863-ft flagship at the anchorage. After blasting his way through he was then to beach the Yamato and use her 18-in guns to shell the US troops on shore. But the mad scheme had no hope of succeeding.

The Yamato was superior in gunpower and armour to any other battleship afloat, but without air cover these assets were

useless. The mission's course was plotted within fifty miles of the coast of Kyushu, with its many airfields, but the Japanese C-in-C made no order for air cover to protect the 'Special Sea Attack Force'. The Yamato's massive anti-aircraft firepower was compromised by low cloud cover. If she was found by US aircraft the greatest battleship of all time would face a terrible test.

On April 6, 1945 she slipped out of the Inland Sea by the Bungo Strait accompanied by a screen of six destroyers. Soon after dawn the next day the Yamato was sighted by the first American air patrols. Zigzagging his ship to avoid submarines and to throw off the hunting carrier air-groups, Admiral Ito received reports at noon of two big aircraft formations heading northwards on interception course. Already the ship's own radar had detected the danger and at 1232 hours formations of some 150 aircraft broke cloud cover and were sighted at about thirteen miles. Immediately the Japanese fleet increased speed to 24 knots, but already US fighters were coming in fast and low using cloud as low as several hundred feet for cover, smothering the Yamato's anti-aircraft batteries with bombs and machine-gun fire. Following the fighters, TBF torpedo bombers came in at wave height as the Japanese fleet formation broke up, each

ship having to take evasive action.

Nine minutes after the first attack the Yamato was struck by two bombs near the aft secondary gun turret, and a few minutes later a torpedo struck the port bow. The American pilots were concentrating on the stricken battleship's port beam and at 1300 hours two more torpedoes struck home, severing the ship's communications. Half an hour later a third wave of about 150 aircraft appeared and the attacking torpedo aircraft scored three hits on the port beam, which gave the Yamato a list beyond the capacity of her counter-flooding arrangements. The starboard engine and boiler rooms were flooded and the great ship's speed fell to a limping seven knots. Now circling, with her rudder jammed, the Japanese ship soaked up bombs and machine-gun fire while her own gunners' aim was thrown off by the ship's ever increasing list to port.

At 1417 hours the tenth torpedo struck, dealing the ship a decisive blow. Admiral Ito transferred to a destroyer and Captain Ariga ordered his men to abandon ship while he was lashed to the Yamato's binnacle. Six minutes later the Yamato's own exploding ammunition ripped the ship apart. She sank within seconds, taking more than 3000 men with her.

Yamato *running full speed trials, 1942*

Yamato

Designed to outrange the guns of any opponent, the mighty Yamato class battleships were rendered obsolescent from the outset by the rise of the aircraft carrier. A third vessel was completed as a carrier, and a fourth was scrapped ehile incomplete

Displacement: 72,800 tons full load *Length:* 263 m *Armament:* 9×460-mm, 12×155-mm, 12 (later 24)×127-mm AA, 24 (later 147)×25-mm AA, 4×12.7-mm AA *Armour:* 400-mm belt, 500/650-mm turrets, 200-mm decks
Max speed: 27½ knots

Yamato class

Yamato	Dec 1941	Sunk by US aircraft 1945
Musashi	Aug 1942	Sunk by US aircraft 1944

Musashi *down at the bows and sinking after a massive air attack during the Battle for Leyte Gulf, October 24, 1944. It took hits from 20 torpedoes and 17 bombs to sink her*

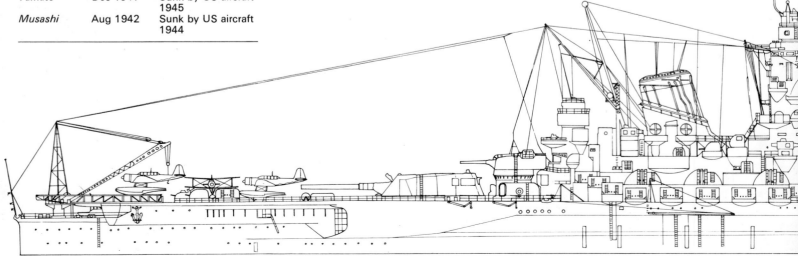

Above: Yamato *fitting out at Kure Naval Yard, 1941. Each 18-in gun weighed over 150 tons and could hurl a 3220-lb shell 45,000 yards*

Fukui

US Navy

Above: The huge target of the Yamato at Leyte Gulf, as seen by an American pilot. The Yamato *survived this battle but her sister was lost. The Japanese tried to build warships that could outfight anything else afloat, but without air cover the fate of the super-battleships was sealed*

The superstructure of the Yamato bristling with 5-in and 25-mm anti-aircraft guns. The Japanese provided blast-proof mountings for the 5-in guns to protect the crew from the phenomenal blast of the 18-in guns which could tear the flesh from the unprotected arm of an exposed gunner. The weight of US air attacks forced them to add 25-mm guns regardless of the risk

THE GIANTS SLIP AWAY

When the Second World War ended in August 1945 the battleship's reign formally ended, although she still had the prestige she had always enjoyed—sufficient to ensure that the Japanese surrender was signed on the quarterdeck of USS *Missouri*, with HMS *Duke of York* nearby as flagship of the British Pacific Fleet. But nearly all were destined, if not for the scrapheap, then at least premature retirement. The Royal Navy at last completed the *Vanguard* in 1946, having spent most of 1944 and 1945 arguing about her anti-aircraft armament. She was a fine ship in every way, even though her 15-in guns had first gone to sea in the battle-cruisers *Courageous* and *Glorious* in 1917. This meant that they had once been fired in anger, in November 1917, despite what her critics said. All the older battleships were scrapped except those of the Americans (who retained their modernised veterans in order to placate Congress), the Russians and the Italians. Under the peace treaty the Italians were allowed to keep the *Andrea Doria* and *Caio Duilio* for training, while the Soviet Union was given the *Giulio Cesare* as reparation for war losses at the hands of Italian submarines in the Black Sea. Sadly the two elegant *Littorios* had to be scrapped, for no better reason than to stop the Russians from demanding one of them. France did better than might be expected, for the *Richelieu* had been overhauled and modernised in the USA in 1944, and it proved feasible to complete the *Jean Bart* in 1949.

A few battleships were kept in service as flagships and for training, but the majority went into the 'mothball fleet'. But the Korean War provided a good excuse to get the rest of the *Iowa* class back into service.

A rare aerial view of the Vanguard *firing a 15-in broadside during gunnery practice*

They performed sterling service in shore bombardment, but when they went back into reserve it was widely assumed that the next move would be to the breakers. Numerous schemes were proposed for using battleships in the 1950s. The obvious one was to replace the big guns with guided missiles, and indeed for many years the Western Press believed that the Russians had completed their big *Sovietski Soyuz* class as missile ships, until the Russians finally admitted that it had been a ponderous leg-pull. Another was to use them as giant oilers and replenishment ships, and indeed during the big NATO exercise 'Mariner' in 1953 the *Iowa* and *Wisconsin* had successfully refuelled all the destroyers in their task force. The incomplete *Kentucky* was suggested as a subject for conversion to a missile ship, but this fell through—like all the other schemes—on grounds of cost. Not only would such a job have been costly, but the running costs would have been exorbitant, for ship and missile systems.

HMS *Vanguard*

The biggest warship ever built in Britain, and the Royal Navy's last battleship, *Vanguard* was originally intended to reinforce the Singapore station and to make use of the 15-in guns in storage since 1925. She never saw action, and expressed her disapproval by running aground on the way to the breakers
Displacement: 51,420 tons max *Length:* ~~248~~ 314 ft 4 in overall *Armament:* 8×15-in, 16×5.2-in, 22×40-mm (final fit) *Armour:* 330/356-mm side, 330-mm main turrets *Max speed:* 29.5 knots

Vanguard class

Name	Completed	Fate
Vanguard	Apr 1946	Scrapped 1960

The USS Missouri *fires a 16-in salvo at targets on the coast of Korea, 1951. A full broadside from her nine 16-in guns weighed over twelve tons*

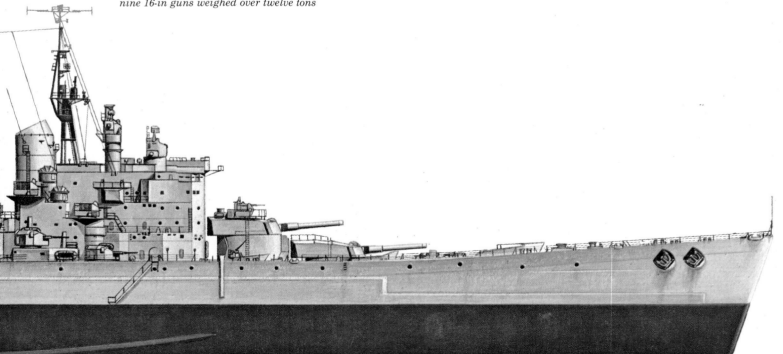

By the 1960s the last battleships were the four *Iowa* class, all in reserve and regarded as stately white elephants. But the Vietnam war was being fought, and one of its clear lessons was that air bombardment did not have enough precision or continuity. An increasingly vociferous lobby, particularly from the US Marine Corps, demanded the re-activation of a battleship to provide cheap and effective fire support. Guided weapons were far too expensive, and air strikes too hard to organize, whereas a battleship could lie off the coast and even resume fire if the initial bombardment had not been fully effective. Eventually the 'big-gun' lobby won the day, and in mid-1967 the *New Jersey* was selected as being in the best condition. The sum of $21 million was spent, mostly on remodelling her upper control tower to take up-to-date communications and electronic-countermeasures gear, but this was offset by saving about 1000 men from her previous complement by eliminating light guns.

The recommissioning of the *New Jersey* on 6 April, 1968 caused many a battleship-lover's heart to flutter, and in one sense the whole idea was almost a gesture of contempt: only the US Navy could dare or even afford to have a battleship fighting in a war of guided weapons and supersonic aircraft. During her tour of duty on the 'gun line' in 1968-69 she served for 120 days, and at one time spent 47 days at sea. She fired 5688 rounds of 16-in shells and more than 15,000 5-in shells; by comparison, in two deployments during the Korean War she had fired only a thousand more 16-in, while in the Second World War she fired 771 rounds.

The *New Jersey*'s comeback did not last long, for she was decommissioned once

Left: A broadside fired at night from the USS New Jersey, *the last operational battleship; is a spectacular reminder of the power of the big gun*

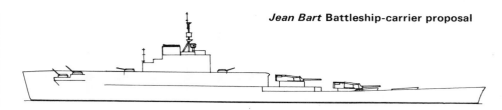

***Jean Bart** Battleship-carrier proposal*

John Roberts

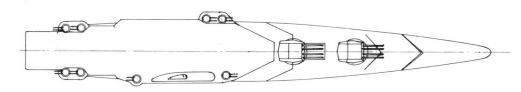

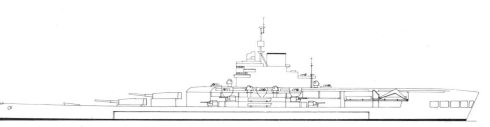

***Lion** class Battleship carrier proposal*

Battleship-Carriers

The last attempt to save the battleship dinosaur from extinction was to mate it with the aircraft carrier. The British produced two designs for hybrid battleship-carriers using the hull of the incomplete French *Jean Bart*, and a second based on the never-built *Lion* class with six 16-in guns. Only the Japanese carried this idea into practice with the *Hyuga* and *Ise* with a flight-deck aft to operate 22 floatplane bombers. The aircraft were never allocated to the ships and both vessels fought at Leyte Gulf as even less effective battleships

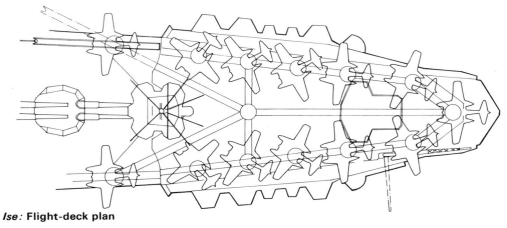

***Ise:** Flight-deck plan*

***Ise:** Profile*

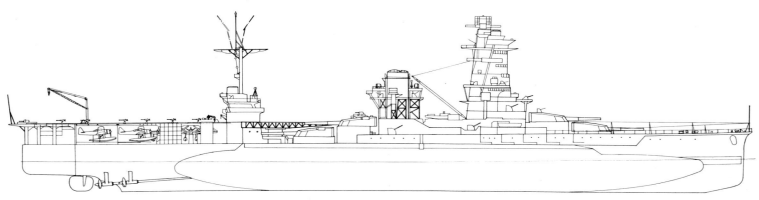

more on 17 December, 1969. The reason was an apparent shortage of 16-in barrel-liners, without which her guns would soon become worn and inaccurate. Ironically, as she was on her way home to decommission a whole field full of gun-liners was discovered in Washington, apparently missed from the inventory some time since 1945. But in a large bureaucracy decisions cannot be reversed easily; the 70 officers and 1556 enlisted men had already been allocated to other ships, and it was not possible to rescind the decision.

Apart from the *Missouri*, which is earmarked for preservation in memory of her role as the platform for the Japanese surrender in 1945, the *Iowa*s will probably not see out the decade. But other battleships

Long gone to breaker's yards or rusting hulks, sunk where they fought in two world wars, all that remains of the mighty battleships are a few museum ships' preserved armaments and fittings, and the plans, drawings and photographs which let research continue. Above is an invitation to the launch of HMS Resolution in Jarrow, 1892

have been preserved—the *Texas, North Carolina, Alabama* and *Massachusetts*—to give future generations some idea of the complexity and majesty of the type. No British battleship has been preserved, although attempts were made to save first the *Warspite* in 1946 and then the *Vanguard* in 1961 as memorials, one because of her unique war record and the other because she was the last. Strangely enough, the first

British ironclad, HMS *Warrior,* is still afloat, having outlasted a whole century of later ships. She acts as a floating jetty at a fuel terminal, and could still be saved to bridge the gap between HMS *Victory* and the American battleships. Togo's flagship at Tusushima, the *Mikasa,* survives at Yokosuka. She was nearly destroyed during an air raid during the Second World War, but was later restored to her former glory and is now the only example of a pre-dreadnought battleship.

The battleship was in its day the most complex mobile structure in existence, and it pushed technology to its limits. But it was also a product of the societies which sponsored it, and was a reflection of all the factors which made up those societies.

Battleships 1950-77

Argentina

Moreno	Scrapped in Italy 1957
Rivadavia	–do–

Brazil

Minas Geraes	Sold 1953 and scrapped in Italy 1954
Sao Paulo	Sold 1951 but lost in Atlantic in tow November 1951

Chile

Almirante Latorre	Scrapped in Japan 1959

France

Richelieu	Scrapped in Italy 1968
Jean Bart	Scrapped in Japan 1969

Italy

Caio Duilio	Scrapped 1958
Andrea Doria	–do–

Great Britain

King George V	Scrapped 1958
Duke of York	–do–
Howe	–do–
Anson	Scrapped 1957
Vanguard	Scrapped 1960

Soviet Union

Oktyabrskaya Revolutsia	Scrapped 1956
Sevastopol	Scrapped about 1957
Petropavlovsk	Salved and scrapped about 1950
Novorossiisk	Sunk by mine (?) in Sevastopol 1956

Turkey

Yavuz	Scrapped 1972

United States

Mississippi	Gunnery trials ship from 1947, and scrapped 1956
Tennessee	Scrapped 1959
California	–do–
Colorado	–do–
Maryland	–do–
West Virginia	Scrapped 1961
North Carolina	State memorial 1961
Washington	Scrapped 1961
South Dakota	Scrapped 1962
Indiana	Scrapped 1964
Massachusetts	State memorial 1965
Alabama	State memorial 1964
Iowa	Still in existence (1977)
New Jersey	–do–
Missouri	–do–
Wisconsin	–do–

Last of the dreadnoughts. The Turkish battle-cruiser Yavuz *(ex-Goeben) guarded Istanbul as a museum ship for many years with only a Petty Officer and his cat as crew—until she was tragically scrapped in 1972*

PICTURE INDEX

Note: Bold entries indicate photograph, otherwise artwork

Further reading

Breyer, S **Battleships and Battle-cruisers 1905-1970**
Dulin, R & Garzke, W **Battleships—US Navy Battleships in World War II**
Ensigns (series) **King George V Class** (No 1), **Queen Elizabeth Class** (No 4), HMS **Hood** (special)
Kennedy, L **Pursuit—The Hunting of the Bismarck**
Lenton, H T **German Warships in the Second World War**
Mayer, S L (editor) **The Japanese War Machine, The Russian War Machine**
Padfield, P **The Battleship Era**
Parkes, O **British Battleships**
Preston, A **Battleships of World War I**
Raven, A & Roberts, J **British Battleships of World War II**
Ships Data (series) **North Carolina, South Dakota**
Warship Profiles (series) **Dreadnought** (No 1) **Graf Spee** (No 4) **Seydlitz** (No 14), **Bismarck** (No 18) **Hood** (No 19), **Tennessee** (No 21), **Furious** (No 23), **Yamato** (No 30), **Scharnhorst** (No 33), **Eagle** (No 35), **Tecumseh** (No 36), **König** (No 37), **Mississippi/Kilkis** (No 39)